The New Century Psalter

The New Century Psalter

Edited by
Burton H. Throckmorton Jr.
and
Arthur G. Clyde

The Pilgrim Press
Cleveland, Ohio

The New Century Psalter

Published 2000

ISBN 0-8298-1240-0

Printed in the United States of America on acid-free paper

Contents

ACKNOWLEDGMENTS

The Daily Lectionary of Psalms in this Psalter is adapted from the two-year Daily Office Lectionary of the Book of Common Prayer of the Episcopal Church.

The editors gratefully acknowledge the Rev. Joseph P. Russell for his counsel on the adaptation of the lectionary.

Burton H. Throckmorton Jr.
Arthur G. Clyde
Editors

FOREWORD

Psalms in the Western World

Today the Hebrew psalms are read and sung or chanted every day of the year, and everywhere on the face of the earth. They make up the heart of both personal and corporate prayer for all of Judaism—Orthodox, Conservative, and Reformed, for all forms of Christianity—Greek, Roman, and Protestant, and for men, women, and children. Through the Divine Office or breviary, psalms are read every day by all priests and nuns of the Roman and Eastern Orthodox churches. This ancient book of hymns and prayers, created for the use of Jews in the Israel of long ago, and probably learned by heart by Jesus as a boy, has survived by centuries the use for which it was prepared, and has become the prayer and hymn book not only for modern Jews, but also for much of the church of the Western world.

The use of psalms in worship threads its way through many centuries and settings. In public worship and religious communities, the psalms were sung in various cycles that would take the worshiper through all the psalms over a period of time. Many Christians knew psalms from memory. The Reformation saw the emergence of a new way of singing psalms, metrical psalmody, introduced by Calvinists and Lutherans. It is in this style that psalm-hymns such as "All people that on earth do dwell" were written. All of this new style of psalmody—psalm paraphrases set to rhythmic tunes—had another characteristic, namely, vernacular language. Whereas for centuries the psalms were sung in the Western church primarily in Latin, the metrical psalms appeared in English, French, German, and other languages. The Puritans sang psalms as they crossed the sea to a new world. Later, in Cambridge, Massachusetts, in 1640, the Bay Psalm Book was published in an attempt by the minister-translators to render the psalms as literally as metrical form would allow. These various metrical psalms in various languages—for example, Psalm 46, paraphrased by Martin Luther as "Ein' feste Burg" and translated into English as "A mighty fortress," and Isaac Watts's English paraphrase of Psalm 90, "O God, our help in ages past"—formed the backbone of seventeenth- and eighteenth-century Protestant hymnals.

Poetic as these metrical psalm renderings may be—and many are sung to this day—they are in fact paraphrases, and often do not correspond closely to the original Hebrew texts. This fact, coupled with a general decline in the use of hymnody in many churches, is part of the background for the reclaiming of psalms in Christian worship for churches in the Reformed traditions. The last quarter of the twentieth century has seen the appearance of new psalters based on various modern translations of the Bible, and often arranged for singing. These psalters restore the biblical language of the psalms to worship in the tradition of the earliest psalm singing in the church, as the Book of Common Prayer has done through the ages. *The New Century Psalter* is very much in the tradition of the earliest psalm singing in the church, and the original psalter of the Bible.

A Psalter for Sunday Worship and Daily Devotions

This psalter has been designed for use in both community and private worship, and for both Sunday and daily use. For reading and singing in Sunday services of worship, this psalter contains all the selections from the psalms designated by the *Revised Common Lectionary* (RCL), the scheme for Sunday readings used in many denominations. In addition, this psalter has been designed for use in personal and corporate worship on a daily basis, as it contains virtually every verse of all of the one hundred fifty psalms of the Bible. Wherever verses of psalms are not part of the Sunday lectionary selection, they have been added within brackets, or sometimes by including a complete version of the psalm after the lectionary selection. This makes it easy for both uses. For Sunday worship, bracketed verses may be skipped; for daily use, they may be included. The RCL Sunday lectionary omits verses from some of the psalms. Most of these verses have been restored in this psalter.

About the Daily Lectionary

For daily use, a daily lectionary, the same one used in the Episcopal *Book of Common Prayer,* is provided at the beginning of the psalms. This scheme of readings—and that is essentially what a lectionary is—leads the worshiper through the entire psalter in seven-week cycles. Thus, this psalter can be a daily devotional for those who wish to pray the psalms and be immersed in the richness of prayer and praise that psalms can provide. For those who wish to add other readings, the seven-week cycle of psalms is compatible with any other scheme of reading through the other books of the Bible. It should be noted here that the essence of the Sunday lectionary scheme is different from the daily reading cycle. Sunday lectionaries are made of selections, harmoniously paired, for preaching and study, with psalms chosen for their relevance to other readings. The intent of reading the psalms daily, in more or less consecutive order, is to participate in the vast range of human experience in covenant with God, and to let God's word flow over us in our daily meditations.

Orders for Prayer

The New Century Psalter contains orders for corporate and individual morning and evening prayer. The Order for Morning Prayer and the Order for Evening Prayer have been pointed so that a group of worshipers may sing the service to one of the many psalm tones provided, beginning on page 226. These psalms can also be spoken (ignoring the points). Following Psalm 150 (p. 199) are some additional musical settings of psalms, of canticles for Morning and Evening Prayer (Magnificat and Song of Zechariah) with responses, and of other canticles. The Daily Devotions for Individual and Family Use contain brief services of prayer for the home. There is one for morning, evening, and close of day. All of these orders for corporate and home use will work very well with the Daily Lectionary of Psalms, provided in the front of this psalter.

The Wording of Psalms in This Psalter

All the psalms in this book are based on the New Revised Standard Version of the Bible, but the wording has been adapted as follows:

(1) It has been adjusted to deal with all dimensions of exclusion that are built into our language—gender, race, disability, etc., and it attempts to modify and to curtail somewhat the maleness of the language used for God in the psalms.

(2) The verses of the psalms have been divided and, in some instances, carefully reworded to attain balanced couplets that are more easily spoken, prayed, and sung.

Daily Lectionary of Psalms

This lectionary provides a way of reading through the book of Psalms in a seven-week cycle (more or less) over the course of a year. The readings are extracted from the lectionary found in the Book of Common Prayer (without the additional readings from scripture). It is a lectionary for a full liturgical year, beginning with the first Sunday in Advent. If the date of Easter is early or late, this will have the same effect on the date of Ash Wednesday and will cause the number of weeks after Epiphany to vary. The user will need to make the adjustment. Since the date of Pentecost moves in the same way, care must be taken in determining which Proper should begin the season after Pentecost. This is easily accomplished with a secular calendar, since the lectionary specifies, for example, Week of the Sunday closest to May 11.

Brackets indicate whole psalms that are optional; parentheses are used for optional verses. The use of an asterisk (*) following Psalm 95 in Lent indicates that it may be used as an optional call to worship (invitatory).

For some, the psalm readings will provide all that is needed for daily devotions. For those who desire to add other readings from scripture, a full lectionary of daily readings can be used, for example, *Book of Common Prayer* or *Between Sundays*. Another option is to reflect on two or three verses of scripture, perhaps from the *Revised Common Lectionary* Sunday readings. Still another way is to use a plan to read through the Bible over a chosen period of time.

Week of 1 Advent

Sunday
Morning 146, 147; *Evening* 111, 112, 113

Monday
Morning 1, 2, 3; *Evening* 4, 7

Tuesday
Morning 5, 6; *Evening* 10, 11

Wednesday
Morning 119:1–24; *Evening* 12, 13, 14

Thursday
Morning 18:1–19; *Evening* 18:20–50

Friday
Morning 16, 17; *Evening* 22

Saturday
Morning 20, 21:1–7 (8–13); *Evening* 110:1–5 (6–7), 116, 117

Week of 2 Advent

Sunday
Morning 148, 149, 150; *Evening* 114, 115

Monday
Morning 25; *Evening* 9, 15

Tuesday
Morning 26, 28; *Evening* 36, 39

Wednesday
Morning 38; *Evening* 119:25–48

Thursday
Morning 37:1–17; *Evening* 37:18–40

Friday
Morning 31; *Evening* 35

Saturday
Morning 30, 32; *Evening* 42, 43

Week of 3 Advent

Sunday
Morning 63:1–8 (9–11), 98; *Evening* 103

Monday
Morning 41, 52; *Evening* 44

Tuesday
Morning 45; *Evening* 47, 48

Wednesday
Morning 119:49–72; *Evening* 49, [53]

Thursday
Morning 50; *Evening* [59, 60] *or* 33

Friday
Morning 40, 54; *Evening* 51

Saturday
Morning 55; *Evening* 138, 139:1–18 (19–24)

Week of 4 Advent

Sunday
Morning 24, 29; *Evening* 8, 84

Monday
Morning 61, 62; *Evening* 112, 115

Tuesday
Morning 66, 67; *Evening* 116, 117

Wednesday
Morning 72; *Evening* 111, 113

Thursday
Morning 80; *Evening* 146, 147

Friday
Morning 93, 96; *Evening* 148, 150

December 24
Morning 45, 46

Christmas Eve
Evening 89:1–29

Christmas Day and Following

Christmas Day
Morning 2, 85; *Evening* 110:1–5 (6–7), 132

First Sunday after Christmas
Morning 93, 96; *Evening* 34

December 26
Morning 28, 30; *Evening* 118

December 27
Morning 97, 98; *Evening* 145

December 28
Morning 2, 26; *Evening* 19, 126

December 29
Morning 18:1–19; *Evening* 18:20–50*

December 30
Morning 20, 21:1–7 (8–13); *Evening* 23, 27

December 31
Morning 46, 48; *Evening* 90

January 1
Morning 103; *Evening* 148

Second Sunday after Christmas
Morning 66, 67; *Evening* 145

January 2
Morning 34; *Evening* 33

January 3
Morning 68; *Evening* 72**

January 4
Morning 85, 87; *Evening* 89:1–29**

January 5
Morning 2, 110:1–5 (6–7)

Eve of Epiphany
Evening 29, 98

Epiphany and Following

Epiphany (January 6)
Morning 46, 97; *Evening* 96, 100

January 7
Morning 103; *Evening* 114, 115

January 8
Morning 117, 118; *Evening* 112, 113

January 9
Morning 121, 122, 123; *Evening* 131, 132

**If today is Saturday, use Psalms 23 and 27 at Evening Prayer.*
***If today is Saturday, use Psalm 136 at Evening Prayer.*

January 10
Morning 138, 139:1–18 (19–24); *Evening* 147

January 11
Morning 148, 150; *Evening* 91, 92

January 12
Morning 98, 99, [100]

Eve of 1 Epiphany
Evening 104

Week of 1 Epiphany

Sunday
Morning 146, 147; *Evening* 111, 112, 113

Monday
Morning 1, 2, 3; *Evening* 4, 7

Tuesday
Morning 5, 6; *Evening* 10, 11

Wednesday
Morning 119:1–24; *Evening* 12, 13, 14

Thursday
Morning 18:1–19; *Evening* 18:20–50

Friday
Morning 16, 17; *Evening* 22

Saturday
Morning 20, 21:1–7 (8–13); *Evening* 110:1–5 (6–7), 116, 117

Week of 2 Epiphany

Sunday
Morning 148, 149, 150; *Evening* 114, 115

Monday
Morning 25; *Evening* 9, 15

Tuesday
Morning 26, 28; *Evening* 36, 39

Wednesday
Morning 38; *Evening* 119:25–48

Thursday
Morning 37:1–17; *Evening* 37:18–40

Friday
Morning 31; *Evening* 35

Saturday
Morning 30, 32; *Evening* 42, 43

Week of 3 Epiphany

Sunday
Morning 63:1–8 (9–11), 98; *Evening* 103

Monday
Morning 41, 52; *Evening* 44

Tuesday
Morning 45; *Evening* 47, 48

Wednesday
Morning 119:49–72; *Evening* 49, [53]

Thursday
Morning 50; *Evening* [59, 60] *or* 118

Friday
Morning 40, 54; *Evening* 51

Saturday
Morning 55; *Evening* 138, 139:1–18 (19–24)

Week of 4 Epiphany

Sunday
Morning 24, 29; *Evening* 8, 84

Monday
Morning 56, 57, [58]; *Evening* 64, 65

Tuesday
Morning 61, 62; *Evening* 68:1–20 (21–23), 24–35

Wednesday
Morning 72; *Evening* 119:73–96

Thursday
Morning [70], 71; *Evening* 74

Friday
Morning 69:1–21 (22–28), 29–36; *Evening* 73

Saturday
Morning 75, 76; *Evening* 23, 27

Week of 5 Epiphany

Sunday
Morning 93, 96; *Evening* 34

Monday
Morning 80; *Evening* 77, [79]

Tuesday
Morning 78:1–39; *Evening* 78:40–72

Wednesday
Morning 119:97–120; *Evening* 81, 82

Thursday
Morning [83] *or* 146, 147; *Evening* 85, 86

Friday
Morning 88; *Evening* 91, 92

Saturday
Morning 87, 90; *Evening* 136

Week of 6 Epiphany

Sunday
Morning 66, 67; *Evening* 19, 46

Monday
Morning 89:1–18; *Evening* 89:19–52

Tuesday
Morning 97, 99, [100]; *Evening* 94, [95]

Wednesday
Morning 101, 109:1–5 (6–20), 21–31; *Evening* 119:121–144

Thursday
Morning 105:1–22; *Evening* 105:23–45

Friday
Morning 102; *Evening* 107:1–32

Saturday
Morning 107:33–43, 108:1–6 (7–13); *Evening* 33

Week of 7 Epiphany

Sunday
Morning 118; *Evening* 145

Monday
Morning 106:1–18; *Evening* 106:19–48

Tuesday
Morning [120], 121, 122, 123; *Evening* 124, 125, 126, [127]

Wednesday
Morning 119:145–176; *Evening* 128, 129, 130

Thursday
Morning 131, 132, [133]; *Evening* 134, 135

Friday
Morning 140, 142; *Evening* 141, 143:1–11 (12)

Saturday
Morning 137:1–6 (7–9), 144; *Evening* 104

Week of 8 Epiphany

Sunday
Morning 146, 147; *Evening* 111, 112, 113

Monday
Morning 1, 2, 3; *Evening* 4, 7

Tuesday
Morning 5, 6; *Evening* 10, 11

Wednesday
Morning 119:1–24; *Evening* 12, 13, 14

Thursday
Morning 18:1–19; *Evening* 18:20–50

Friday
Morning 16, 17; *Evening* 22

Saturday
Morning 20, 21:1–7 (8–13); *Evening* 110:1–5 (6–7), 116, 117

Week of Last Epiphany

Sunday
Morning 148, 149, 150; *Evening* 114, 115

Monday
Morning 25; *Evening* 9, 15

Tuesday
Morning 26, 28; *Evening* 36, 39

Ash Wednesday
Morning 95* & 32, 143; *Evening* 102, 130

Thursday
Morning 37:1–17; *Evening* 37:18–40
Friday
Morning 95* & 31; *Evening* 35
Saturday
Morning 30, 32; *Evening* 42, 43

Week of 1 Lent
Sunday
Morning 63:1–8 (9–11), 98; *Evening* 103
Monday
Morning 41, 52; *Evening* 44
Tuesday
Morning 45; *Evening* 47, 48
Wednesday
Morning 119:49–72; *Evening* 49, [53]
Thursday
Morning 50; *Evening* [59, 60] *or* 19, 46
Friday
Morning 95* & 40, 54; *Evening* 51
Saturday
Morning 55; *Evening* 138, 139:1–18 (19–24)

Week of 2 Lent
Sunday
Morning 24, 29; *Evening* 8, 84
Monday
Morning 56, 57, [58]; *Evening* 64, 65
Tuesday
Morning 61, 62; *Evening* 68:1–20 (21–23), 24–35
Wednesday
Morning 72; *Evening* 119:73–96
Thursday
Morning [70], 71; *Evening* 74
Friday
Morning 95* & 69:1–21 (22–28), 29–36; *Evening* 73
Saturday
Morning 75, 76; *Evening* 23, 27

Week of 3 Lent
Sunday
Morning 93, 96; *Evening* 34
Monday
Morning 80; *Evening* 77, [79]
Tuesday
Morning 78:1–38; *Evening* 78:39–72
Wednesday
Morning 119:97–120; *Evening* 81, 82
Thursday
Morning [83] *or* 42, 43; *Evening* 85, 86
Friday
Morning 95* & 88; *Evening* 91, 92
Saturday
Morning 87, 90; *Evening* 136

Week of 4 Lent
Sunday
Morning 66, 67; *Evening* 19, 46
Monday
Morning 89:1–18; *Evening* 89:19–52
Tuesday
Morning 97, 99, [100]; *Evening* 94, [95]
Wednesday
Morning 101, 109:1–5 (6–20), 21–31; *Evening* 119:121–144
Thursday
Morning 69:1–21 (22–28), 29–36; *Evening* 73
Friday
Morning 95* & 102; *Evening* 107:1–32
Saturday
Morning 107:33–43, 108:1–6 (7–13); *Evening* 33

Week of 5 Lent
Sunday
Morning 118; *Evening* 145
Monday
Morning 31; *Evening* 35

Tuesday
Morning [120], 121, 122, 123; *Evening* 124, 125, 126, [127]

Wednesday
Morning 119:145–176; *Evening* 128, 129, 130

Thursday
Morning 131, 132, [133]; *Evening* 140, 142

Friday
Morning 95* & 22; *Evening* 141, 143:1–11 (12)

Saturday
Morning 137:1–6 (7–9), 144; *Evening* 42, 43

Holy Week
Palm Sunday
Morning 24, 29; *Evening* 103

Monday
Morning 51:1–17 (18–19); *Evening* 69:1–23

Tuesday
Morning 6, 12; *Evening* 94

Wednesday
Morning 55; *Evening* 74

Maundy Thursday
Morning 102; *Evening* 142, 143

Good Friday
Morning 95* & 22; *Evening* 40:1–13 (14–17), 54

Holy Saturday
Morning 95* & 88; *Evening* 27

Easter Week
Easter Day
Morning 148, 149, 150; *Evening* 113, 114, *or* 118

Monday
Morning 93, 98; *Evening* 66

Tuesday
Morning 103; *Evening* 111, 114

Wednesday
Morning 97, 99; *Evening* 115

Thursday
Morning 146, 147; *Evening* 148, 149

Friday
Morning 136; *Evening* 118

Saturday
Morning 145; *Evening* 104

Week of 2 Easter
Sunday
Morning 146, 147; *Evening* 111, 112, 113

Monday
Morning 1, 2, 3; *Evening* 4, 7

Tuesday
Morning 5, 6; *Evening* 10, 11

Wednesday
Morning 119:1–24; *Evening* 12, 13, 14

Thursday
Morning 18:1–19; *Evening* 18:20–50

Friday
Morning 16, 17; *Evening* 134, 135

Saturday
Morning 20, 21:1–7 (8–13); *Evening* 110:1–5 (6–7), 116, 117

Week of 3 Easter
Sunday
Morning 148, 149, 150; *Evening* 114, 115

Monday
Morning 25; *Evening* 9, 15

Tuesday
Morning 26, 28; *Evening* 36, 39

Wednesday
Morning 38; *Evening* 119:25–48

Thursday
Morning 37:1–17; *Evening* 37:18–40

Friday
Morning 105:1–22; *Evening* 105:23–45

Saturday
Morning 30, 32; *Evening* 42, 43

Week of 4 Easter
Sunday
Morning 63:1–8 (9–11), 98; *Evening* 103

Monday
Morning 41, 52; *Evening* 44

Tuesday
Morning 45; *Evening* 47, 48

Wednesday
Morning 119:49–72; *Evening* 49, [53]

Thursday
Morning 50; *Evening* [59, 60] *or* 114, 115

Friday
Morning 40, 54; *Evening* 51

Saturday
Morning 55; *Evening* 138, 139:1–18 (19–24)

Week of 5 Easter
Sunday
Morning 24, 29; *Evening* 8, 84

Monday
Morning 56, 57, [58]; *Evening* 64, 65

Tuesday
Morning 61, 62; *Evening* 68:1–20 (21–23), 24–35

Wednesday
Morning 72; *Evening* 119:73–96

Thursday
Morning [70], 71; *Evening* 74

Friday
Morning 106:1–18; *Evening* 106:19–48

Saturday
Morning 75, 76; *Evening* 23, 27

Week of 6 Easter
Sunday
Morning 93, 96; *Evening* 34

Monday
Morning 80; *Evening* 77, [79]

Tuesday
Morning 78:1–39; *Evening* 78:40–72

Wednesday
Morning 119:97–120

Eve of Ascension
Evening 68:1–20

Ascension Day
Morning 8, 47; *Evening* 24, 96

Friday
Morning 85, 86; *Evening* 91, 92

Saturday
Morning 87, 90; *Evening* 136

Week of 7 Easter
Sunday
Morning 66, 67; *Evening* 19, 46

Monday
Morning 89:1–18; *Evening* 89:19–52

Tuesday
Morning 97, 99, [100]; *Evening* 94, [95]

Wednesday
Morning 101, 109:1–5 (6–20), 21–31; *Evening* 119:121–144

Thursday
Morning 105:1–22; *Evening* 105:23–45

Friday
Morning 102; *Evening* 107:1–32

Saturday
Morning 107:33–43, 108:1–6 (7–13)

Eve of Pentecost
Evening 33

The Day of Pentecost
Morning 118; *Evening* 145

For the weekdays that follow, use the psalms of the numbered Proper (1 through 6) which corresponds most closely to the date of Pentecost.

Eve of Trinity Sunday
Evening 104

Trinity Sunday
Morning 146, 147; *Evening* 111, 112, 113

For the weekdays that follow, use the psalms of the numbered Proper (2 through 7) which corresponds most closely to the date of Trinity Sunday.

The Season after Pentecost

Proper 1 *Week of the Sunday closest to May 11*

Monday
Morning 106:1–18; *Evening* 106:19–48

Tuesday
Morning [120], 121, 122, 123; *Evening* 124, 125, 126, [127]

Wednesday
Morning 119:145–176; *Evening* 128, 129, 130

Thursday
Morning 131, 132, [133]; *Evening* 134, 135

Friday
Morning 140, 142; *Evening* 141, 143:1–11 (12)

Saturday
Morning 137:1–6 (7–9), 144; *Evening* 104

Proper 2 *Week of the Sunday closest to May 18*

Monday
Morning 1, 2, 3; *Evening* 4, 7

Tuesday
Morning 5, 6; *Evening* 10, 11

Wednesday
Morning 119:1–24; *Evening* 12, 13, 14

Thursday
Morning 18:1–19; *Evening* 18:20–50

Friday
Morning 16, 17; *Evening* 22

Saturday
Morning 20, 21:1–7 (8–13); *Evening* 110:1–5 (6–7), 116, 117

Proper 3 *Week of the Sunday closest to May 25*

Sunday
Morning 148, 149, 150; *Evening* 114, 115

Monday
Morning 25; *Evening* 9, 15

Tuesday
Morning 26, 28; *Evening* 36, 39

Wednesday
Morning 38; *Evening* 119:25–48

Thursday
Morning 37:1–17; *Evening* 37:18–40

Friday
Morning 31; *Evening* 35

Saturday
Morning 30, 32; *Evening* 42, 43

Proper 4 *Week of the Sunday closest to June 1*

Sunday
Morning 63:1–8 (9–11), 98; *Evening* 103

Monday
Morning 41, 52; *Evening* 44

Tuesday
Morning 45; *Evening* 47, 48

Wednesday
Morning 119:49–72; *Evening* 49, [53]

Thursday
Morning 50; *Evening* [59, 60] *or* 8, 84

Friday
Morning 40, 54; *Evening* 51

Saturday
Morning 55; *Evening* 138, 139:1–18 (19–24)

Proper 5 *Week of the Sunday closest to June 8*

Sunday
Morning 24, 29; *Evening* 8, 84

Monday
Morning 56, 57, [58]; *Evening* 64, 65

Tuesday
Morning 61, 62; *Evening* 68:1–20 (21–23), 24–35

Wednesday
Morning 72; *Evening* 119:73–96

Thursday
Morning [70], 71; *Evening* 74

Friday
Morning 69:1–21 (22–28), 29–36; *Evening* 73

Saturday
Morning 75, 76; *Evening* 23, 27

Proper 6 *Week of the Sunday closest to June 15*

Sunday
Morning 93, 96; *Evening* 34

Monday
Morning 80; *Evening* 77, [79]

Tuesday
Morning 78:1–39; *Evening* 78:40–72

Wednesday
Morning 119:97–120; *Evening* 81, 82

Thursday
Morning [83] *or* 34; *Evening* 85, 86

Friday
Morning 88; *Evening* 91, 92

Saturday
Morning 87, 90; *Evening* 136

Proper 7 *Week of the Sunday closest to June 22*

Sunday
Morning 66, 67; *Evening* 19, 46

Monday
Morning 89:1–18; *Evening* 89:19–52

Tuesday
Morning 97, 99, [100]; *Evening* 94, [95]

Wednesday
Morning 101, 109:1–5 (6–20), 21–31; *Evening* 119:121–144

Thursday
Morning 105:1–22; *Evening* 105:23–45

Friday
Morning 102; *Evening* 107:1–32

Saturday
Morning 107:33–43, 108:1–6 (7–13); *Evening* 33

Proper 8 *Week of the Sunday closest to June 29*

Sunday
Morning 118; *Evening* 145

Monday
Morning 106:1–18; *Evening* 106:19–48

Tuesday
Morning [120], 121, 122, 123; *Evening* 124, 125, 126, [127]

Wednesday
Morning 119:145–176; *Evening* 128, 129, 130

Thursday
Morning 131, 132, [133]; *Evening* 134, 135

Friday
Morning 140, 142; *Evening* 141, 143:1–11 (12)

Saturday
Morning 137:1–6 (7–9), 144; *Evening* 104

Proper 9 *Week of the Sunday closest to July 6*

Sunday
Morning 146, 147; *Evening* 111, 112, 113

Monday
Morning 1, 2, 3; *Evening* 4, 7

Tuesday
Morning 5, 6; *Evening* 10, 11

Wednesday
Morning 119:1–24; *Evening* 12, 13, 14

Thursday
Morning 18:1–19; *Evening* 18:20–50

Friday
Morning 16, 17; *Evening* 22

Saturday
Morning 20, 21:1–7 (8–13); *Evening* 110:1–5 (6–7), 116, 117

Proper 10 *Week of the Sunday closest to July 13*

Sunday
Morning 148, 149, 150; *Evening* 114, 115

Monday
Morning 25; *Evening* 9, 15

Tuesday
Morning 26, 28; *Evening* 36, 39

Wednesday
Morning 38; *Evening* 119:25–48

Thursday
Morning 37:1–17; *Evening* 37:18–40

Friday
Morning 31; *Evening* 35

Saturday
Morning 30, 32; *Evening* 42, 43

Proper 11 *Week of the Sunday closest to July 20*

Sunday
Morning 63:1–8 (9–11), 98; *Evening* 103

Monday
Morning 41, 52; *Evening* 44

Tuesday
Morning 45; *Evening* 47, 48

Wednesday
Morning 119:49–72; *Evening* 49, [53]

Thursday
Morning 50; *Evening* [59, 60] *or* 66, 67

Friday
Morning 40, 54; *Evening* 51

Saturday
Morning 55; *Evening* 138, 139:1–18 (19–24)

Proper 12 *Week of the Sunday closest to July 27*

Sunday
Morning 24, 29; *Evening* 8, 84

Monday
Morning 56, 57, [58]; *Evening* 64, 65

Tuesday
Morning 61, 62; *Evening* 68:1–20 (21–23), 24–35

Wednesday
Morning 72; *Evening* 119:73–96

Thursday
Morning [70], 71; *Evening* 74

Friday
Morning 69:1–21 (22–28), 29–36; *Evening* 73

Saturday
Morning 75, 76; *Evening* 23, 27

Proper 13 *Week of the Sunday closest to August 3*

Sunday
Morning 93, 96; *Evening* 34

Monday
Morning 80; *Evening* 77, [79]

Tuesday
Morning 78:1–39; *Evening* 78:40–72

Wednesday
Morning 119:97–120; *Evening* 81, 82

Thursday
Morning [83] *or* 145; *Evening* 85, 86

Friday
Morning 88; *Evening* 91, 92

Saturday
Morning 87, 90; *Evening* 136

Proper 14 *Week of the Sunday closest to August 10*

Sunday
Morning 66, 67; *Evening* 19, 46

Monday
Morning 89:1–18; *Evening* 89:19–52

Tuesday
Morning 97, 99, [100]; *Evening* 94, [95]

Wednesday
Morning 101, 109:1–5 (6–20), 21–31; *Evening* 119:121–144

Thursday
Morning 105:1–22; *Evening* 105:23–45

Friday
Morning 102; *Evening* 107:1–32

Saturday
Morning 107:33–43, 108:1–6 (7–13); *Evening* 33

Proper 15 *Week of the Sunday closest to August 17*

Sunday
Morning 118; *Evening* 145

Monday
Morning 106:1–18; *Evening* 106:19–48

Tuesday
Morning [120], 121, 122, 123; *Evening* 124, 125, 126, [127]

Wednesday
Morning 119:145–176; *Evening* 128, 129, 130

Thursday
Morning 131, 132, [133]; *Evening* 134, 135

Friday
Morning 140, 142; *Evening* 141, 143:1–11 (12)

Saturday
Morning 137:1–6 (7–9), 144; *Evening* 104

Proper 16 *Week of the Sunday closest to August 24*

Sunday
Morning 146, 147; *Evening* 111, 112, 113

Monday
Morning 1, 2, 3; *Evening* 4, 7

Tuesday
Morning 5, 6; *Evening* 10, 11

Wednesday
Morning 119:1–24; *Evening* 12, 13, 14

Thursday
Morning 18:1–19; *Evening* 18:20–50

Friday
Morning 16, 17; *Evening* 22

Saturday
Morning 20, 21:1–7 (8–13); *Evening* 110:1–5 (6–7), 116, 117

Proper 17 *Week of the Sunday closest to August 31*

Sunday
Morning 148, 149, 150; *Evening* 114, 115

Monday
Morning 25; *Evening* 9, 15

Tuesday
Morning 26, 28; *Evening* 36, 39

Wednesday
Morning 38; *Evening* 119:25–46

Thursday
Morning 37:1–17; *Evening* 37:18–40

Friday
Morning 31; *Evening* 35

Saturday
Morning 30, 32; *Evening* 42, 43

Proper 18 *Week of the Sunday closest to September 7*

Sunday
Morning 63:1–8 (9–11), 98; *Evening* 103

Monday
Morning 41, 52; *Evening* 44

Tuesday
Morning 45; *Evening* 47, 48

Wednesday
Morning 119:49–72; *Evening* 49, [53]

Thursday
Morning 50; *Evening* [59, 60] *or* 93, 96

Friday
Morning 40, 54; *Evening* 51

Saturday
Morning 55; *Evening* 138, 139:1–18 (19–24)

Proper 19 *Week of the Sunday closest to September 14*

Sunday
Morning 24, 29; *Evening* 8, 84

Monday
Morning 56, 57, [58]; *Evening* 64, 65

Tuesday
Morning 61, 62; *Evening* 68:1–20 (21–23), 24–35

Wednesday
Morning 72; *Evening* 119:73–96

Thursday
Morning [70], 71; *Evening* 74

Friday
Morning 69:1–21 (22–28), 29–36; *Evening* 73

Saturday
Morning 75, 76; *Evening* 23, 27

Proper 20 *Week of the Sunday closest to September 21*

Sunday
Morning 93, 96; *Evening* 34

Monday
Morning 80; *Evening* 77, [79]

Tuesday
Morning 78:1–39; *Evening* 78:40–72

Wednesday
Morning 119:97–120; *Evening* 81, 82

Thursday
Morning [83] *or* 116, 117; *Evening* 85, 86

Friday
Morning 88; *Evening* 91, 92

Saturday
Morning 87, 90; *Evening* 136

Proper 21 *Week of the Sunday closest to September 28*

Sunday
Morning 66, 67; *Evening* 19, 46

Monday
Morning 89:1–18; *Evening* 89:19–52

Tuesday
Morning 97, 99, [100]; *Evening* 94, [95]

Wednesday
Morning 101, 109:1–5 (6–20), 21–31; *Evening* 119:121–144

Thursday
Morning 105:1–22; *Evening* 105:23–45

Friday
Morning 102; *Evening* 107:1–32

Saturday
Morning 107:33–43, 108:1–6 (7–13); *Evening* 33

Proper 22 *Week of the Sunday closest to October 5*

Sunday
Morning 118; *Evening* 145

Monday
Morning 106:1–18; *Evening* 106:19–48

Tuesday
Morning [120], 121, 122, 123; *Evening* 124, 125, 126, [127]

Wednesday
Morning 119:145–176; *Evening* 128, 129, 130

Thursday
Morning 131, 132, [133]; *Evening* 134, 135

Friday
Morning 140, 142; *Evening* 141, 143:1–11 (12)

Saturday
Morning 137:1–6 (7–9), 144; *Evening* 104

Proper 23 *Week of the Sunday closest to October 12*

Sunday
Morning 146, 147; *Evening* 111, 112, 113

Monday
Morning 1, 2, 3; *Evening* 4, 7

Tuesday
Morning 5, 6; *Evening* 10, 11

Wednesday
Morning 119:1–24; *Evening* 12, 13, 14

Thursday
Morning 18:1–19; *Evening* 18:20–50

Friday
Morning 16, 17; *Evening* 22

Saturday
Morning 20, 21:1–7 (8–13); *Evening* 110:1–5 (6–7), 116, 117

Proper 24 *Week of the Sunday closest to October 19*

Sunday
Morning 148, 149, 150; *Evening* 114, 115

Monday
Morning 25; *Evening* 9, 15

Tuesday
Morning 26, 28; *Evening* 36, 39

Wednesday
Morning 38; *Evening* 119:25–48

Thursday
Morning 37:1–17; *Evening* 37:18–40

Friday
Morning 31; *Evening* 35

Saturday
Morning 30, 32; *Evening* 42, 43

Proper 25 *Week of the Sunday closest to October 26*

Sunday
Morning 63:1–8 (9–11), 98; *Evening* 103

Monday
Morning 41, 52; *Evening* 44

Tuesday
Morning 45; *Evening* 47, 48

Wednesday
Morning 119:49–72; *Evening* 49, [53]

Thursday
Morning 50; *Evening* [59, 60] *or* 103

Friday
Morning 40, 54; *Evening* 51

Saturday
Morning 55; *Evening* 138, 139:1–18 (19–24)

Proper 26 *Week of the Sunday closest to November 2*

Sunday
Morning 24, 29; *Evening* 8, 84

Monday
Morning 56, 57, [58]; *Evening* 64, 65

Tuesday
Morning 61, 62; *Evening* 68:1–20 (21–23), 24–35

Wednesday
Morning 72; *Evening* 119:73–96

Thursday
Morning [70], 71; *Evening* 74

Friday
Morning 69:1–21 (22–28), 29–36; *Evening* 73

Saturday
Morning 75, 76; *Evening* 23, 27

Proper 27 *Week of the Sunday closest to November 9*

Sunday
Morning 93, 96; *Evening* 34

Monday
Morning 80; *Evening* 77, [79]

Tuesday
Morning 78:1–39; *Evening* 78:40–72

Wednesday
Morning 119:97–120; *Evening* 81, 82

Thursday
Morning [83] *or* 23, 27; *Evening* 85, 86

Friday
Morning 88; *Evening* 91, 92

Saturday
Morning 87, 90; *Evening* 136

Proper 28 *Week of the Sunday closest to November 16*

Sunday
Morning 66, 67; *Evening* 19, 46

Monday
Morning 89:1–18; *Evening* 89:19–52

Tuesday
Morning 97, 99, [100]; *Evening* 94, [95]

Wednesday
Morning 101, 109:1–5 (6–20), 21–31; *Evening* 119:121–144

Thursday
Morning 105:1–22; *Evening* 105:23–45

Friday
Morning 102; *Evening* 107:1–32

Saturday
Morning 107:33–43, 108:1–6 (7–13); *Evening* 33

Proper 29 *Week of the Sunday closest to November 23*

Sunday
Morning 118; *Evening* 145

Monday
Morning 106:1–18; *Evening* 106:19–48

Tuesday
Morning [120], 121, 122, 123; *Evening* 124, 125, 126, [127]

Wednesday
Morning 119:145–176; *Evening* 128, 129, 130

Thursday
Morning 131, 132, [133]; *Evening* 134, 135

Friday
Morning 140, 142; *Evening* 141, 143:1–11 (12)

Saturday
Morning 137:1–6 (7–9), 144; *Evening* 104

Orders for Prayer

Order for Morning Prayer

The practice of Christian morning prayer came from our Jewish heritage. This service of prayer is based on traditions of early Christian daily public worship. Appropriate for any gathering for morning worship, morning prayer can be adapted for use in the home. A daily lectionary may be used to provide scripture selections.

Opening Sentence

All may stand or, if desired, remain seated throughout.

O God, opén my lips.
And my mouth shall procláim your praise.

Doxology

The following or other praise of the Trinity may be said or sung. Alleluia is omitted in the season of Lent.

Praise to the holy and undivided Trinitý, one God:
as it was in the beginning, is now, and will be forevér. Amen.

Allélluia!
Allélluia!

Throughout Lent
Praise to ýou, O Christ,
Sovereign of etérnal Glory.

Morning Hymn or Canticle (Optional)

A morning hymn or canticle may be sung.

Morning Psalm

One of the following psalms, or others, may be used: Psalm 51, 63, 67, or 95.

Psalms

An additional psalm for the day or other psalms may be sung or said. Following each psalm is a period of silence for reflection.

Reading from Scripture

One or more readings from scripture are announced and read, followed by

A
The word of truth.
Thanks be to God.

B *following a Gospel reading*
This is the good news.
Praise to you, O Christ.

After a silence for reflection following the reading of scripture, an appropriate meditation or a reading other than scripture may be offered. Silence may follow.

Canticle of Zechariah

May be sung or spoken.

Blessed be the Sovereign Gód of Israel,
who has looked favorably on the people ánd redeemed them.
God has raised up a mighty savíor for us
in the house of God's śervant David;
as God spoke through the mouth of the holy prophets fŕom of old,
that we would be saved from our enemies and from the hand of áll who hate us.
Thus God has śhown the mercy
promised tó our ancestors,

and has remembered God's holy covenant,
the oath that God swore to our ancestor Abraham,
to grant us that we, being rescued from the hands of our enemies,
might serve God without fear, in holiness and righteousness
before God all our days.
And you, child, will be called the prophet of the Most High,
for you will go before God to prepare God's ways;
to give knowledge of salvation to the people
by the forgiveness of their sins.
By the tender mercy of our God,
the dawn from on high will break upon us,
to give light to those who sit in night and in the shadow of death,
to guide our feet into the way of peace.

Prayers

One of the following prayers for mercy (A, B, C, or D) may be said.

A

God be with you.
And also with you.
(Let us pray, saying "Christ have mercy on us.")
That there may be purpose and fulfillment, O God, in all that we do,
Christ have mercy on us.
That we may show others this day the love that you have taught us,
Christ have mercy on us.
That the church throughout the world may respond to your call
for peace and justice,
Christ have mercy on us.
That those who are in need be helped and comforted,
Christ have mercy on us.
(Other intercessions may be added.)
That we may be strengthened by your grace for the tasks of this day,
Christ have mercy on us.

B

Prayer of Our Savior

One of the following versions or another version may be said.

A

Our Father in heaven,
hallowed be your name,
your kingdom come,
your will be done,
on earth as in heaven.
Give us today our daily bread.
Forgive us our sins
as we forgive those who sin against us.
Save us from the time of trial
and deliver us from evil.
For the kingdom, the power,
and the glory are yours,
now and for ever. Amen.

B

Our Father-Mother, who is in the heavens,
may your name be made holy,
may your dominion come,
may your will be done,
on the earth as it is in heaven.
Give us today the bread we need;
and forgive us our debts,
as we have forgiven our debtors;
and do not put us to the test,
but rescue us from evil.
For yours is the dominion, and the power,
and the glory forever. Amen.

Collect

God bé with you.
And alśo with you.

One of the following or others may be used.

General
Almighty God, give us faith to live this day not knowing where it will lead, but with the assurance that your love and guidance are with us always; through Jesus Christ. **Amen.**

Advent
Stir up our hearts, O God, to prepare the way for the coming of the Promised One. Help us to spend our days open to the presence of Christ in our lives. **Amen.**

Christmastide
Almighty God, you have given us the Word in flesh. Let the Word be the wisdom for all that we do in our lives; through Jesus Christ, this Word, who reigns with you and the Holy Spirit, one God, now and forever. **Amen.**

Epiphany
Almighty God, as you have led us to your Child by a star, lead us to seek faithfully your presence in our lives this day; through Jesus Christ, the light of the world. **Amen.**

Lent
Most merciful God, all have sinned and fall short of your glory; but you have given us your only begotten Child that we may have eternal life. Keep us ever mindful of this gift that we may gratefully serve you all of our days. **Amen.**

Eastertide
Almighty God, in Christ you have embraced all of life through the one who is the way, the truth, and the life. Pour out your grace upon us that we may love all of life as you have loved us. **Amen.**

A concluding hymn may be sung. (Optional)

May the God of hope fill you with all joy and peace in believing, so that you may abound in hope by the power of the Holy Spirit.

Let ús bless God.
Thanks bé to God.

Order for Evening Prayer

The practice of Christian evening prayer came from our Jewish heritage. This service of prayer is based on traditions of early Christian daily public worship. Appropriate for any gathering for evening worship, this order for prayer can be adapted for use in the home. In the earliest tradition, lamps are lighted as the hymn of praise is sung to Christ, the radiant light. If evening prayer is the final prayer of the night, a penitential prayer may be said following the opening sentence. A daily lectionary may be used to provide scripture selections.

Service of Light

For the lighting of candles or lamps (optional)

Jesus Christ is the light óf the world.
The light shines in the deepest night,
and the night did not óvercome it.
Stay with us now, for ít is evening,
and the day is álmost over.
Let your light dispérse the shadows
and shine withín us here.

Evening Hymn

A hymn is sung when the candles or lamps have been lit. "O Holy Radiance," p. 213, "O Wisdom," p. 214, or another evening hymn may be used. If the preceding Service of Light is not used, Evening Prayer may begin with the Opening Sentence and Doxology, and an evening hymn may be sung before the Evening Psalm.

Opening Sentence

All may stand or, if desired, remain seated throughout.

O God, come tó my aid.
Hear my voice when I cŕy to you.

Doxology

The following or other praise of the Trinity may be said or sung. Alleluia may be spoken or sung, and is omitted in the season of Lent.

Praise to the holy and undivided Trinitý, one God:
as it was in the beginning, is now, and will be forevér. Amen.

Alléluia!
Alléluia!

Throughout Lent

Praise to yóu, O Christ,
Sovereign of etérnal Glory.

Evening Psalm

Psalm 141 is said or sung. (See p. 188 or 205.) In keeping with the intention of Psalm 141, incense may be used. Following the psalm, the people may be seated.

Psalm

Following the evening psalm, one or more psalms may be said or sung, especially Psalms 110–117; 120–133; 135–147. Following each psalm is a period of silence for reflection.

Reading from Scripture

One or more readings from scripture are announced and read, followed by

A

God have mercý on us
Thanks bé to God.

B

The wórd of truth.
Thanks bé to God.

C *following a Gospel reading.*

This is thé good news.
Praise to yóu, O Christ.

After a silence for reflection following the reading of scripture, an appropriate meditation or a reading other than scripture may be offered. Silence may follow.

THE SONG OF MARY

May be sung or spoken.

My soul magnifies the Sovereign,
and my spirit rejoices in God my Savior;
for God has looked with favor on the lowliness of God's servant.
Surely, from now on all generations will call me blessed;
for the Mighty One has done great things for me,
the Mighty One whose name is holy.
God's mercy is for those who fear God
from generation to generation.
God has shown great strength;
and has scattered the proud in the thoughts of their hearts.
God has brought down the powerful from their thrones,
and lifted up the lowly;
God has filled the hungry with good things,
and sent the rich away empty.
God has helped God's servant Israel,
in remembrance of God's mercy,
according to the promise made to our ancestors,
to Abraham and Sarah and to their descendants forever.

PRAYERS

One of the following prayers for mercy (A, B, C, or D) may be said.

A

God be with you.
And also with you.

(Let us pray, saying "O God, hear our prayer.")
For the peace from on high and for our salvation, let us pray,
O God, hear our prayer.

For the welfare of all churches, and for those who lead us in the faith,
O God, hear our prayer.

For our nation and our community, and for those preside in public offices,
O God, hear our prayer.

For all who hunger, are sick, and in pain,
O God, hear our prayer.

(Other intercessions may be added.)
For a peaceful evening and safety this night,
O God, hear our prayer.

B

C

D

Prayer of Our Savior

One of the following versions or another version may be said.

A

Our Father in heaven,
hallowed be your name,
your kingdom come,
your will be done,
on earth as in heaven.
Give us today our daily bread.
Forgive us our sins
as we forgive those who sin against us.
Save us from the time of trial
and deliver us from evil.
For the kingdom, the power,
and the glory are yours,
now and for ever. Amen.

B

Our Father-Mother, who is in the heavens,
may your name be made holy.
may your dominion come,
and your will be done,
on the earth as it is in heaven.
Give us today the bread we need;
and forgive us our debts,
as we have forgiven our debtors;
and do not put us to the test,
but rescue us from evil.
For yours is the dominion, and the power,
and the glory forever. Amen.

Collect

God be with you.
And also with you.

The following or others may be used.

General
Almighty God, you have brought us to the ending of this day; release us from all chains of strife and draw us close with your gentle bands of peace. **Amen.**

Advent
Almighty God, as you have sent the Word to be the light of the world, let that light shine in our hearts that we may be filled with the joy and peace that you alone can provide. **Amen.**

Christmastide
Almighty God, may the light that shines from the cradle in Bethlehem be the light in our hearts that guides us and protects us; we pray in the name of the Christ, who is the way, the truth, and the light. **Amen.**

Epiphany
Eternal Light, you have shone your glory upon us in Christ, the Word made flesh. May our lives ever be a reflection of your gift of salvation to us. **Amen.**

Lent
O Jesus, Sun of Salvation, shine in our inmost beings this night; be the lamp to our way, and our beacon of hope. We pray in the name of Christ, the light of the world. **Amen.**

Eastertide
Almighty God, you have given us the gift of eternal life in the risen Christ. May the glorious light of the resurrection shine within us forevermore, through Jesus Christ we pray. **Amen.**

A concluding hymn may be sung. (Optional)

A
Let us bless God.
Thanks be to God.

B
May God bless us and protect us.
May God bring us to everlasting light.
Amen.

Daily Devotions for Individual and Family Use

Morning

O God, open my lips
and my mouth shall proclaim your praise.
Create in me a clean heart, O God,
and put a new and right spirit within me.
Do not cast me away from your presence,
and do not take your Holy Spirit from me.
Restore to me the joy of your salvation,
and sustain in me a willing spirit.

Psalm

(A psalm from the daily lectionary may be used, followed by a time of silence and meditation.)

(Additional readings and a hymn may be used.)

Prayers

(Prayers may be said for oneself and for others.)

The Prayer of Our Savior

(One of the following versions or another version may be said.)

A

Our Father in heaven,
hallowed be your name,
your kingdom come,
your will be done,
on earth as in heaven.
Give us today our daily bread.
Forgive us our sins
as we forgive those who sin against us.
Save us from the time of trial
and deliver us from evil.
For the kingdom, the power,
and the glory are yours,
now and for ever. Amen.

B

Our Father-Mother, who is in the heavens,
may your name be made holy,
may your dominion come,
may your will be done,
on the earth as it is in heaven.
Give us today the bread we need;
and forgive us our debts,
as we have forgiven our debtors;
and do not put us to the test,
but rescue us from evil.
For yours is the dominion, and the
power, and the glory forever. Amen.

Collect

O God, I give you hearty thanks for the rest of the past night and for the gift of a new day, with its opportunities of pleasing you. Grant that I may so pass its hours in the perfect freedom of your service, that at eventide I may again give thanks unto you; through Jesus Christ our Sovereign. Amen.

OR

Almighty and everlasting God, our Sovereign, who has safely brought me to the beginning of this day: defend me in the same with your mighty power; and grant that this day I fall into no sin, nor run into any kind of danger, but that all my doings, being ordered by your governance, may be righteous in your sight; through Jesus Christ our Savior. Amen.

Evening

(A lamp or candle may be lit. In early Christian worship lamps were lighted as a hymn of praise was sung to Christ, the radiant light.)

(If the lamp or candle is not used, devotions may begin with "O God, come to my aid . . .")

For the Lighting of Lamps

Jesus Christ is the light of the world.
The light shines in the deepest night,
    and the night did not overcome it.
Stay with me now, for it is evening,
    and the day is almost over.
Let your light disperse the shadows
    and shine within me here.

(The following hymn, the Phos Hilaron, may be said or sung. See page 213 for a musical setting.)

O holy radiance, joyous light,
    O splendid glory shining bright,
Immortal Father, heavenly One,
    O blessed Jesus Christ, the Sun:

We see the sunshine fade to night,
    and welcoming the evening light,
To Father, Son, and Spirit raise
    our hymns of wonder, love, and praise.

Unceasingly our tongues shall laud
    your worth, Begotten One of God,
O Breath of life; let all proclaim
    the glory of your wondrous name.

(If a lamp or candle is not lit, devotions may begin here.)

O God, come to my aid.
Hear my voice when I cry to you.

Psalm

(A psalm from the daily lectionary may be used, followed by a time of silence and meditation.)
(Additional readings may be used. A hymn may be used.)

Prayers

(Prayers may be said for oneself and for others, and prayers of thanksgiving for the day. If this is the final time of devotions for the day, the following confession may be said.)

Have mercy on me, O God, according to your steadfast love; according to your abundant mercy blot out my transgressions. Wash me thoroughly from my iniquity, and cleanse me from my sin. Amen.

OR

Merciful and eternal God, who is always more ready to hear than we to pray, and prepared to give more than we either desire or deserve, pour down upon us the abundance of your mercy, forgiving us those things of which our conscience is afraid, and giving us those good things which we are not worthy to ask, but through the merits and mediation of Jesus Christ, your Child, our Savior. Amen.

The Prayer of Our Savior

(One of the following versions or another version may be said.)

A

Our Father in heaven,
hallowed be your name,
your kingdom come,
your will be done,
on earth as in heaven.
Give us today our daily bread.
Forgive us our sins
as we forgive those who sin against us.
Save us from the time of trial
and deliver us from evil.
For the kingdom, the power,
and the glory are yours,
now and for ever. Amen.

B

Our Father-Mother, who is in the heavens,
may your name be made holy,
may your dominion come,
may your will be done,
on the earth as it is in heaven.
Give us today the bread we need;
and forgive us our debts,
as we have forgiven our debtors;
and do not put us to the test,
but rescue us from evil.
For yours is the dominion, and the
power, and the glory forever. Amen.

Collect

O God, support us all the day long, until the shadows lengthen and the evening comes, and the busy world is hushed, and the fever of life is over, and our work is done. Then in your mercy grant us a safe lodging, and a holy rest, and peace at the last, through Jesus Christ our Savior. Amen.

OR

Most holy God, the source of all good desires, all right judgments, and all just works: Give to us, your servants, that peace which the world cannot give, so that our minds may be fixed on the doing of your will, and that we, being delivered from the fear of all enemies, may live in peace and quietness; through the mercies of Christ Jesus our Savior. Amen.

Close of Day

Come, bless God, all you servants of God, who stand by night in the house of God! Lift up your hands to the holy place, and bless the Most High.

Psalm

(A psalm from the daily lectionary may be used, or Psalm 4 or 91, followed by a time of silence and meditation.)

(Additional readings may be used. A hymn may be used.)

Prayer

Have mercy on me, O God, according to your steadfast love; according to your abundant mercy blot out my transgressions. Wash me thoroughly from my iniquity, and cleanse me from my sin. Amen.

OR

O Sovereign God, bring us at our last awakening into the house and gate of heaven, to enter into that gate and dwell in that house, where there shall be no dimness nor dazzling, but one equal light; no voice nor silence, but one equal music; no fears nor hopes, but one equal possession; no ends nor beginnings, but one equal eternity; in the habitation of your glory and dominion, world without end. Amen.

(Prayers may be said for oneself and for others, and prayers of thanksgiving for the day.)

The Prayer of Our Savior

(One of the following versions or another version may be said.)

A

Our Father in heaven,
hallowed be your name,
your kingdom come,
your will be done,
on earth as in heaven.
Give us today our daily bread.
Forgive us our sins
as we forgive those who sin against us.
Save us from the time of trial
and deliver us from evil.
For the kingdom, the power,
and the glory are yours,
now and for ever. Amen.

B

Our Father-Mother, who is in the heavens,
may your name be made holy,
may your dominion come,
may your will be done,
on the earth as it is in heaven.
Give us today the bread we need;
and forgive us our debts,
as we have forgiven our debtors;
and do not put us to the test,
but rescue us from evil.
For yours is the dominion, and the
power, and the glory forever. Amen.

Collect

Be present, O merciful God, and protect me through the silent hours of this night, so that even though I am weary of the changes and chances of this fleeting world, I may rest upon your eternal changelessness; through Jesus Christ, our Savior. Amen.

Song of Trust

Antiphon (Response)
Save me when I am waking, and defend me when I am sleeping,
that when I awake I may watch with Christ,
and when I sleep I may rest in peace.

O God, now you are dismissing your servant in peace,
according to your word;
for my eyes have seen your salvation,
which you have prepared in the presence of all peoples,
a light for revelation to the Gentiles
and for glory to your people Israel.
(Repeat antiphon)

Antiphon (Response)
Save me when I am waking, and defend me when I am sleeping,
that when I awake I may watch with Christ,
and when I sleep I may rest in peace.

Psalms

Psalm 1

Response — *Antiphon: Judy Hunnicutt, 1994*

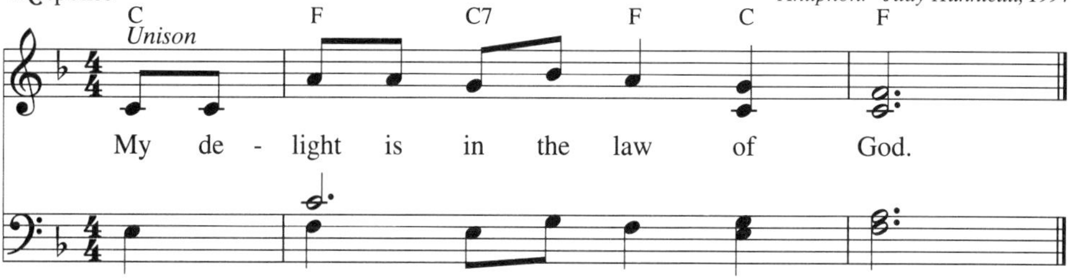

℟

[1]Happy are those who do not follow
the advice óf the wicked,
or take the path that sinners tread,
or sit in the śeat of scoffers;

[2]but their delight is in the ĺaw of God,
and on God's law they meditate dáy
and night.

[3]They are like trees planted by śtreams
of water,
which yield their fruit ín its season,

and their leaves dó not wither.
In all that they dó they prosper.

[4]The wicked áre not so,
but are like chaff that the wind
d́rives away.

[5]Therefore the wicked will not stand ín
the judgment,
nor sinners in the congregation óf
the righteous;

[6]for God watches over the way óf the
righteous,
but the way of the wićked will
perish. ℟

Psalm 2

Response — *Antiphon: Carolyn Jennings, 1994*

℟

[1]Why do the natíons conspire,
and the peoples ṕlot in vain?

[2]The rulers of the earth set themselves,
and the leaders take counśel together,

℟ Happy are all who take refuge in God.

against God and those God has
anointed, saying,

3 “Let us burst their bonds asunder,
and cast their cords from us.”

4 The one who sits in the heavens
laughs;
God has them in derision. ℟

5 Then God will speak to them in
wrath,
and terrify them in fury, saying,

6 “I have set my ruler on Zion,
my holy hill.”

7 I will tell of the decree of God:
God said to me, “You are my child;
today I have begotten you.

8 “Ask of me, and I will make the
nations your heritage,
and the ends of the earth your
possession. ℟

9 “You shall break them with a rod of
iron,
and dash them in pieces like a
potter's vessel.”

10 Now therefore, O rulers, be wise;
be warned, O leaders of the earth.

11 Serve God with fear, with trembling
12 kiss God's feet,
or God will be angry, and you will
perish in the way;

for God's wrath is quickly kindled.
Happy are all who take refuge in
God. ℟

(May be sung with double tone.)

Psalm 3

℟esponse

Antiphon: Marty Haugen, 1994

℟

1 O, how many are my foes!
Many are rising against me;

2 many are saying to me,
“There is no help for you in God.”

3 But you, O God, are a shield around me,
my glory, and the one who lifts up my
head.

4 I cry aloud to God
who answers me from the holy hill. ℟

5 I lie down and sleep;
I wake again, for God sustains me.

6 I am not afraid of ten thousands of people
who have set themselves against me all
around.

[7]Rise up, O God! Deliver me, Ó my God!
For you strike all my enemies on the cheek; you break the teeth óf the wicked.

[8]Deliverance belóngs to God;
may your blessing be ón your people! ℟

(May be sung with double tone.)

Psalm 4

℟esponse

Antiphon: *Peter Niedmann, 1994*

℟

[1]Answer me ẃhen I call,
O God óf my right!
You gave me room when I was ín distress.
Be gracious to me, and h́ear my prayer.

[2]How long, you people, shall my honor śuffer shame?
How long will you love vain words, and seek áfter lies?

[3]But kńow that God has set apart the faith́ful for God;
God hears ẃhen I call. ℟

[4]When you are disturbed, d́o not sin;
ponder it on your beds, ánd be silent.

[5]Offer right sacrifices, and put your t́rust in God.
[6]There are many who say, "O that we might śee some good!
Let the light of your face shine on ús, O God!"

[7]You have put gladness in my heart
more than when their grain and ẃine abound.

[8]I will both lie down and śleep in peace;
for you alone, O God, make me lie d́own in safety. ℟

(May be sung with double tone.)

Psalm 5

Response *Antiphon: Martie McMane, 1994*

R.

[1]Give ear to my words, O God;
give heed to my sighing.

[2]Listen to the sound of my cry,
my Sovereign and my God, for to you I pray.

[3]O God, in the morning you hear my voice;
in the morning I plead my case to you, and watch.

[4]For you are not a God who delights in wickedness;
evil will not sojourn with you. R.

[5]The boastful will not stand before your eyes;
you hate all evildoers.

[6]You destroy those who speak lies;
God abhors the bloodthirsty and deceitful.

[7]But I, through the abundance of your steadfast love, will enter your house,
I will bow down toward your holy temple in awe of you.

[8]Lead me, O God, in your righteousness because of my enemies;
make your way straight before me. R.

[9]For there is no truth in their mouths;
their hearts are destruction;

their throats are open graves;
they flatter with their tongues.

[10]Make them bear their guilt, O God;
let them fall by their own counsels;

because of their many transgressions cast them out,
for they have rebelled against you. R.

[11]But let all who take refuge in you rejoice;
let them ever sing for joy.

Spread your protection over them,
so that those who love your name may exult in you.

[12]For you bless the righteous, O God;
you cover them with favor as with a shield. R.

(Unbracketed verses may be sung with double tone.)

Psalm 6

Response

Antiphon: Robert Fryson, 1994

℟

1 O God, do not rebuke me in your anger,
or discipline me in your wrath.

2 Be gracious to me, O God, for I am languishing;
O God, heal me, for my bones are shaking with terror.

3 My soul also is struck with terror,
while you, O God—how long?

4 Turn, O God, save my life;
deliver me for the sake of your steadfast love.

5 For in death there is no remembrance of you;
in Sheol who can give you praise? ℟

6 I am weary with my moaning;
every night I flood my bed with tears;
I drench my couch with my weeping.

7 My eyes waste away because of grief;
they grow weak because of all my foes.

8 Depart from me, all you workers of evil,
for God has heard the sound of my weeping.

9 God has heard my supplication;
God accepts my prayer.

10 All my enemies shall be ashamed and struck with terror;
they shall turn back, and in a moment be put to shame. ℟

Psalm 7

Antiphon: Marty Haugen, 1994

Response

℟

1 O God my God, in you I take refuge;
save me from all my pursuers, and deliver me,

2 or like a lion they will tear me apart;
they will drag me away, with no one to rescue.

3 O God my God, if I have done this,
if there is wrong in my hands,

4 if I have repaid my ally with harm
or plundered my foe without cause, ℟

5 then let the enemy pursue and overtake me,
trample my life to the ground, and lay my soul in the dust.

6 Rise up, O God, in your anger;
lift yourself up against the fury of my enemies;

awake, O my God;
you have appointed a judgment.

7 Let the assembly of the peoples be gathered around you,
and over it take your seat on high. ℟

8 God judges the peoples;
judge me, O God, according to my righteousness and according to the integrity that is in me.

9 O let the evil of the wicked come to an end,
but establish the righteous, you who test the minds and hearts, O righteous God.

10 God, who saves the upright in heart, is my shield.
11 God is a righteous judge, and a God who has indignation every day.

12 If one does not repent,
God will sharpen the sword; ℟

God has bent and strung the bow,
13 and has prepared deadly weapons, making arrows into fiery shafts.

14 See how people conceive evil, and are pregnant with mischief, and bring forth lies.
15 They make a pit, digging it out, and fall into the hole that they have made.

16 Their mischief returns upon their own heads,
and on their own heads their violence descends.

17 I will give to God the thanks due to God's righteousness,
and sing praise to the name of God, the Most High. ℟

(May be sung with double tone.)

Psalm 8

℟esponse

Antiphon: Lee Dengler, 1994

℟

1 O God, our Sovereign, how majestic
is your name in all the earth!
You have set your glory above the heavens.

2 Out of the mouths of babes and
infants you have founded a bulwark
because of your foes,
to silence the enemy and the avenger.

3When I look at your heavens, the work of your fingers,
the moon and the stars that you have established;

4what are human beings that you are mindful of them,
mortals that you care for them? ℟

5Yet you have made them a little lower than God,
and crowned them with glory and honor.

6You have given them dominion over the works of your hands;
you have put all things under their feet,

7all sheep and oxen, and also the beasts of the field,
8the birds of the air, and the fish of the sea, whatever passes along the paths of the seas.

9O God, our Sovereign,
how majestic is your name in all the earth! ℟

(May be sung with double tone.)

Psalm 9

℟esponse

Antiphon: Elaine Kirkland, 1994

1I will give thanks to God with my whole heart;
I will tell of all your wonderful deeds.

2I will be glad and exult in you;
I will sing praise to your name, O Most High.

3When my enemies turned back,
they stumbled and perished before you.

4For you have maintained my just cause;
you have sat on the throne giving righteous judgment.

5You have rebuked the nations and destroyed the wicked;
you have blotted out their name forever and ever.

6The enemies have vanished in everlasting ruins; their cities you have rooted out;
the very memory of them has perished.

7But God sits enthroned forever,
and has established God's throne for judgment.

8God judges the world with righteousness,
and God judges the peoples with equity.

℟

9God is a stronghold for the oppressed,
a stronghold in times of trouble.

10And those who know your name put their trust in you,
for you, O God, have not forsaken those who seek you.

11Sing praises to God, who dwells in Zion.
Declare God's deeds among the peoples.

12For God who avenges blood is mindful of them;
God does not forget the cry of the afflicted. ℟

13Be gracious to me, O God.
See what I suffer from those who hate me;

you are the one who lifts me up from the gates of death,
14so that I may recount all your praises, and, in the gates of daughter Zion, rejoice in your deliverance.

15The nations have sunk in the pit that they have made;
in the net that they hid has their own foot been caught.

16God has made God known,
God has executed judgment; the wicked are snared in the work of their own hands. ℟

17The wicked shall depart to Sheol,
all the nations that forget God.

18For the needy shall not always be forgotten,
nor the hope of the poor perish forever.

19Rise up, O God! Do not let mortals prevail;
let the nations be judged before you.

20Put them in fear, O God;
let the nations know that they are only human. ℟

(May be sung with double tone.)

Psalm 10

Response *Antiphon: Da id Hurd, 1994*

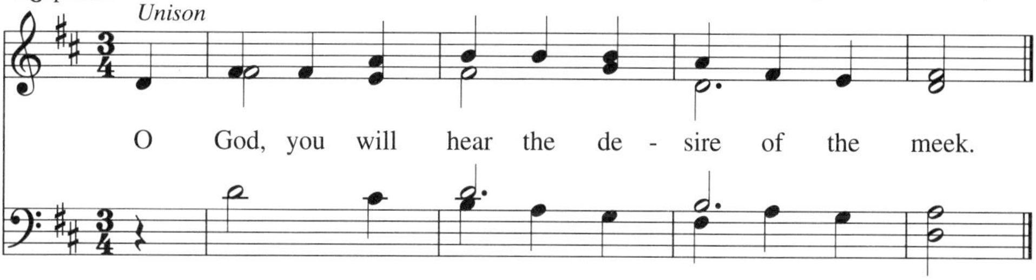

℟

1 Why, O God, do you stand far off?
Why do you hide yourself in times of trouble?

2 In arrogance the wicked persecute the poor—
let them be caught in the schemes they have devised.

3 For the wicked boast of the desires of their heart,
those greedy for gain curse and renounce God.

4 In the pride of their countenance the wicked say, "God will not seek us out";
all their thoughts are, "There is no God." ℟

5 Their ways prosper at all times; your judgments are on high, out of their sight;
as for their foes, the wicked scoff at them.

6 They think in their heart, "We shall not be moved;
throughout all generations we shall not meet adversity."

7 Their mouths are filled with cursing and deceit and oppression;
under their tongues are mischief and iniquity.

8 They sit in ambush in the villages;
in hiding places they murder the innocent. ℟

Their eyes stealthily watch for the helpless;
9 they lurk in secret like a lion in its lair;

they lurk that they may seize the poor;
they seize the poor and drag them off in their net.

10 They stoop, they crouch, and the helpless fall by their might.
11 They think in their heart, "God has forgotten, has looked away, and will never see it."

12 Rise up, O God; O God, lift up your hand;
do not forget the oppressed. ℟

13 Why do the wicked renounce God,
and say in their hearts, "You will not call us to account"?

14 But you do see! Indeed you note trouble and grief,
that you may take it into your hands;

the helpless commit themselves to you;
you have been the helper of the orphan.

15 Break the arm of the wicked and evildoers;
seek out their wickedness until you find no more.

16 God is sovereign forever and ever;
the nations shall perish from the land of God.

℟ O God, you will hear the desire of the meek.

17 O God, you will hear the desire of the meek;
you will strengthen their heart,
you will incline your ear 18 to do justice for the orphan and the oppressed,
so that those from earth may strike terror no more. ℟

Psalm 11

℟esponse

Antiphon: Carolyn Jennings, 1994

℟

1 In God I take refuge;
how can you say to me, "Flee like a bird to the mountains;

2 for look, the wicked bend the bow, they have fitted their arrow to the string,
to shoot in the night at the upright in heart.

3 If the foundations are destroyed,
what can the righteous do?"

4 God is in God's holy temple;
God's throne is in heaven. ℟

God's eyes behold,
the gaze of God examines humankind.

5 God tests the righteous and the wicked,
and the soul of God hates the lover of violence.

6 God will rain coals of fire and sulfur on the wicked;
a scorching wind shall be the portion of their cup.

7 For God is righteous, and loves righteous deeds;
the upright shall behold the face of God. ℟

(May be sung with double tone.)

Psalm 12

Response *Antiphon: Emma Lou Diemer, 1994*

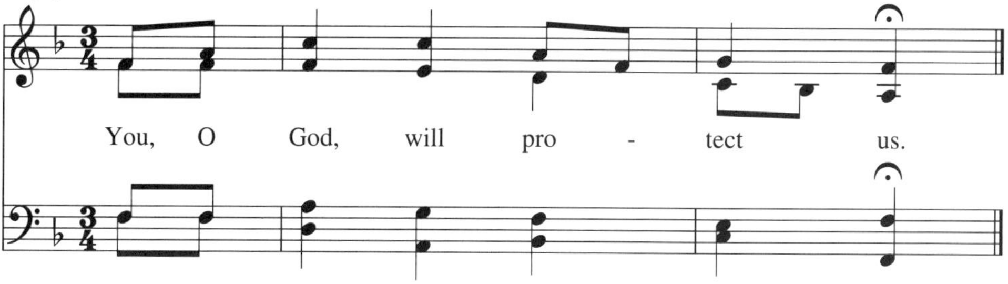

R

[1]Help, O God, for there is no longer anyone who is godly;
the faithful have disappeared from humankind.

[2]They utter lies to each other;
they speak with flattering lips and a double heart.

[3]May God cut off all flattering lips,
the tongue that makes great boasts—

[4]those who say, "With our tongues we will prevail;
our lips are our own—who is our master?" R

[5]God says, "Because the poor are despoiled, because the needy groan, I will now rise up";
"I will place them in the safety for which they long."

[6]The promises of God are promises that are pure,
silver refined in a furnace on the ground, purified seven times.

[7]You, O God, will protect us;
you will guard us from this generation forever.

[8]On every side the wicked prowl,
as vileness is exalted among humankind. R

(May be sung with double tone.)

Psalm 13

Response *Antiphon: Da id Hurd, 1994*

[1]How long, O God? Will you forget me forever?
How long will you hide your face from me?

[2]How long must I bear pain in my soul, and have sorrow in my heart all day long?

℟ Consider and answer me, O God, my God!

How long shall my enemy be
exalted over me?

[3]Consider and answer me, O God, my God!
Give light to my eyes, or I will sleep the sleep of death,

[4]and my enemy will say, "I have prevailed";
my foes will rejoice because I am shaken.

[5]But I trusted in your steadfast love;
my heart shall rejoice in your salvation.

[6]I will sing to God,
because God has dealt bountifully with me. ℟

Psalm 14

℟esponse

Antiphon: Hyeon Jeong, 1994

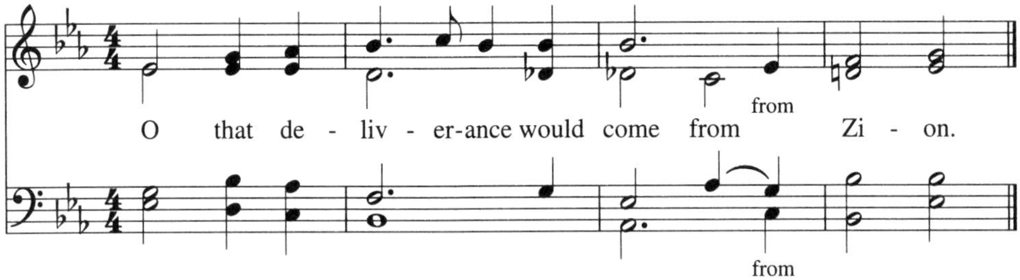

℟

[1]Fools say in their hearts, "There is no God."
They are corrupt, they do abominable deeds; there is no one who does good.

[2]God looks down from heaven on humankind
to see if there are any who are wise, who seek after God.

[3]They have all gone astray, they are all alike perverse;
there is no one who does good, no, not one.

[4]Have they no knowledge, all the evildoers who eat up my people as they eat bread,
and do not call upon God? ℟

[5]There they shall be in great terror,
for God is with the company of the righteous.

[6]You would confound the plans of the poor,
but God is their refuge.

[7]O that deliverance for Israel
would come from Zion!

When God restores the fortunes of God's people,
Jacob will rejoice; Israel will be glad. ℟

(May be sung with double tone.)

Psalm 15

Response

Antiphon: Emma Lou Diemer, 1994

℟

[1]O God, who may abide in your tent?
Who may dwell on your holy hill?

[2]Those who walk blamelessly,
and do what is right,

who speak the truth from their heart,
[3]and do not slander with their tongue,

who do no evil to their friends,
nor take up a reproach against their neighbors; ℟

[4]in whose eyes the wicked are despised,
but who honor those who fear God;

who stand by their oath
even to their hurt;

[5]who do not lend money at interest,
and do not take a bribe against the innocent.

Those who do these things
shall never be moved. ℟

(May be sung with double tone.)

Psalm 16

Response

Antiphon: Carolyn Jennings, 1994

[1]Protect me, O God,
for in you I take refuge.

[2]I say to God, "You are my God;
I have no good apart from you."

[3]As for the holy ones in the land,
they are the noble, in whom is all my delight.

[4]Those who choose another god
multiply their sorrows; ℟

℟ In your right hand are pleasures forevermore.

their drink offerings of blood I will not pour out
or take their names upon my lips.

5 God is my chosen portion and my cup;
you hold my lot.

6 The boundary lines have fallen for me in pleasant places;
I have a goodly heritage.

7 I bless God who gives me counsel;
in the night also my heart instructs me. ℟

8 I keep God always before me;
because God is at my right hand,
I shall not be moved.

9 Therefore my heart is glad, and my soul rejoices;
my body also rests secure.

10 For you do not give me up to Sheol,
or let your faithful one see the Pit.

11 You show me the path of life. In your presence there is fullness of joy;
in your right hand are pleasures forevermore. ℟

(May be sung with double tone.)

Psalm 17

℟esponse

Antiphon: Jane Marshall, 1994

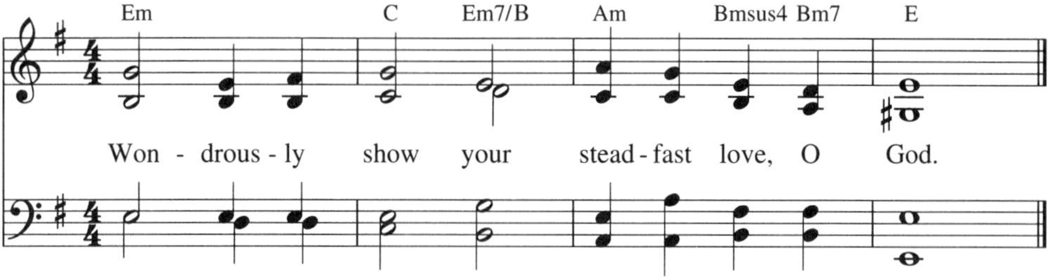

℟

1 Hear a just cause, O God; attend to my cry;
give ear to my prayer from lips free of deceit.

2 From you let my vindication come;
let your eyes see the right.

3 If you try my heart, if you visit me by night, if you test me, you will find no wickedness in me;
my mouth does not transgress.

4 As for what others do,
by the word of your lips I have avoided the ways of the violent.

℟

5 My steps have held fast to your paths;
my feet have not slipped.

6 I call upon you, for you will answer me, O God;
incline your ear to me, hear my words.

7 Wondrously show your steadfast love,
O savior of those who seek refuge from their adversaries at your mighty hand.

8 Guard me as the apple of the eye; hide me in the shadow of your wings,
9 from the wicked who despoil me,
my deadly enemies who surround me.

10 They close their hearts to pity;
with their mouths they speak arrogantly.

11 They track me down; now they surround me;
they set their eyes to cast me to the ground.

12 They are like a lion eager to tear,
like a young lion lurking in ambush. ℟

13 Rise up, O God, confront them, overthrow them!
By your sword deliver my life from the wicked;

14 by your hand, O God, deliver me from mortals,
from mortals whose portion in life is in this world.

May their bellies be filled with what you have stored up for them;
may their children have more than enough; may they leave a surplus for their little ones.

15 As for me, I shall behold your face in righteousness;
when I awake I shall be satisfied, beholding your likeness. ℟

Proper 13 [18] A vs. 1–7, 15; Proper 27 [32] C vs. 1–9.

℟

Psalm 18

Antiphon: Emma Lou Diemer, 1994

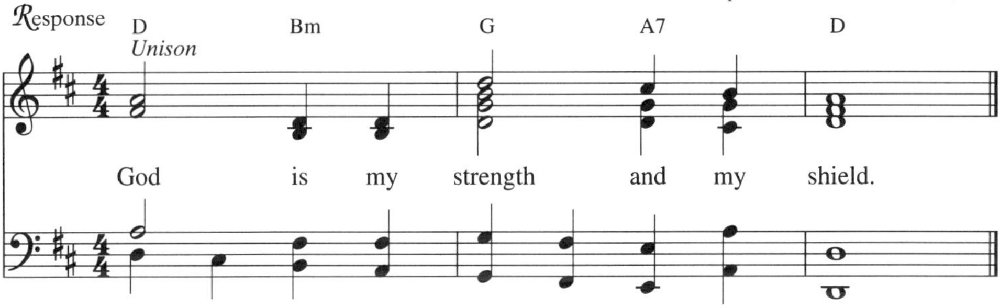

℟

1 I love you, O God, my strength.
2 my rock, my fortress, and my deliverer.

God is my rock in whom I take refuge,
my shield, and the horn of my salvation, my stronghold.

3 I call upon God, who is worthy to be praised,
so I shall be saved from my enemies.

4 The cords of death encompassed me;
the torrents of perdition assailed me;

5 the cords of Sheol entangled me;
the snares of death confronted me. ℟

6 I called upon God in my distress;
to my God I cried for help.

God heard my voice from the temple,
and my cry reached the ears of God.

7 Then the earth reeled and rocked;
the foundations also of the mountains trembled and quaked, because of God's anger.

8 Smoke came from God's nostrils, and devouring fire from God's mouth;
glowing coals flamed forth from God.

9 God bent the heavens, and came down,
with thick darkness beneath the feet. ℟

℟. God is my strength and my shield.

10God rode on a cherúb, and flew,
coming swiftly on the wings óf the wind.

11God made the níght a covering,
and clouds of water fór a canopy.

12Out of the brightness that went befóre God,
hailstones and coals of fire broke thróugh the clouds.

13God also thundered ín the heavens,
and the voice of the Most Hígh broke forth.

14God sent out arrows, and scáttered them;
God flashed forth lightníngs, and routed them. ℟.

15Then the channels of the sea were seen, at your rebuke the foundations of the wórld laid bare
at the blast of the breath of your nostríls, O God.

16God reached down from on hígh and took me;
God drew me out of míghty waters.

17God delivered me from my strong enemy, and from thóse who hated me;
for they were too mightý for me.

18They confronted me in the day of mý calamity;
but God was mý support.

19God brought me out into á broad place;
and delighting in me, Gód delivered me. ℟.

20God rewarded me according tó my righteousness,
and recompensed me according to the cleanness óf my hands.

21For I have képt God's ways,
and have not wickedly departed fróm my God.

22For all God's ordinances wére before me,
and God's statutes I did dísobey.

23I was blameless befóre God,
and kept mysélf from guilt.

24Therefore God has repaid me according tó my righteousness,
according to the cleanness óf my hands. ℟.

25With the loyal you show yóurself loyal;
with the blameless you show yóurself blameless;

26with the pure you show yóurself pure;
and with the crooked you show yoursélf perverse.

27For you deliver a húmble people,
but the haughty eyes yóu bring down.

28It is you who líght my lamp;
God, my God, illumínes my night.

29By you I can crúsh an army,
and by my God I can leap óver a wall.

30The way of this God is perfect; the promise of this Gód proves true;
God is a shield for all who take refúge in God. ℟.

31For who is God except the Most High?
Who is a rock besídes our God—
32the God who girded me with strength, and made mý way safe,

33who made my feet like the feet óf a deer,
and set me secure ón the heights?

34God trains my hánds for war,
so that my arms can bend a bów of bronze.

℟ *God is my strength and my shield.*

35 You have given me the shield of your
salvation,
and your strong hand has supported
me; your help has made me great.

36 You gave me a wide place for my steps,
and my feet did not slip. ℟

37 I pursued my enemies and overtook
them;
and did not turn back until they were
consumed.

38 I struck them down, so that they were
not able to rise;
they fell under my feet.

39 For you girded me with strength for the
battle;
you made my assailants sink under me.

40 You made my enemies turn their backs
to me,
and those who hated me I destroyed. ℟

41 They cried for help, but there was no
one to save them;
they cried to God, but God did not
answer them.

42 I beat them as fine as dust before the
wind;
I cast them out like the mire of the
streets.

43 You delivered me from strife with the
peoples; you made me head of the
nations;
people whom I had not known served
me.

44 As soon as they heard of me they
obeyed me;
foreigners came cringing to me.

45 Foreigners lost heart,
and came trembling out of their
strongholds. ℟

46 God lives! Blessed be my rock,
and exalted be the God of my
salvation,

47 the God who gave me vengeance and
subdued peoples under me;
48 who delivered me from my enemies;

indeed, you exalted me above my
adversaries;
you delivered me from the violent.

49 For this I will extol you, O God, among
the nations,
and sing praises to your name.

50 Great triumphs you give to your king,
and show steadfast love to your
anointed, to David and his descendants
forever. ℟

Proper 21 [26] B vs. 7–14.

Psalm 19

℟esponse *Antiphon: Jean Slates Hawk, 1994*

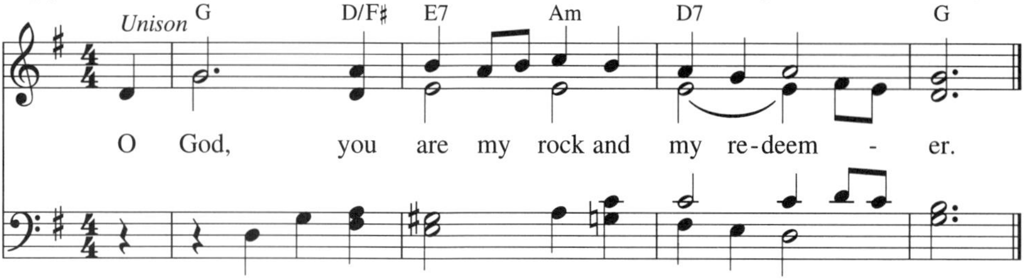

1 The heavens are telling the glory of God;
and the firmament proclaims God's handiwork.

2 Day to day pours forth speech,
and night to night declares knowledge.

3 There is no speech, nor are there words;
their voice is not heard;

4 yet their voice goes out through all the earth,
and their words to the end of the world.

In the heavens God has set a tent for the sun,
5 which comes out like a beloved from a wedding canopy, and like an athlete runs its course with joy.

6 Its rising is from the end of the heavens,
and its circuit to the end of them,
and nothing is hid from its heat. ℟

7 The law of God is perfect, reviving the soul;
the decrees of God are sure, making wise the simple;

8 the precepts of God are right, rejoicing the heart;
the commandment of God is clear, enlightening the eyes;

9 the fear of God is pure, enduring forever;
the ordinances of God are true and righteous altogether.

10 More to be desired are they than gold, even much fine gold;
sweeter also than honey, and drippings of the honeycomb.

11 Moreover by them is your servant warned;
in keeping them there is great reward.

12 But who can detect their errors?
Clear me from hidden faults.

13 Keep back your servant also from the insolent;
do not let them have dominion over me.

Then I shall be blameless,
and innocent of great transgression.

14 Let the words of my mouth and the meditation of my heart be acceptable to you,
O God, my rock and my redeemer.
℟

Proper 21 [26] B vs. 7–14.

Psalm 20

℟esponse

Antiphon: Vérne de la Peña, 1994

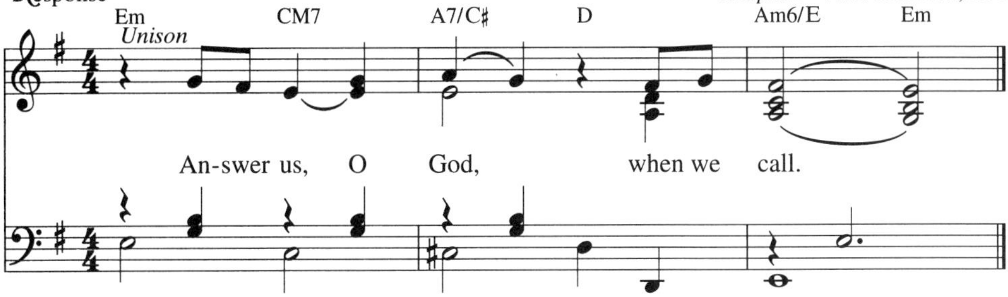

[1]May God answer you in the day of trouble!
The name of the God of Jacob protect you!

[2]May God send you help from the sanctuary,
and give you support from Zion.

[3]May God remember all your offerings,
and regard with favor your burnt sacrifices.

[4]May God grant you your heart's desire,
and fulfill all your plans. ℟

[5]May we shout for joy over your victory, and in the name of our God set up our banners.
May God fulfill all your petitions.

[6]Now I know that God will help God's anointed,
and will answer them from God's holy heaven with mighty victories by God's strong hand.

[7]Some take pride in chariots, and some in horses,
but our pride is in the name of the Sovereign our God.

[8]They will collapse and fall, but we shall rise and stand upright.
[9]Give victory to the ruler, O God;
answer us when we call. ℟

(May be sung with double tone.)

Psalm 21

Response

Antiphon: Judy Hunnicutt, 1994

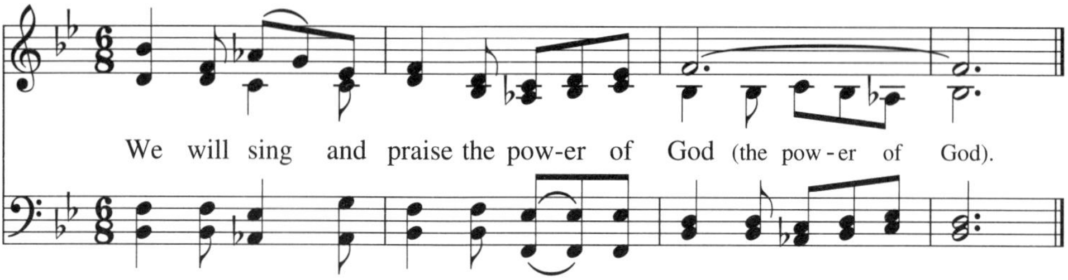

R

1 In your strength, O God, the ruler
rejoices,
and greatly exults in your help!

2 You have satisfied the desire of the
ruler's heart,
and have not withheld the request of
the ruler's lips.

3 For you meet the ruler with rich blessings,
and set a crown of fine gold on the
ruler's head.

4 The ruler asked you for life, and you
gave it—
length of days forever and ever. R

5 Through your help, great is the ruler's
glory,
upon whose head you bestow splendor
and majesty.

6 You bestow on the ruler blessings
forever;
you make the ruler glad with the joy of
your presence.

7 For the ruler trusts in God,
and through the steadfast love of the
Most High shall not be moved. R

8 Your hand will find out all your enemies;
your strong hand will find out those
who hate you.

9 You will make them like a fiery furnace
when you appear.
God will swallow them up in wrath,
and fire will consume them.

10 You will destroy their offspring from
the earth,
and their children from among
humankind.

11 If they plan evil against you,
if they devise mischief, they will not
succeed.

12 For you will put them to flight;
you will aim at their faces with your
bows.

13 Be exalted, O God, in your strength!
We will sing and praise your power. R

Psalm 22

Antiphon: Marty Haugen, 1994

℟esponse

℟

1 My God, my God, why have ýou forsaken me?
Why are you so far from helping me, from the words óf my groaning?

2 O my God, I cry by day, but you dó not answer;
and by night, but f́ind no rest.

3 Yet you are holy, enthroned on the praisés of Israel.
4 In you our ancestors trusted; they trusted, and ýou delivered them.

5 To you they cried, ánd were saved;
in you they trusted, and were not ṕut to shame. ℟

6 But I am a worm, ánd not human;
scorned by others, and despised b́y the people.

7 All who śee me mock at me;
they make mouths at me, they śhake their heads;

8 "Commit your ćause to God;
let God deliver—let God rescue the one in whom Ǵod delights!" ℟

9 Yet it was you who took me f́rom the womb;
you kept me safe on my ḿother's breast.

10 On you I was cast f́rom my birth,
and since my mother bore me you have b́een my God.

11 Do not be f́ar from me,
for trouble is near and there is no óne to help.

12 Many bulls encircle me, strong bulls of Baśhan surround me;
13 they open wide their mouths at me, like a ravening and ŕoaring lion.

14 I am poured out like water, and all my bones are óut of joint;
my heart is like wax; it is melted withín my breast;

15 my mouth is dried up ĺike a potsherd,
and my tongue sticks to my jaws;
you lay me in the dúst of death. ℟

16 For dogs are áll around me;
a company of evildoérs encircles me.

My hands and f́eet have shriveled;
17 I can count áll my bones.

18 They stare and gloat óver me;
they divide my clothes among themselves, and for my clothing t́hey cast lots.

19 O God, do not be f́ar away!
O my help, come quickly t́o my aid!

℟ O God, do not be far away; O God, do not be far away.

[20]Deliver my soul from the sword,
my life from the power of the dog!

[21]Save me from the mouth of the lion!
From the horns of the wild oxen
you have rescued me.

[22]I will tell of your name to my
brothers and sisters;
in the midst of the congregation
I will praise you: ℟

[23]You who fear God, praise God!
All you offspring of Jacob, glorify
God;

stand in awe of God,
all you offspring of Israel!

[24]For God did not despise or abhor
the affliction of the afflicted;
God did not hide God's face from
me, but heard when I cried to God.
℟

[25]From you comes my praise in the
great congregation;
my vows I will pay before those
who fear God.

[26]The poor shall eat and be satisfied;
those who seek God shall praise
God. May your hearts live forever!

[27]All the ends of the earth shall
remember and turn to God;
and all the families of the nations
shall worship before God.

[28]For dominion belongs to God,
and God rules over the nations. ℟

[29]To God, indeed, shall all who sleep in
the earth bow down;
before God shall bow all who go
down to the dust, and I shall live
for God.

[30]Posterity will serve God;
future generations will be told
about God,

[31]and proclaim God's deliverance to a
people yet unborn,
saying that God has done it. ℟

Good Friday ABC, the entire Psalm; Lent 2 B vs. 23–31; Easter 5 B vs. 25–31; Proper 23 [28] B vs. 1–15; Proper 7 [12] C vs. 19–28.

Psalm 23

℟esponse

Antiphon: Carolyn Jennings, 1994

[1]God is my shepherd, I shall not want.
[2]God makes me lie down in green
pastures, and leads me beside still
waters;

[3]God restores my soul,
and leads me in right paths for the
sake of God's name.

4Even though I walk through the darkest valley, I fear no evil;
for you are with me; your rod and your staff—they comfort me.

5You prepare a table before me in the presence of my enemies;
you anoint my head with oil; my cup overflows.

6Surely goodness and mercy shall follow me all the days of my life,
and I shall dwell in the house of God my whole life long. ℟

Psalm 24

Antiphon: Peter Niedmann, 1994

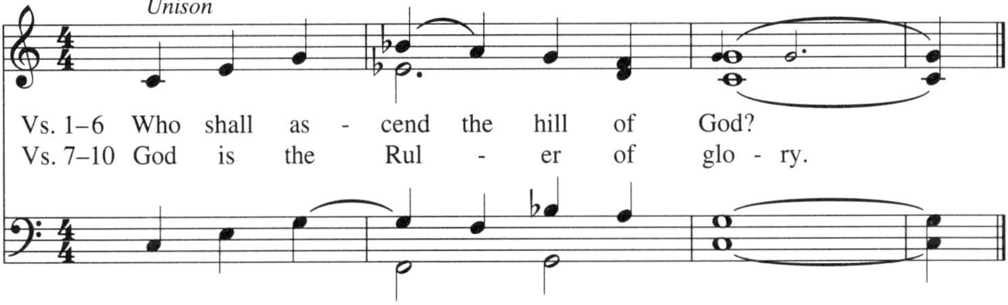

℟

1The earth is God's and all that is in it,
the world, and those who live in it;

2for God has founded it on the seas,
and established it on the rivers.

3Who shall ascend the hill of God?
And who shall stand in God's holy place?

4Those who have clean hands and pure hearts,
who do not lift up their souls to what is false, and do not swear deceitfully.

5They will receive blessing from God,
and vindication from the God of their salvation.

6Such is the company of those who seek God,
who seek the face of the God of Jacob. ℟

7Lift up your heads, O gates! and be lifted up, O ancient doors!
that the Ruler of glory may come in.

8Who is the Ruler of glory?
God, strong and mighty, God, mighty in battle.

9Lift up your heads, O gates! and be lifted up, O ancient doors!
that the Ruler of glory may come in.

10Who is this Ruler of glory?
The Sovereign of hosts—God is the Ruler of glory. ℟

Presentation ABC vs. 7–10 (Alt.).

Psalm 25

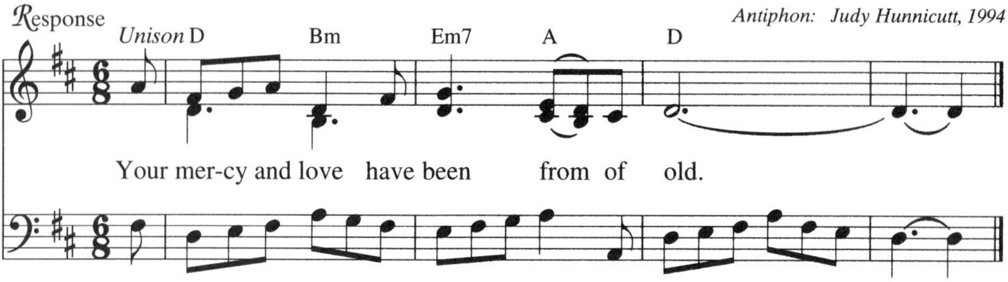

℟

1 To you, O God,
I lift up my soul.

2 O my God, in you I trust; do not let me be put to shame;
do not let my enemies exult over me.

3 Do not let those who wait for you be put to shame;
let them be ashamed who are wantonly treacherous.

4 Make me to know your ways, O God;
teach me your paths. ℟

5 Lead me in your truth, and teach me, for you are the God of my salvation;
for you I wait all day long.

6 Be mindful of your mercy, O God, and of your steadfast love,
for they have been from of old.

7 Do not remember the sins of my youth
or my transgressions;

according to your steadfast love remember me,
for your goodness' sake, O God! ℟

8 Good and upright is God;
therefore God instructs sinners in the way.

9 God leads the humble in what is right,
and teaches the humble God's way.

10 All the paths of God are steadfast love and faithfulness,
for those who keep God's covenant and God's decrees. ℟

11 For your name's sake, O God,
pardon my guilt, for it is great.

12 Who are they that fear God?
God will teach them the way that they should choose.

13 They will abide in prosperity,
and their children shall possess the land.

14 The friendship of God is for those who fear God,
who makes the covenant known to them.

15 My eyes are ever toward God,
for God will pluck my feet out of the net. ℟

16 Turn to me and be gracious to me,
for I am lonely and afflicted.

17 Relieve the troubles of my heart,
and bring me out of my distress.

18 Consider my affliction and my trouble,
and forgive all my sins.

19 Consider how many are my foes,
and with what violent hatred they hate me.

20 O guard my life, and deliver me;
do not let me be put to shame, for I take refuge in you.

21 May integrity and uprightness preserve me, for I wait for you.
22 Redeem Israel, O God, out of all its troubles. ℟

Proper 21 [26] A vs. 1–9.

Psalm 26

℟esponse *Antiphon: Elaine Kirkland, 1994*

℟

1 Vindicate me, O God, for I have walked in my integrity,
and I have trusted in God without wavering.

2 Prove me, O God, and try me;
test my heart and mind.

3 For your steadfast love is before my eyes,
and I walk in faithfulness to you.

4 I do not sit with the worthless,
nor do I consort with hypocrites; ℟

5 I hate the company of evildoers,
and will not sit with the wicked.

6 I wash my hands in innocence,
and go around your altar, O God,

7 singing aloud a song of thanksgiving,
and telling all your wondrous deeds.

8 O God, I love the house in which you dwell,
and the place where your glory abides. ℟

9 Do not sweep me away with sinners,
nor my life with the bloodthirsty,

10 those in whose hands are evil devices,
and whose right hands are full of bribes.

11 But as for me, I walk in my integrity;
redeem me, and be gracious to me.

12 My foot stands on level ground;
in the great congregation I will bless God. ℟

Proper 17 [22] A vs. 1–8. (May be sung with double tone.)

Psalm 27

Response

Antiphon: Lee Dengler, 1994

R

1 God is my light and my salvation;
whom shall I fear?
God is the stronghold of my life; of
whom shall I be afraid?

2 When evildoers assail me to devour
my flesh—
my adversaries and foes—they
shall stumble and fall.

3 Though an army encamp against me,
my heart shall not fear.
Though war rise up against me, yet
I will be confident.

4 One thing I asked of God, that will
I seek after:
to live in the house of God all the
days of my life, R

to behold the beauty of God, and to
inquire in God's temple.
5 For God will hide me in God's
shelter in the day of trouble;

God will conceal me under the cover
of God's tent;
God will set me high on a rock.

6 Now my head is lifted up above my
enemies all around me,
and I will offer in God's tent
sacrifices with shouts of joy;

I will sing and make melody to God.

7 Hear, O God, when I cry aloud, be
gracious to me and answer me! R

8 "Come," my heart says, "seek God's
face!"
Your face, O God, do I seek.

9 Do not hide your face from me.
Do not turn your servant away in
anger, you who have been my help.

Do not cast me off, do not forsake
me,
O God of my salvation!

10 If my father and mother forsake me,
God will take me up. R

11 Teach me your way, O God,
and lead me on a level path because
of my enemies.

12 Do not give me up to the will of my
adversaries, for false witnesses have
risen against me,
and they are breathing out violence.

13 I believe that I shall see the goodness
of God
in the land of the living.

14 Wait for God, be strong;
let your heart take courage, wait for
God! R

Epiphany 3 [3] A vs. 1, 4–9.

(May be sung with double tone.)

Psalm 28

℟esponse

Antiphon: Emma Lou Diemer, 1994

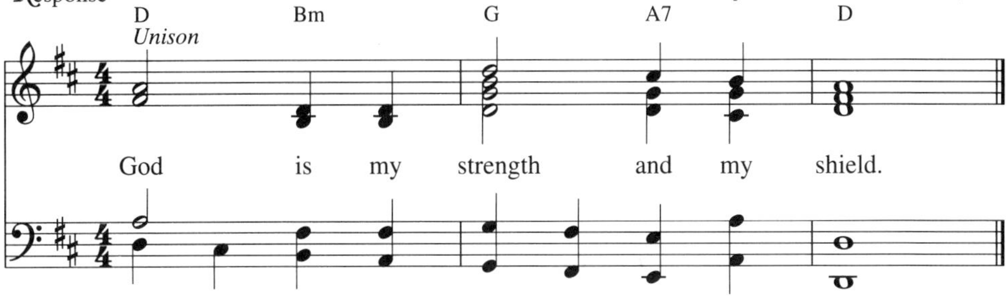

℟

1 To you, O God, I call;
my rock, do not refuse to hear me,

for if you are silent to me,
I shall be like those who go down to the Pit.

2 Hear the voice of my supplication, as I cry to you for help,
as I lift up my hands toward your most holy sanctuary.

3 Do not drag me away with the wicked,
with those who are workers of evil,
who speak peace with their neighbors,
while mischief is in their hearts. ℟

4 Repay them according to their work,
and according to the evil of their deeds;

repay them according to the work of their hands;
render them their due reward.

5 Because they do not regard the works of God, or what God's hands have done,
God will break them down and build them up no more.

6 Blessed be God,
for God has heard the sound of my pleadings. ℟

7 God is my strength and my shield;
my heart trusts in God;

so I am helped, and my heart exults,
and with my song I give God thanks.

8 The God is the strength of God's people,
the saving refuge of God's anointed.

9 O save your people, and bless your heritage;
be their shepherd, and carry them forever. ℟

(May be sung with double tone.)

Psalm 29

℟esponse

Antiphon: Da id Hurd, 1994

℟

[1]Ascribe to God, O heav́enly beings,
ascribe to God glóry and strength.

[2]Ascribe to God the glory óf God's
name;
worship God in hóly splendor.

[3]The voice of God is óver the waters;
the God of glory thunders, God,
over míghty waters.

[4]The voice of Gód is powerful;
the voice of God is fúll of majesty.
℟

[5]The voice of God b́reaks the cedars;
God breaks the ced́ars of Lebanon.

[6]God makes Lebanon skip líke a calf,
and Sirion like a ýoung wild ox.

[7]The voice of God f́lashes forth
in f́lames of fire.

[8]The voice of God śhakes the
wilderness;
God shakes the wilderńess of
Kadesh. ℟

[9]The voice of God causes the oaks to
whirl, and strips the f́orest bare;
and in God's temple áll say,
"Glory!"

[10]God sits enthroned óver the flood;
God sits enthroned as rulér forever.

[11]May God give strength t́o the people!
May God bless the peoṕle with
peace! ℟

Psalm 30

℟esponse

Antiphon: Martie McMane, 1994

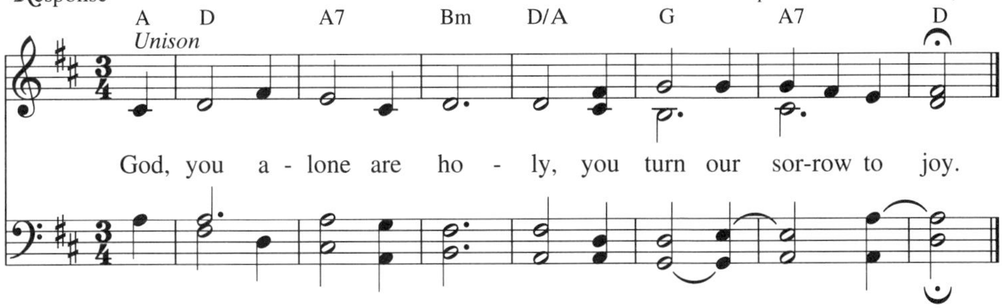

℟

[1]I will extol you, O God, for you have drawn me up,
and did not let my foes rejoice over me.

[2]O God, my God, I cried to you for help,
and you have healed me.

[3]O God, you brought up my soul from Sheol,
restored me to life from among those gone down to the Pit.

[4]Sing praises to God, O you God's faithful ones,
and give thanks to God's holy name. ℟

[5]For God's anger is but for a moment; God's favor is for a lifetime.
Weeping may linger for the night, but joy comes with the morning.

[6]As for me, I said in my prosperity,
"I shall never be moved."

[7]By your favor, O God, you had established me as a strong mountain;
you hid your face; I was dismayed.

[8]To you, O God, I cried,
and to you I made supplication: ℟

[9]"What profit is there in my death, if I go down to the Pit?
Will the dust praise you? Will it tell of your faithfulness?

[10]"Hear, O God, and be gracious to me!
O God, be my helper!"

[11]You have turned my mourning into dancing;
you have taken off my sackcloth and clothed me with joy,

[12]so that my soul may praise you and not be silent.
O God, my God, I will give thanks to you forever. ℟

(May be sung with double tone.)

Psalm 31a

℟esponse

Antiphon: Robert Train Adams, 1994

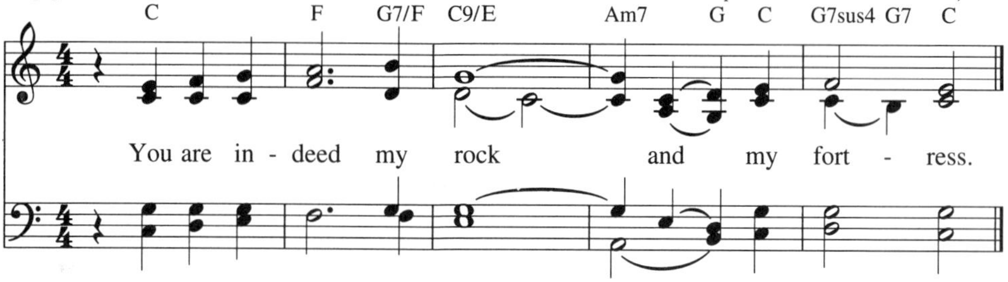

℟

1 In you, O God, I seek refuge; do not let me ever be put to shame;
in your righteousness deliver me.

2 Incline your ear to me; rescue me speedily.
Be a rock of refuge for me, a strong fortress to save me.

3 You are indeed my rock and my fortress;
for your name's sake lead me and guide me,

4 take me out of the net that is hidden for me,
for you are my refuge.

5 Into your hand I commit my spirit;
you have redeemed me, O God, O faithful God.

15 My times are in your hand;
deliver me from the hand of my enemies and persecutors.

16 Let your face shine upon your servant;
save me in your steadfast love. ℟

19 O how abundant is your goodness that you have laid up for those who fear you,
and accomplished for those who take refuge in you, in the sight of everyone!

20 In the shelter of your presence you hide them from human plots;
you hold them safe under your shelter from contentious tongues.

21 Blessed be God, who has wondrously shown steadfast love to me
when I was beset as a city under siege.

22 I had said in my alarm, "I am driven far from your sight."
But you heard my supplications when I cried out to you for help.

23 Love God, all you God's saints.
God preserves the faithful, but abundantly repays the one who acts haughtily.

24 Be strong, and let your heart take courage,
all you who wait for God. ℟

Holy Saturday ABC vs. 1–4, 15–16; Easter 5 A vs. 1–5, 15–16; Proper 4 [9] A vs. 1–5, 19–24.

Psalm 31b

Antiphon: Robert Train Adams, 1994

Response

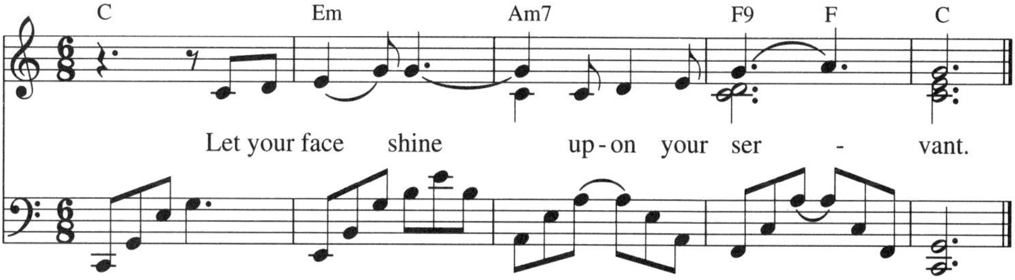

(Selection for Palm/Passion Sunday)

℟

9 Be gracious to me, O God, for I am in distress;
my eye wastes away from grief, my soul and body also.

10 For my life is spent with sorrow, and my years with sighing;
my strength fails because of my misery, and my bones waste away.

11 I am the scorn of all my adversaries, a horror to my neighbors, an object of dread to my acquaintances;
those who see me in the street flee from me.

12 I have passed out of mind like one who is dead;
I have become like a broken vessel.

℟

13 For I hear the whispering of many— terror all around!—
as they scheme together against me,
as they plot to take my life.

14 But I trust in you, O God;
I say, "You are my God."

15 My times are in your hand;
deliver me from the hand of my enemies and persecutors.

16 Let your face shine upon your servant;
save me in your steadfast love. ℟

(May be sung with double tone.)

Psalm 31 (Complete)

(Use antiphon for Psalm 31a on facing page.)

℟

1 In you, O God, I seek refuge; do not let me ever be put to shame;
in your righteousness deliver me.

2 Incline your ear to me; rescue me speedily.
Be a rock of refuge for me, a strong fortress to save me.

3 You are indeed my rock and my fortress;
for your name's sake lead me and guide me,

4 take me out of the net that is hidden for me,
for you are my refuge. ℟

℟ You are indeed my rock and my fortress.

5 Into your hand I commit my spirit;
you have redeemed me, O God, O faithful God.

6 You hate those who pay regard to worthless idols,
but I trust in God.

7 I will exult and rejoice in your steadfast love,
because you have seen my affliction;

you have taken heed of my adversities,
8 and have not delivered me into the hand of the enemy;
you have set my feet in a broad place. ℟

9 Be gracious to me, O God, for I am in distress;
my eye wastes away from grief, my soul and body also.

10 For my life is spent with sorrow, and my years with sighing;
my strength fails because of my misery,
and my bones waste away.

11 I am the scorn of all my adversaries, a horror to my neighbors, an object of dread to my acquaintances;
those who see me in the street flee from me.

12 I have passed out of mind like one who is dead;
I have become like a broken vessel. ℟

13 For I hear the whispering of many—terror all around!—
as they scheme together against me, as they plot to take my life.

14 But I trust in you, O God;
I say, "You are my God."

15 My times are in your hand;
deliver me from the hand of my enemies and persecutors.

16 Let your face shine upon your servant;
save me in your steadfast love. ℟

17 Do not let me be put to shame, O God, for I call on you;
let the wicked be put to shame; let them go dumbfounded to Sheol.

18 Let the lying lips be stilled that speak insolently against the righteous,
those lips that speak with pride and contempt.

19 O how abundant is your goodness that you have laid up for those who fear you,
and accomplished for those who take refuge in you, in the sight of everyone!

20 In the shelter of your presence you hide them from human plots;
you hold them safe under your shelter from contentious tongues. ℟

21 Blessed be God, who has wondrously shown steadfast love to me
when I was beset as a city under siege.

22 I had said in my alarm, "I am driven far from your sight."
But you heard my supplications when I cried out to you for help.

23 Love God, all you God's saints.
God preserves the faithful, but abundantly repays the one who acts haughtily.

24 Be strong, and let your heart take courage,
all you who wait for God. ℟

(May be sung with double tone.)

Psalm 32

Response *Antiphon: Emma Lou Diemer, 1994*

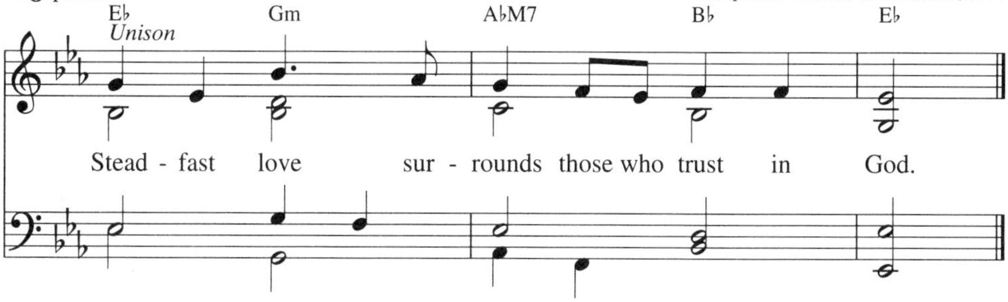

R

1 Happy are those whose transgression
is forgiven,
whose sin is covered.

2 Happy are those to whom God
imputes no iniquity,
and in whose spirit there is no
deceit.

3 While I kept silence, my body
wasted away
through my groaning all day long.

4 For day and night your hand was
heavy upon me;
my strength was dried up as by the
heat of summer. R

5 Then I acknowledged my sin to you,
and I did not hide my iniquity;

I said, "I will confess my
transgressions to God,"
and you forgave the guilt of my
sin.

6 Therefore let all who are faithful offer
prayer to you;
at a time of distress, the rush of
mighty waters shall not reach them.

7 You are a hiding place for me; you
preserve me from trouble;
you surround me with glad cries of
deliverance. R

8 I will instruct you and teach you the
way you should go;
I will counsel you with my eye
upon you.

9 Do not be like a horse or a mule,
without understanding,
whose temper must be curbed with
bit and bridle, else it will not stay
near you.

10 Many are the torments of the wicked,
but steadfast love surrounds those
who trust in God.

11 Be glad in God and rejoice, O
righteous,
and shout for joy, all you upright
in heart. R

Proper 26 [31] C vs. 1–7. (If all verses are used, may be sung with double tone.)

Psalm 33

℟esponse

Antiphon: Robert Fryson, 1994

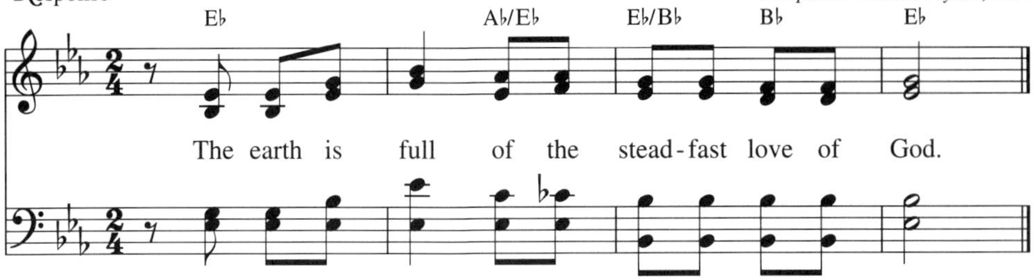

℟

1 Rejoice in God, O you righteous.
Praise befits the upright.

2 Praise God with the lyre;
make melody to God with the harp of ten strings.

3 Sing to God a new song;
play skillfully on the strings, with loud shouts.

4 For the word of God is upright,
and all God's work is done in faithfulness. ℟

5 God loves righteousness and justice;
the earth is full of the steadfast love of God.

6 By the word of God the heavens were made,
and all their host by the breath of God's mouth.

7 God gathered the waters of the sea as in a bottle;
God put the deeps in storehouses.

8 Let all the earth fear God;
let all the inhabitants of the world stand in awe of God. ℟

9 For God spoke, and it came to be;
God commanded, and it stood firm.

10 God brings the counsel of the nations to nothing;
God frustrates the plans of the peoples.

11 The counsel of God stands forever,
the thoughts of God's heart to all generations.

12 Happy is the nation whose God is the Sovereign,
the people whom God has chosen as God's own heritage.

13 God looks out from heaven;
God sees all humankind.

14 From where God sits enthroned, God watches all the inhabitants of the earth—
15 God who fashions the hearts of them all, and observes all their deeds.

16 A ruler is not saved by a great army;
a warrior is not delivered by great strength.

17 The war horse is a vain hope for victory,
and by its great might it cannot save. ℟

18 Truly the eye of God is on those who fear God,
on those who hope in God's steadfast love,

19 to deliver their soul from death,
and to keep them alive in famine.

20 Our soul waits for God,
who is our help and shield.

21 Our heart is glad in God,
because we trust in God's holy name.

22 Let your steadfast love, O God,
be upon us,
even as we hope in you. ℟

Proper 5 [10] A vs. 1–12; Proper 14 [19] C vs. 12–22.

Psalm 34

℟esponse *Antiphon: Jane Marshall, 1994*

Unison

℟esponse *(To be sung on All Saints Day)* *Antiphon: Jane Marshall, 1994*

Unison

℟

1 I will bless God at all times;
God's praise shall continually be in my mouth.

2 My soul makes its boast in God;
let the humble hear and be glad.

3 O magnify God with me,
and let us exalt God's name together.

4 I sought God, and God answered me,
and delivered me from all my fears.

℟

5 Look to God, and be radiant;
so your faces shall never be ashamed.

6 This poor soul cried, and was heard by God,
and was saved from every trouble.

7 The angel of God encamps around those who fear God;
God's angel delivers them.

8 O taste and see that God is good;
happy are those who take refuge in God. ℟

℟ O let us exalt God's name forever. *℟ Happy are those who take refuge in God. (All Saints)*

9 O fear God, all you holy ones of God,
for those who fear God have no want.

10 The young lions suffer want and hunger,
but those who seek God lack no good thing.

11 Come, O children, listen to me;
I will teach you the fear of God.

12 Which of you desires life, and covets many days to enjoy good?
13 Keep your tongue from evil, and your lips from speaking deceit. ℟

14 Depart from evil, and do good;
seek peace, and pursue it.

15 The eyes of God are on the righteous,
God's ears are open to their cry.

16 The face of God is against evildoers,
to cut off the remembrance of them from the earth.

17 When the righteous cry for help, God hears,
and rescues them from all their troubles. ℟

18 God is near to the brokenhearted,
and saves the crushed in spirit.

19 Many are the afflictions of the righteous,
but God rescues them from them all.

20 God keeps all their bones;
not one of them will be broken.

21 Evil brings death to the wicked,
and those who hate the righteous will be condemned.

22 God redeems the life of those who serve God;
none of those who take refuge in God will be condemned.

All Saints A vs. 1–10, 22; Proper 14 [19] B vs. 1–8; Proper 15 [20] B vs. 9–14; Proper 16 [21] B vs. 15–22; Proper 25 [30] B vs. 1–8, (19–22).

Psalm 35

℟esponse

Antiphon: Marty Haugen, 1994

℟

1 Contend, O God, with those who contend with me;
fight against those who fight against me!

2 Take hold of shield and buckler,
and rise up to help me!

3 Draw the spear and javelin against my pursuers;
say to my soul, "I am your salvation."

4 Let those who seek my life be shamed.
Let those who plot evil against me be turned back and confounded.

℟

5 Let them be like chaff before the wind,
with God's angel driving them on.

6 Let their way be obscure and slippery,
with God's angel pursuing them.

7 For unprovoked they hid their net for me;
unprovoked they dug a pit for my life.

8 Let ruin come on them unawares. And
let the net that they hid ensnare them;
let them fall in it and be destroyed. ℟

9 Then my soul shall rejoice in God,
and exult in God's deliverance.

10 All my bones shall say, "O God, who is
like you?

You deliver the weak from those too
strong for them, the weak and needy
from those who exploit them."

11 Malicious witnesses rise up;
they ask me of things I know nothing
about.

12 They repay me evil for good;
desolation is in my soul. ℟

13 But as for me, when they were sick, I
wore sackcloth;
I afflicted myself with fasting.

I prayed with head bowed on my bosom,
14 as though I grieved for a friend or a
brother;
I went about as one who laments for a
mother, bowed down and in mourning.

15 But at my stumbling they gathered in
glee, they gathered together against me;
unknown assailants mocked me
without ceasing;

16 they degraded me more and more,
gnashing at me with their teeth. ℟

17 How long, O God, will you look on?
Rescue me from their ravages, my life
from those lions!

18 Then I will thank you in the great
congregation;
in the mighty throng I will praise you.

19 Do not let my treacherous enemies
rejoice over me,
or those who hate me for no reason
look at me with disdain.

20 For they do not speak peace,
but they conceive deceitful words
against those who are peaceful in the
land. ℟

21 They open wide their mouths to accuse
me;
they say, "Hurray! We have seen it
with our own eyes."

22 You have seen, O God; do not be silent!
O God, do not be far from me!

23 Wake up! Rouse yourself for my
defense,
for my cause, my God and my Sovereign!

24 Vindicate me, O Sovereign, my God,
according to your righteousness,
and do not let them rejoice over me. ℟

25 Do not let them say to themselves,
"Hurray, we have our heart's desire!"
Do not let them say, "We have
swallowed you up."

26 Let all those who rejoice at my calamity
be put to shame and confusion;
let those who gloat over me be covered
with shame and dishonor.

27 Let those who desire my vindication
shout for joy and be glad,
and say evermore, "Great is God, who
delights in the welfare of God's servant."

28 Then my tongue shall tell of your
righteousness
and of your praise all the day long. ℟

(May be sung with double tone.)

Psalm 36

℟esponse

Antiphon: Jean Slates Hawk, 1994

℟

5 Your steadfast love, O God, extends
to the heavens,
your faithfulness to the clouds.

6 Your righteousness is like the mighty
mountains, your judgments are like
the great deep;
you save humans and animals alike,
O God.

7 How precious is your steadfast love,
O God!
All people may take refuge in the
shadow of your wings.

8 They feast on the abundance of your
house,
and you give them drink from the
river of your delights. ℟

9 For with you is the fountain of life;
in your light we see light.

10 O continue your steadfast love to
those who know you,
and your salvation to the upright
of heart!

11 Do not let the foot of the arrogant
tread on me,
or the hand of the wicked drive me
away. ℟

Monday in Holy Week ABC vs. 5–11; Epiphany 2 [2] C vs. 5–10.

Psalm 37a

℞esponse

Antiphon: Vérne de la Peña, 1994

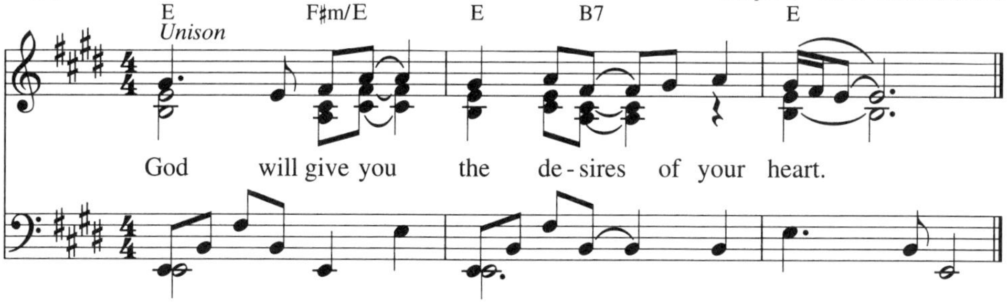

℞

1 Do not fret because of the wicked; do not be envious of wrongdoers,
  2 for they will soon fade like the grass, and wither like the green herb.

3 Trust in God, and do good;
  so you will live in the land, and enjoy security.

4 Take delight in God,
  who will give you the desires of your heart.

5 Commit your way to God;
  trust in God, and God will act. ℞

6 God will make your vindication shine like the light,
  and the justice of your cause like the day at noon.

7 Be still before God, and wait patiently;
  do not fret over those who prosper in their way, over those who carry out evil devices.

8 Refrain from anger, and forsake wrath.
  Do not fret—it leads only to evil.

9 For the wicked shall be cut off,
  but those who wait for God shall inherit the land. ℞

10 Yet a little while, and the wicked will be no more;
  though you look diligently for their place, they will not be there.

11 But the meek shall inherit the land,
  and delight themselves in abundant prosperity.

12 The wicked plot against the righteous,
  and gnash their teeth at them;

13 but God laughs at the wicked,
  seeing that their day is coming. ℞

14 The wicked draw the sword and bend their bows to bring down the poor and needy,
  to kill those who walk uprightly;

15 their sword shall enter their own heart,
  and their bows shall be broken.

16 Better is a little that the righteous person has
  than the abundance of many wicked.

17 For the arms of the wicked shall be broken,
  but God upholds the righteous.

39 The salvation of the righteous is from God,
  who is their refuge in the time of trouble.

40God helps them and rescues them;
God rescues them from the wicked,
and saves them, because they take refuge in God. ℞

℞ God will give you the desires of your heart.

Epiphany 7 [7] C all verses; Proper 22 [27] C vs. 1–9.

(Unbracketed verses may be sung with double tone.)

Psalm 37b

℞

18God knows the days of the blameless,
and their heritage will abide forever;

19they are not put to shame in evil times,
in the days of famine they have abundance.

20But the wicked perish, and the enemies of God are like the glory of the pastures—they vanish;
like smoke they vanish away.

21The wicked borrow, and do not pay back,
but the righteous are generous and keep giving;

22for those blessed by God shall inherit the land,
but those cursed by God shall be cut off. ℞

23God makes our steps firm,
whenever God delights in our way;

24though we stumble, we shall not fall headlong,
for God holds us by the hand.

25I have been young, and now am old,
yet I have not seen the righteous forsaken or their children begging bread.

26They are ever giving liberally and lending,
and their children become a blessing.

27Depart from evil, and do good;
so you shall abide forever. ℞

28For God loves justice,
and will not forsake those who are faithful.

The righteous shall be kept safe forever,
but the children of the wicked shall be cut off.

29The righteous shall inherit the land,
and live in it forever.

30The mouths of the righteous utter wisdom,
and their tongues speak justice.

31The law of their God is in their hearts;
their steps do not slip. ℞

32The wicked watch for the righteous,
and seek to kill them.

33God will not abandon them to their power,
or let them be condemned when they are brought to trial.

34Wait for God, and keep to the way of God, who will exalt you to inherit the land;
you will look on the destruction of the wicked.

35I have seen the wicked oppressing,
and towering like a cedar of Lebanon.

36 Again I passed by, and they wére no more;
though I sought them, they could nót be found. ℟

37 Mark the blameless, and beh́old the upright,
for there is posterity fór the peaceable.

38 But transgressors shall be altogethér destroyed;
the posterity of the wicked shall b́e cut off.

39 The salvation of the righteous ís from God,
who is their refuge in the t́ime of trouble.

40 God helps them and ŕescues them;
God rescues them from the wicked,
and saves them, because they take refúge in God. ℟

Psalm 38

℟esponse

Antiphon: Marty Haugen, 1994

℟

1 O God, do not rebuke me ín your anger,
or discipline me ín your wrath.

2 For your arrows h́ave sunk into me,
and your hand h́as come down on me.

3 There is no soundness in my body because of your índignation;
there is no health in my bones because óf my sin.

4 For my iniquities have gone óver my head;
they weigh like a burden too heav́y for me. ℟

5 My wounds smell f́oul and fester
because óf my foolishness;

6 I am utterly bowed d́own and prostrate;
all day long I go áround mourning.

7 For my loins are f́illed with burning,
and there is no health ín my flesh.

8 I am utterly ś pent and crushed;
I groan because of the anguish óf my heart.

9 O God, all my longing is ḱnown to you;
my sighing is not hidd́en from you. ℟

10 My heart throbs, and ḿy strength fails,
and the light of my éyes has left me.

11 My friends and companions stand aloof from ḿy affliction,
and my neighbors ś tand far off.

12 Those who seek my life ĺay their snares;
those who seek to hurt me threaten my ruin, and plot treachery all t́he day long.

℟ O God,do not be far away, O God, do not be far away.

13 But I am like those who are deaf, I do
not hear;
like those who are mute, who cannot
speak.

14 Truly, I am like one who does not hear,
and in whose mouth is no retort. ℟

15 But it is for you, O God, that I wait;
it is you, O God my God, who will
answer.

16 For I pray, "Only do not let them rejoice
over me,
those who exalt when I take a wrong
step."

17 For I am ready to fall,
and my pain is ever with me.

18 I confess my iniquity;
I am sorry for my sin. ℟

19 Those who are my foes without cause
are mighty,
and many are those who hate me for
no reason.

20 Those who render me evil for good are
my adversaries
because I try to do good.

21 Do not forsake me, O God;
O my God, do not be far from me;

22 make haste to help me,
O God, my salvation. ℟

Psalm 39

℟esponse

Antiphon: Martie McMane, 1994

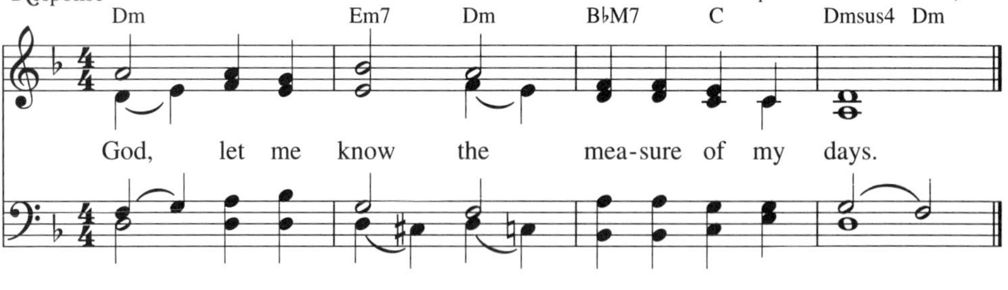

℟

1 I said, "I will guard my ways
that I may not sin with my tongue;

I will keep a muzzle on my mouth
as long as the wicked are in my
presence."

2 I was silent and still;
I held my peace to no avail;

my distress grew worse,
3 my heart became hot within me.

While I mused, the fire burned;
then I spoke with my tongue: ℟

4 "God, let me know my end, and what is
the measure of my days,
how fleeting is my life.

5 You have made my days a mere
handbreadth long,
and my whole life is as nothing in
your sight.

Surely everyone stands as a mere breath.
6 Surely everyone goes about like a
shadow.

Surely they are in turmoil for nothing;
they heap up, and do not know who
will gather. ℟

7 And now, O God, what do I wait for?
My hope is in you.

8 Deliver me from all my transgressions.
Do not make me the scorn of the fool.

9 I am silent; I do not open my mouth,
for it is you who have done it all.

10 Remove from me your beatings;
I am worn down by the blows of your hand. ℞

11 You chastise mortals in punishment for sin;
like a moth, you eat away what is dear to them. Surely everyone is a mere breath.

12 Hear my prayer, O God, and give ear to my cry;
do not be deaf to my weeping.

For I am your passing guest,
an alien, like all my forebears.

13 Turn your gaze away from me,
that I may smile again, before I depart and am no more." ℞

Psalm 40

Antiphon: Marty Haugen, 1994

℞

1 I waited patiently for God,
who inclined to me and heard my cry.

2 God drew me up from the desolate pit, out of the miry bog;
God set my feet upon a rock,
making my steps secure.

3 God put a new song in my mouth, a song of praise to our God.
Many will see and fear, and put their trust in God.

4 Happy are those who make God their trust,
who do not turn to the proud, to those who go astray after false gods. ℞

5 You have multiplied, O God my God, your wondrous deeds and your thoughts toward us;
none can compare with you.

Were I to proclaim and tell of them,
they would be more than can be counted.

6 Sacrifice and offering you do not desire, but you have given me an open ear.
Burnt offering and sin offering you have not required.

R I delight to do your will, O my God, I delight to do your will.

7Then I said, "Here I am;
in the scroll of the book it is written of me. R

8"I delight to do your will, O my God;
your law is within my heart."

9I have told the glad news of deliverance in the great congregation;
see, I have not restrained my lips,
as you know, O God.

10I have not hidden your saving help within my heart,
I have spoken of your faithfulness and your salvation;

I have not concealed your steadfast love and your faithfulness,
I have not concealed them from the great congregation.

11Do not, O God, withhold your mercy from me;
let your steadfast love and your faithfulness keep me safe forever. R

12For evils have encompassed me without number;
my iniquities have overtaken me, until I cannot see;

they are more than the hairs of my head,
and my heart fails me.

13Be pleased, O God, to deliver me;
O God, make haste to help me. R

14Let all those be put to shame and confusion who seek to snatch away my life;
let those be turned back and brought to dishonor who desire my hurt.

15Those who say to me, "Aha!"
—let them be appalled with shame.

16But may all who seek you rejoice and be glad in you;
may those who love your salvation say continually, "God is great!"

17As for me, I am poor and needy,
but God takes thought of me.

You are my help and my deliverer;
do not delay, O my God. R

Epiphany 2 [2] A vs. 1–11; Annunciation ABC vs. 5–10 (Alt.).

Psalm 41

Response *Antiphon: Peter Niedmann, 1994*

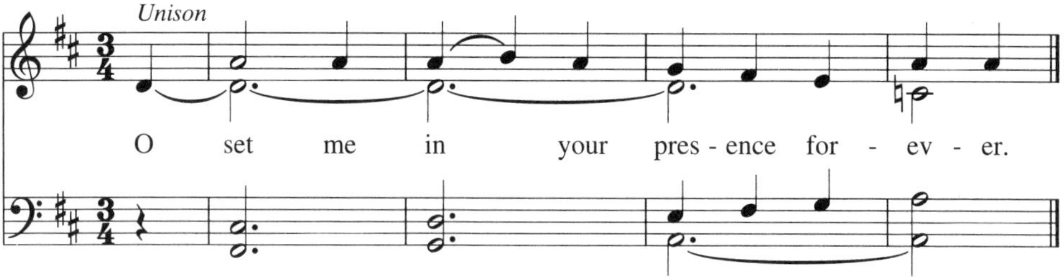

R

1Happy are those who consider the poor;
God delivers them in the day of trouble.

2God protects them and keeps them alive; they are called happy in the land.
You do not give them up to the will of their enemies.

3 God sustains them on their sickbed;
in their illness you heal all their infirmities.

4 As for me, I said, "O God, be gracious to me;
heal me, for I have sinned against you." ℞

5 My enemies wonder in malice when I will die,
and when my name will perish.

6 And when they come to see me, they utter empty words, while their hearts gather mischief;
when they go out, they tell it abroad.

7 All who hate me whisper together about me; they imagine the worst for me.
8 They think that a deadly thing has fastened on me, that I will not rise again from where I lie.

9 Even my friend in whom I trusted, who ate of my bread,
has exalted at my misfortune. ℞

10 But you, O God, be gracious to me,
and raise me up, that I may repay them.

11 By this I know that you are pleased with me;
because my enemy has not triumphed over me.

12 But you have upheld me because of my integrity,
and set me in your presence forever.

13 Blessed be the Sovereign, the God of Israel,
from everlasting to everlasting.
Amen and Amen. ℞

(May be sung with double tone.)

Psalms 42, 43

℞esponse

Antiphon: Carolyn Jennings, 1994

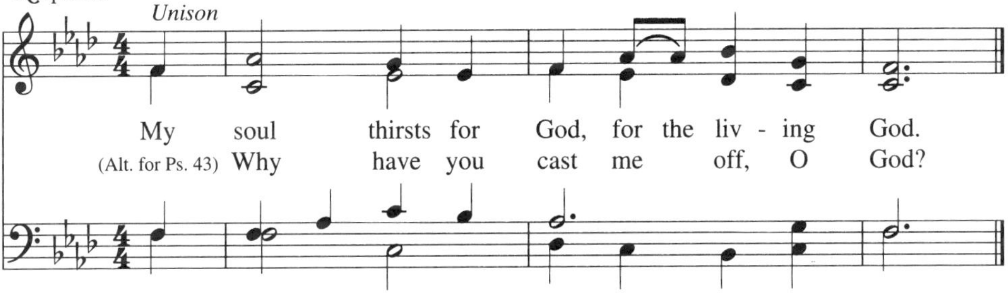

℞

1 As a deer longs for flowing streams
so my soul longs for you, O God.

2 My soul thirsts for God, for the living God.
When shall I come and behold the face of God?

3 My tears have been my food day and night,
While people say to me continually, "Where is your God?"

4 These things I remember,
as I pour out my soul:

how I went with the throng, and led them in procession to the h́ouse of God,
with glad shouts and songs of thanksgiving, a multitude ḱeeping festival. ℟

5 Why are you cast down, O my soul, and why are you disquiet́ed within me?
Hope in God; for I shall again praise God, my help 6 ánd my God.

My soul is cast d́own within me;
therefore I remember you from the Land of Jordan and of Hermon, f́rom Mount Mizar.

7 Deep calls to deep at the thunder óf your cataracts;
all your waves and your billows h́ave gone over me. ℟

8 By day God commands God's śteadfast love,
and at night God's song is with me,
a prayer to the God óf my life. ℟

9 I say to God, my rock, "Why have ýou forgotten me?
Why must I walk about mournfully because the enemý oppresses me?"

10 As with a deadly wound in my body, my adverśaries taunt me,
while they say to me continually, "Where ís your God?"

11 Why are you cast down, Ó my soul?
Why are you disquiet́ed within me?

Hope in God; for I shall again ṕraise the one,
who is my help ánd my God. ℟

(Psalm 43)

℟

1 Vindicate me, O God, and defend my cause against an unǵodly people;
from those who are deceitful and unj́ust deliver me!

2 For you are the God in whom Í take refuge;
why have you ćast me off?

Why must I walk ábout mournfully because of the oppression óf the enemy?

3 O send out your light and your truth; lét them lead me;
let them bring me to your holy hill and t́o your dwelling.

4 Then I will go to the altar of God, to God my exćeeding joy;
and I will praise you with the harp, O Ǵod, my God.

5 Why are you cast down, Ó my soul,
and why are you disquiet́ed within me?

Hope in God; for I shall again ṕraise the one,
who is my help ánd my God. ℟

Psalms 42 and 43 Easter Vigil ABC and Proper 7 [12] C; Psalm 43 Proper 26 [31] A.

Psalm 44

Antiphon: Carolyn Jennings, 1994

℟

[1]We have heard with our ears, O God,
our ancestors have told us, what deeds you performed in their days, in the days of old:

[2]you with your own hand drove out the nations,
but our ancestors you planted;

you afflicted the peoples,
but our ancestors you set free;

[3]for not by their own sword did they win the land,
nor did their own arm give them victory;

but it was by your strong hand, and your arm, and the light of your countenance,
for you delighted in them. ℟

[4]You are my Sovereign and my God;
you command victories for Jacob.

[5]Through you we push down our foes;
through your name we tread down our assailants.

[6]For not in my bow do I trust,
nor can my sword save me.

[7]But you have saved us from our foes,
and have put to confusion those who hate us. ℟

[8]In God we have boasted continually,
and we will give thanks to your name forever.

[9]Yet you have rejected us and abased us,
and have not marched with our armies.

[10]You made us turn back from the foe,
and our enemies have gotten the spoils.

[11]You have made us like sheep for slaughter,
and have scattered us among the nations.

[12]You have sold your people for a trifle,
demanding no high price for them. ℟

[13]You have made us the taunt of our neighbors,
the derision and scorn of those around us.

[14]You have made us a byword among the nations,
a laughingstock among the peoples.

[15]All day long my disgrace is before me,
and shame has covered my face

[16]at the words of the taunters and revilers,
at the sight of the enemy and the avenger. ℟

[17]All this has come upon us,
yet we have not forgotten you, or been false to your covenant.

[18]Our heart has not turned back,
nor have our steps departed from your way,

℟ Why have you cast me off, O God?

19 yet you have crushed us in the haunt of jackals,
and covered us in heavy shadows.

20 If we had forgotten the name of our God,
or spread out our hands to a strange god,

21 would not God discover this?
For God knows the secrets of the heart.

22 Because of you we are being killed all the day long,
and accounted as sheep for the slaughter. ℟

23 Rouse yourself! Why do you sleep, O God?
Awake, do not cast us off forever!

24 Why do you hide your face?
Why do you forget our affliction and oppression?

25 For we sink down to the dust;
our bodies cling to the ground.

26 Rise up, come to our help.
Redeem us for the sake of your steadfast love. ℟

Psalm 45

℟esponse *Antiphon: Judy Hunnicutt, 1994*

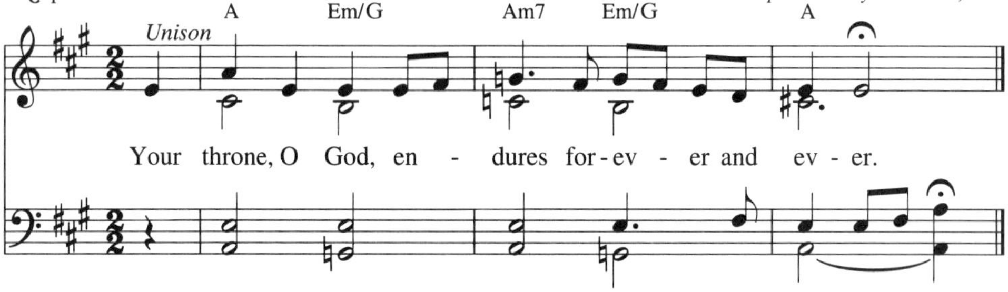

℟

1 My heart overflows with a goodly theme; I address my verses to the king;
my tongue is like the pen of a ready scribe.

2 You are the most handsome of men; grace is poured upon your lips;
therefore God has blessed you forever.

3 Gird your sword on your thigh, O mighty one,
in your glory and majesty.

4 In your majesty ride on victoriously for the cause of truth and to defend the right;
let your right hand teach you dread deeds. ℟

5 Your arrows are sharp in the heart of the king's enemies;
the peoples fall under you.

6 Your throne, O God, endures forever and ever.
Your royal scepter is a scepter of equity;

7 you love righteousness and hate wickedness.
Therefore God, your God, has anointed you with the oil of gladness beyond your companions;

[8]your robes are all fragrant with myrrh and aloes and cassia.
From ivory palaces stringed instruments make you glad; ℟

[9]daughters of kings are among those who serve you,

at your right hand stands the queen in gold of Ophir.

[10]Hear, O daughter, consider and incline your ear;

forget your people and your parents' house,

[11]and the king will desire your beauty.
Since he is your lord, bow to him;

[12]the people of Tyre will seek your favor with gifts,

the richest of the people [13]with all kinds of wealth. ℟

The princess is clothed in her chamber with gold-woven robes;
[14]in many-colored robes she is led to the king;

behind her the virgins, her companions, follow.
[15]With joy and gladness they are led along as they enter the palace of the king.

[16]In the place of ancestors you, O king, shall have descendants;
you will make them nobles in all the earth.

[17]I will cause your name to be celebrated in all generations;
therefore the peoples will praise you forever and ever. ℟

Annunciation ABC (Alt.) all verses; Proper 9 [14] A vs. 10–17; Proper 17 [22] B vs. 1–2, 6–9. (If all verses are used, may be sung with double tone.)

Psalm 46

℟esponse

Antiphon: Lee Dengler, 1994

℟

[1]God is our refuge and strength,
a very present help in trouble.

[2]Therefore we will not fear, though the earth should change,
though the mountains shake in the heart of the sea;

[3]though its waters roar and foam,
though the mountains tremble with its tumult.

[4]There is a river whose streams make glad the city of God,
the holy habitation of the Most High. ℟

R̸ The God of hosts is with us, therefore we will not fear.

5 God is in the midst of the city; it shall not be moved;
God will help it when the morning dawns.

6 The nations are in an uproar, the empires totter;
God's voice resounds and the earth melts.

7 The God of hosts is with us;
the God of Jacob is our refuge.

8 Come, behold the works of God;
see what desolations God has brought on the earth. R̸

9 God makes wars cease to the end of the earth;
God breaks the bow, and shatters the spear; God burns the shields with fire.

10 "Be still, and know that I am God!
I am exalted among the nations, I am exalted in the earth."

11 The God of hosts is with us;
the God of Jacob is our refuge. R̸

Psalm 47

Response

Antiphon: Elaine Kirkland, 1994

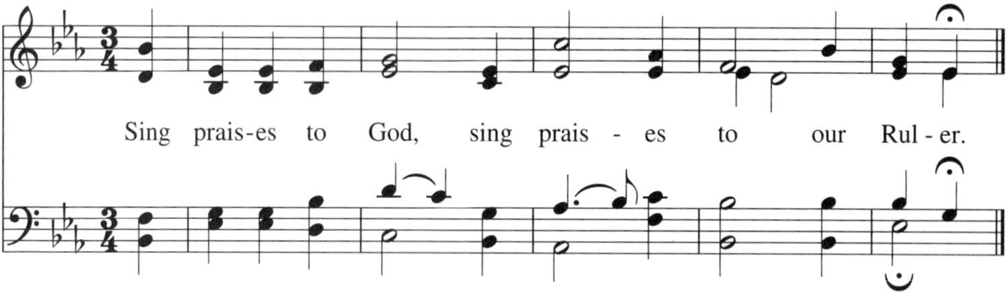

R̸

1 Clap your hands, all you peoples;
shout to God with loud songs of joy.

2 For God, the Most High, is awesome,
a great ruler over all the earth.

3 God subdued peoples under us, and nations under our feet.
4 God chose our heritage for us, the pride of Jacob whom God loves.

5 God has gone up with a shout,
God has gone up with the sound of a trumpet. R̸

6 Sing praises to God, sing praises;
sing praises to our Ruler, sing praises.

7 For God is the ruler of all the earth;
sing praises with a psalm.

8 God is ruler over the nations;
God sits on God's holy throne.

9 The nobles of the peoples gather
as the people of the God of Sarah and Abraham.

For the shields of the earth belong to God;
God is highly exalted. R̸

Psalm 48

℟esponse

Antiphon: Martie McMane, 1994

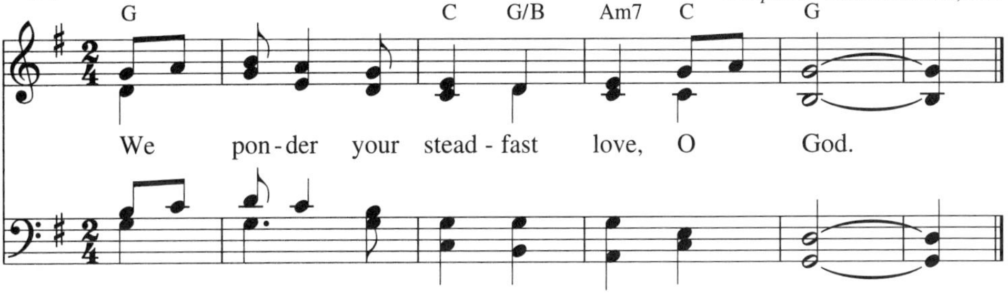

℟

1 Great is God and greatly to be praised
in the city of our God.

God's holy mountain, 2 beautiful in elevation,
is the joy of all the earth,

Mount Zion, in the far north,
the city of the great Ruler.
3 Within its citadels God is a sure defense. ℟

4 Then the rulers assembled,
they came on together.
5 As soon as they saw it, they were astounded; they were in panic, they took to flight;

6 trembling took hold of them there,
pains as of a woman in labor,
7 as when an east wind shatters the ships of Tarshish.

8 As we have heard, so have we seen in the city of the God of hosts,
in the city of our God, which God establishes forever.

9 We ponder your steadfast love, O God,
in the midst of your temple. ℟

10 Your name, O God, like your praise,
reaches to the ends of the earth.
Your right hand is filled with victory.

11 Let Mount Zion be glad,
let the towns of Judah rejoice
because of your judgments.

12 Walk about Zion, go all around it, count its towers,
13 consider well its ramparts;
go through its citadels,

that you may tell the next generation 14 that this is God,
our God forever and ever.
God will be our guide forever. ℟

Psalm 49

Response *Antiphon: David Hurd, 1994*

℟

1 Hear this, all you peoples; give ear,
all inhabitants of the world,
2 both low and high, rich and
poor together.

3 My mouth shall speak wisdom;
the meditation of my heart
shall be understanding.

4 I will incline my ear to a proverb;
I will solve my riddle to the
music of the harp. ℟

5 Why should I fear in times of trouble,
when the iniquity of my persecutors
surrounds me,

6 those who trust in their wealth
and boast of the abundance of
their riches?

7 Truly, no ransom avails for one's life,
there is no price one can give
to God for it.

8 For the ransom of life is costly,
and can never suffice
9 that one should live on forever
and never see the grave. ℟

10 When we look at the wise, they die;
the foolish and stupid perish
together and leave their wealth to
others.

11 Their graves are their homes forever,
their dwelling places to all
generations, though they named
lands their own.

12 Mortals cannot abide in their pomp;
they are like the animals that
perish. ℟

13 Such is the fate of the foolhardy,
the end of those who are pleased with
their lot.

14 Like sheep they are appointed for Sheol;
Death shall be their shepherd;

straight to the grave they descend, and
their form shall waste away;
Sheol shall be their home.

15 But God will ransom my soul from the
power of Sheol,
for God will receive me. ℟

16 Do not be afraid when some become
rich,
when the wealth of their houses
increases.

17 For when they die they will carry
nothing away;
their wealth will not go down after
them.

18 Though in their lifetime they count
themselves happy—
for you are praised when you do well
for yourself—

19 they will go to the company of their
ancestors,
who will never again see the light.

20 Mortals cannot abide in their pomp;
they are like the animals that perish. ℟

Psalm 50

℟esponse

Antiphon: Hyeon Jeong, 1994

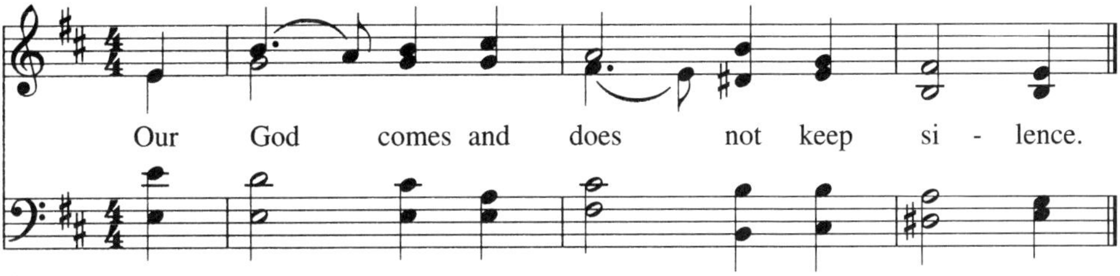

℟

1 The mighty one, God the Sovereign,
speaks and summons the earth:
from the rising of the sun to
its setting.

2 Out of Zion, the perfection of beauty,
God shines forth.
3 Our God comes and does not
keep silence,

before God is a devouring fire,
and a mighty tempest all around. ℟

4 God calls to the heavens above
and to the earth,
that God may judge God's
people:

5 "Gather to me my faithful ones,
who made a covenant with me
by sacrifice!"

6 The heavens declare God's
righteousness,
for God indeed is judge. ℟

7 "Hear, O my people, and I will speak,
O Israel, I will testify against
you for I am God, your God.

8 Not for your sacrifices do I
rebuke you;
your burnt offerings
are continually before me. ℟

9 I will not accept a bull from your
house, or goats from your folds.
10 For every animal of the forest is
mine, the cattle on a thousand hills.

11 I know all the birds of the air,
and all that moves in the field
is mine.

12 If I were hungry,
I would not tell you,
for the world and all that is
in it is mine. ℟

13 Do I eat the flesh of bulls,
or drink the blood of goats?

14 Offer to God a sacrifice of
thanksgiving,
and pay your vows to
the Most High.

15 Call on me in the day of trouble;
I will deliver you,
and you shall glorify me." ℟

16 But to the wicked God says:
"What right have you to recite my
statutes, or take my covenant on your
lips?

R Our God comes and does not keep silence.

17 For you hate discipline,
and you cast my words behind you.

18 You make friends with a thief when you see one,
and you keep company with adulterers.

19 You give your mouth free rein for evil,
and your tongue frames deceit.

20 You sit and speak against your kin;
you slander your own mother's child.
R

21 These things you have done and I have been silent;
you thought that I was one just like yourself.

But now I rebuke you,
and lay the charge before you.

22 Mark this, then, you who forget God,
or I will tear you apart, and there will be no one to deliver.

23 Those who bring thanksgiving as their sacrifice honor me;
to those who go the right way I will show the salvation of God." R

Proper 5 [10] A vs. 7–15; Epiphany Last and Transfiguration B vs. 1–6; Proper 14 [19] C vs. 1–8, 22–23

Psalm 51

Response

Antiphon: Emma Lou Diemer, 1994

R

1 Have mercy on me, O God,
according to your steadfast love;
according to your abundant mercy
blot out my transgressions.

2 Wash me thoroughly from my iniquity, and cleanse me from my sin.
3 For I know my transgressions,
and my sin is ever before me.

4 Against you, you alone, have I sinned, and done what is evil in your sight,
so that you are justified in your sentence and blameless when you pass judgment.

5 Indeed, I was born guilty,
a sinner when my mother conceived me. R

6 You desire truth in the inward being;
therefore teach me wisdom in my secret heart.

[7]Purge me with hyssop,
and I shall be clean;
wash me, and I shall be
purer than snow.

[8]Let me hear joy and gladness;
let the bones that you have
crushed rejoice.

[9]Hide your face from my sins,
and blot out all my iniquities. ℟

[10]Create in me a clean heart, O God,
and put a new and right spirit
within me.

[11]Do not cast me away from
your presence,
and do not take your
holy spirit from me.

[12]Restore to me the joy of your
salvation,
and sustain in me a willing spirit.

[13]Then I will teach transgressors
your ways,
and sinners will return to you. ℟

[14]Deliver me from bloodshed, O God,
O God of my salvation,
and my tongue will sing aloud
of your deliverance.

[15]O God, open my lips,
and my mouth will declare
your praise.

[16]For you have no delight in sacrifice;
if I were to give a burnt offering,
you would not be pleased.

[17]The sacrifice acceptable to God
is a troubled spirit;
a broken and contrite heart, O God,
you will not despise. ℟

[18]Do good to Zion in your good pleasure;
rebuild the walls of Jerusalem,

[19]then you will delight in right sacrifices, in
burnt offerings and whole burnt
offerings;
then bulls will be offered on your altar.
℟

Ash Wednesday ABC vs. 1–17; Lent 5 B vs. 1–12 (Alt.);
Proper 13 [18] B vs. 1–12; Proper 19 [24] C vs. 1–10.
(If only verses 1–17 are used, may be sung with double tone.)

Psalm 52

℟esponse

Antiphon: Jane Marshall, 1994

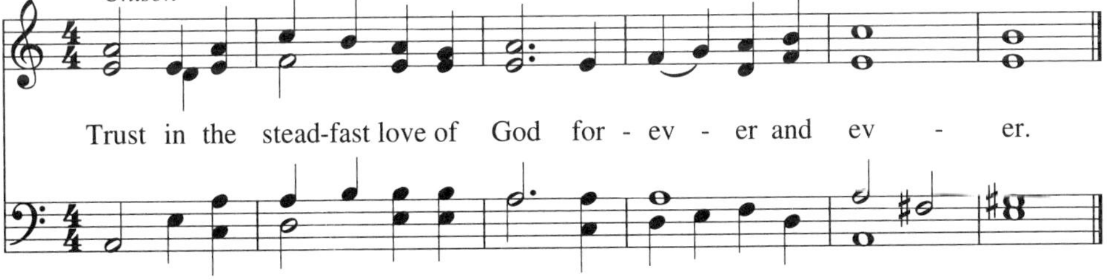

℟

[1]Why do you boast, O mighty one,
of mischief done against the godly?

All day long [2]you are plotting
destruction.

Your tongue is like a sharp razor,
you worker of treachery.

[3]You love evil more than good, and
lying more than speaking the truth.

4 You love all words that devour,
O deceitful tongue.

5 But God will break you down forever;
God will snatch and tear you from your tent and uproot you from the land of the living. ℟

6 The righteous will see, and fear,
and will laugh at the evildoer, saying,
7 "See the one who would not take refuge in God, but trusted in abundant riches, and sought refuge in wealth!"

8 But I am like a green olive tree
in the house of God.
I trust in the steadfast love of God
forever and ever.

9 I will thank you forever,
because of what you have done.
In the presence of the faithful I will proclaim your name,
for your name is good. ℟

Psalm 53

℟esponse

Antiphon: Hyeon Jeong, 1994

℟

1 Fools say in their hearts, "There is no God."
They are corrupt, they commit abominable acts; there is no one who does good.

2 God looks down from heaven on humankind
to see if there are any who are wise,
who seek after God.

3 They have all fallen away, they are all alike perverse;
there is no one who does good, no, not one.

4 Have they no knowledge, those evildoers,
who eat up my people as they eat bread, and do not call upon God? ℟

5 There they shall be in great terror,
in terror such as has never been.

For God will scatter the bones of the ungodly;
they will be put to shame, for God has rejected them.

6 O that deliverance for Israel
would come from Zion!

When God restores the fortunes of God's people,
Jacob will rejoice; Israel will be glad. ℟

(May be sung with double tone.)

Psalm 54

Response

Antiphon: Robert Fryson, 1994

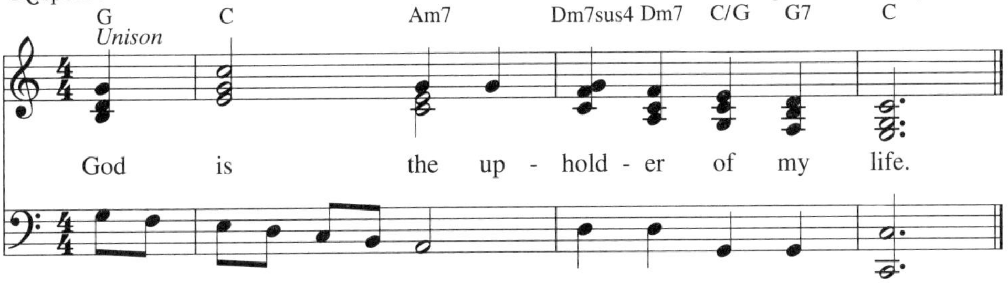

℟

1 Save me, O God, by your name,
and vindicate me by your might.

2 Hear my prayer, O God;
give ear to the words of my mouth.

3 For the insolent have risen against me,
the ruthless seek my life;
they do not set God before them.

4 But surely, God is my helper;
God is the upholder of my life. ℟

5 God will repay my enemies for their evil.
In your faithfulness,
put an end to them.

6 With a freewill offering I will sacrifice to you;
I will give thanks to your name,
O God, for it is good.

7 For God has delivered me from every trouble,
and my eye has looked in triumph on my enemies. ℟

Psalm 55

Response

Antiphon: Hyeon Jeong, 1994

℟

1 Give ear to my prayer, O God;
do not hide yourself from my supplication.

2 Attend to me, and answer me;
I cannot rest from complaining.

I am distraught 3 by the noise of the enemy,
because of the clamor of the wicked.

For they bring trouble upon me,
and in anger they cherish enmity against me. ℟

℟ O that I had the wings of a dove.

4My heart is in anguish within me,
the terrors of death have fallen upon me.

5Fear and trembling come upon me,
and horror overwhelms me.

6And I say, "O that I had wings like a dove!
I would fly away and be at rest;

7truly, I would flee far away;
I would lodge in the wilderness; ℟

8I would hurry to find a shelter for myself
from the raging wind and tempest."

9Confuse, O God, confound their speech;
for I see violence and strife in the city.

10Day and night they encircle it along its walls,
and iniquity and trouble are within it;

11ruin is in its midst;
oppression and fraud do not depart from its marketplace. ℟

12It is not enemies who taunt me—I could bear that;
it is not adversaries who deal insolently with me—I could hide from them.

13But it is you, my equal, my companion,
my familiar friend, 14with whom I kept
pleasant company;
we walked in the house of God with the throng.

15Let death come upon them; let them go down alive to Sheol;
for evil is in their homes and in their hearts.

16But I call upon God,
and God will save me. ℟

17Evening and morning and at noon I utter my complaint and moan,
and God will hear my voice.

18God will redeem me unharmed from the battle that I wage,
for many are arrayed against me.

19God, who is enthroned from of old, will hear, and will humble them
—because they do not change, and do not fear God.

20My companion laid hands on a friend
and violated a covenant with me, ℟

21with speech smoother than butter,
but with a heart set on war;

with words that were softer than oil,
but in fact were drawn swords.

22Cast your burden on God who will sustain you;
and will never permit the righteous to be moved.

23But you, O God, will cast them down into the lowest pit;
the bloodthirsty and treacherous shall not live out half their days. But I will trust in you. ℟

(May be sung with double tone.)

Psalm 56

Response

Antiphon: Emma Lou Diemer, 1994

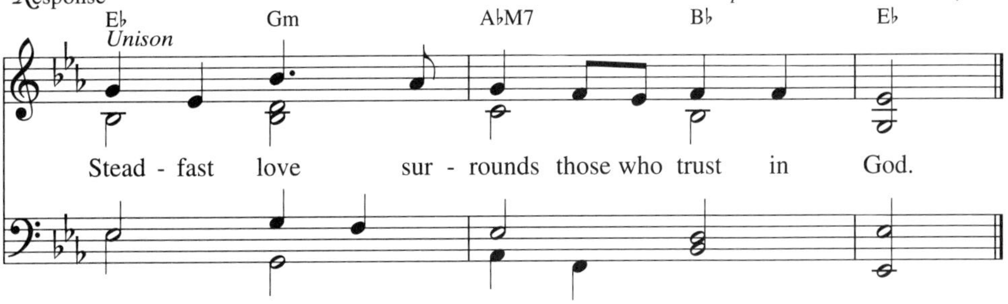

℟

1 Be gracious to me, O God, for people trample on me;
all day long foes oppress me;

2 my enemies trample on me all day long,
for many fight against me.

O Most High, 3 when I am afraid,
I put my trust in you.

4 In God, whose word I praise, in God I trust;
I am not afraid; what can mortals do to me? ℟

5 All day long people seek to injure my cause;
all their thoughts are against me for evil.

6 They stir up strife,
they lurk, they watch my steps.

As they hoped to have my life, 7 so repay them for their crime;
in wrath cast down the peoples, O God!

8 You have kept count of my tossings;
put my tears in your bottle. Are they not in your record? ℟

9 Then my enemies will retreat in the day when I call.
This I know, that God is for me.

10 In God, whose word I praise,
in the Most High, whose word I praise,

11 in God I trust; I am not afraid.
What can a mere mortal do to me?

12 My vows to you I must perform, O God;
I will render thank offerings to you.

13 For you have delivered my soul from death, and my feet from falling,
so that I may walk before God in the light of life. ℟

Psalm 57

℟esponse

Antiphon: Marty Haugen, 1994

℟

1 Be merciful to me, O God,
be merciful to me,
for in you my soul takes refuge;

in the shadow of your wings I will take refuge,
until the destroying storms pass by.

2 I cry to God Most High,
to God whose purpose is fulfilled for me.

3 God will send from heaven and save me,
putting to shame those who trample on me.
God will send forth God's steadfast love and faithfulness. ℟

4 I lie down among lions that greedily devour human prey;
their teeth are spears and arrows,
their tongues sharp swords.

5 Be exalted, O God, above the heavens.
Let your glory be over all the earth.

6 People set a net for my steps;
my soul was bowed down.

They dug a pit in my path,
but they have fallen into it themselves. ℟

7 My heart is steadfast, O God,
my heart is steadfast. I will sing and make melody.

8 Awake, my soul! Awake, O harp and lyre!
I will awake the dawn.

9 I will give thanks to you, O God, among the peoples;
I will sing praises to you among the nations.

10 For your steadfast love is as high as the heavens;
your faithfulness extends to the clouds.

11 Be exalted, O God, above the heavens,
and let your glory be over all the earth. ℟

Psalm 58

Antiphon: Marty Haugen, 1994

Response

R.

1 Do you indeed decree what is right, you gods?
Do you judge people fairly?

2 No, in your hearts you devise wrongs;
your hands deal out violence on earth.

3 The wicked go astray from the womb;
they err from their birth, speaking lies.

4 They have venom like the venom of a serpent,
like the deaf adder that stops its ear,

5 so that it does not hear the voice of snake charmers
or of the cunning weaver of spells. R.

6 O God, break the teeth in their mouths;
tear out the fangs of the young lions, O God!

7 Let them vanish like water that runs away;
like grass let them be trodden down and wither.

8 Let them be like the snail that dissolves into slime;
like the stillborn child that never sees the sun.

9 Sooner than your pots can feel the heat of thorns, whether green or ablaze,
may God sweep them away!

10 The righteous will rejoice when they see vengeance done;
they will bathe their feet in the blood of the wicked.

11 People will say, "Surely there is a reward for the righteous;
surely there is a God who judges on earth." R.

Psalm 59

℟esponse *Antiphon: Robert Train Adams, 1994*

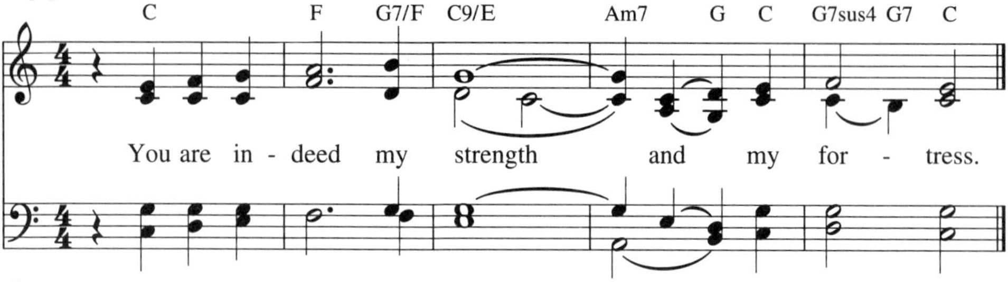

℟

[1]Deliver me from my enemies, Ó my God;
protect me from those who rise úp against me.

[2]Deliver me from those who work evil;
save me from the bloodthirsty.

[3]Even now they lie in wait for my life;
the mighty stir up strife against me.

For no transgression or sin of mine, O God,
[4]for no fault of mine, they run ánd make ready. ℟

Rouse yourself, come to my help and see!
[5]You, Sovereign God of hosts, are Gód of Israel.

Awake to punish áll the nations;
spare none of those who treacherously plot evil.

[6]Each evening they come back,
howling like dogs and prowling abóut the city.

[7]There they are, bellowing with their mouths, with sharp words ón their lips
—for "Who," they think, "will hear us?" ℟

[8]But you laugh at them, O God;
you hold all the nations ín derision.

[9]O my strength, Í will watch for you;
for you, O God, áre my fortress.

[10]In steadfast love my Gód will meet me;
my God will let me look in triumph ón my enemies.

[11]Do not kill them, or my people may forget;
make them totter by your power, and bring them down, Ó God, our shield. ℟

[12]For the sin of their mouths, the words óf their lips,
let them be trapped ín their pride.

For the cursing and lies that they utter,
[13]consume them in wrath;
consume them until they áre no more.

Then it will be known to the ends óf the earth
that God rules óver Jacob.

[14]Each evening they come back,
howling like dogs and prowling abóut the city. ℟

[15]They roam abóut for food,
and growl if they do not get their fill.

[16]But I will sing óf your might;
I will sing aloud of your steadfast love ín the morning.

For you have been a fortress for me
and a refuge in the day of my distress.

17 O my strength, I will sing praises to you,
for you, O God, are my fortress, the God who shows me steadfast love. ℟

(May be sung with double tone.)

Psalm 60

℟esponse

Antiphon: Jane Marshall, 1994

℟

1 O God, you have rejected us and broken our defenses;
you have been angry; now restore us!

2 You have caused the land to quake; you have torn it open;
repair the cracks in it, for it is tottering.

3 You have made your people suffer hard things;
you have given us wine to drink that made us stagger.

4 You have raised a banner for those who fear you,
to rally them out of bowshot. ℟

5 Give victory with your strong hand, and answer us,
so that those whom you love may be rescued.

6 God has promised from the sanctuary:
"With exultation I will divide up Shechem, and portion out the Valley of Succoth.

7 Gilead is mine, and Manasseh is mine;
Ephraim is my helmet; Judah is my scepter.

8 Moab is my washbasin; on Edom I throw my sandal;
over Philistia I shout in triumph." ℟

9 Who will bring me to the fortified city?
Who will lead me to Edom?

10 Have you not rejected us, O God?
You do not march, O God, with our armies.

11 O grant us help against the foe,
for human help is worthless.

12 With God we shall do valiantly;
it is God who will tread down our foes. ℟

(May be sung with double tone.)

Psalm 61

℟esponse *Antiphon: Vérne de la Peña, 1994*

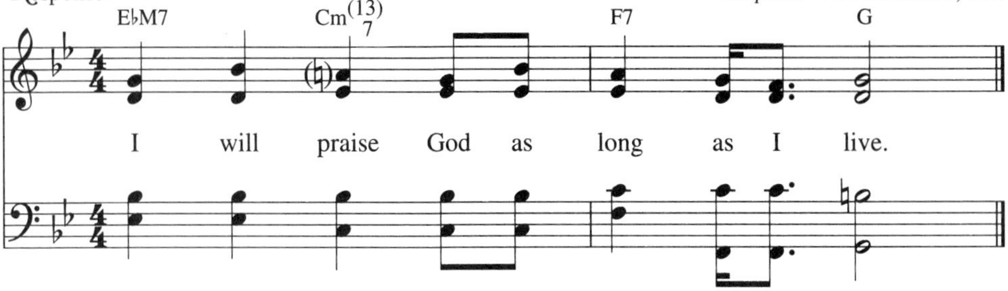

℟

[1]Hear my cry, O God;
listen to my prayer.

[2]From the end of the earth I call to you,
when my heart is faint.
Lead me to the rock that is higher than I;

[3]for you are my refuge,
a strong tower against the enemy.

[4]Let me abide in your tent forever,
find refuge under the shelter of your wings. ℟

[5]For you, O God, have heard my vows;
you have given me the heritage of those who fear your name.

[6]Prolong the life of the ruler;
may the ruler's years endure to all generations!

[7]May the ruler be enthroned forever before God,
and be guarded by your steadfast love and faithfulness!

[8]So I will always sing praises to your name,
as I pay my vows day after day. ℟

(May be sung with double tone.)

Psalm 62

℟esponse *Antiphon: Jean Slates Hawk, 1994*

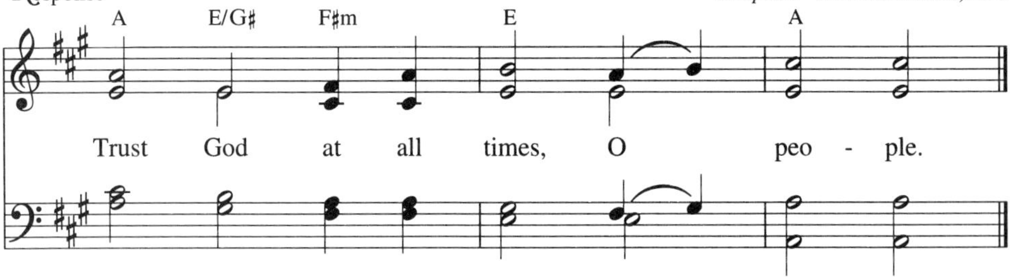

℟

[5]For God alone my soul waits in silence,
for my hope is from God.

[6]God alone is my rock
and my salvation, my fortress;
I shall not be shaken.

7 On God rests my deliverance
ánd my honor;
my mighty rock, my refuge ís
in God.

8 Trust in God at all tímes, O people;
pour out your heart before God
who is a réfuge for us. ℟

9 Those of low estate are but a breath,
those of high estate are á delusion;
in the balances they go up; they
are together lighter thán a breath.

10 Put no confidence in extortion,
and set no vain hópes on robbery;
if riches increase, do not set
your héart on them.

11 Once Gód has spoken;
twice háve I heard this:

that power belóngs to God,
12 and steadfast love belongs to yóu,
O God.

For you repáy to all
according tó their work. ℟

Psalm 63

℟esponse

Antiphon: Vérne de la Peña, 1994

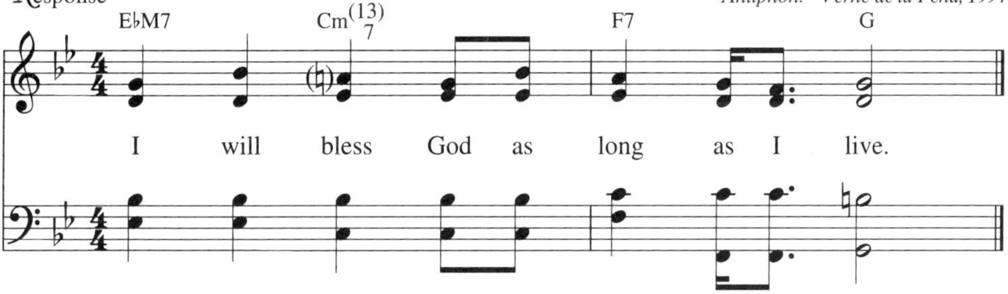

℟

1 O God, you áre my God.
I seek you, my soul thírsts for you;

my flesh fáints for you,
as in a dry and weary land where
there ís no water.

2 So I have looked upon you ín the
sanctuary,
beholding your pówer and glory.

3 Because your steadfast love is bettér
than life,
my líps will praise you.

4 So I will bless you as long ás I live;
I will lift up my hands and call ón
your name. ℟

5 My soul is satisfied as with á rich
feast,
and my mouth praises you with
jóyful lips

6 when I think of you ón my bed,
and meditate on you in the watches
óf the night;

7 for you have béen my help,
and in the shadow of your wings I
síng for joy.

8 My soul clíngs to you;
your mighty hánd upholds me. ℟

9 But those who seek to destróy my life
shall go down into the depths óf the
earth;

℟ I will bless God as long as I live.

[10]they shall be given over to the power of the sword,
they shall be prey for jackals.

[11]But the ruler shall rejoice in God; all who swear by God shall exult,
for the mouths of liars will be stopped.
℟

Psalm 64

℟esponse

Antiphon: David Hurd, 1994

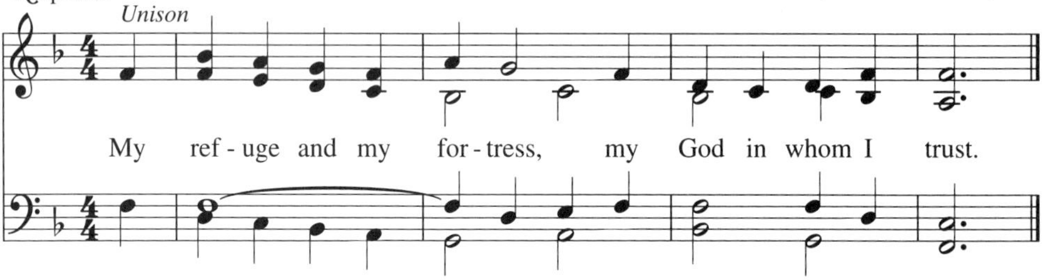

℟

[1]Hear my voice, O God, in my complaint;
preserve my life from the dread enemy.

[2]Hide me from the secret plots of the wicked,
from the scheming of evildoers,

[3]who sharpen their tongues like swords,
who aim bitter words like arrows,

[4]shooting from ambush at the blameless;
they shoot suddenly and without fear.

[5]They hold fast to their evil purpose;
they talk of laying snares secretly,
thinking, "Who can see us? ℟

[6]Who can search out our crimes?
We have thought out a cunningly conceived plot."
For the human heart and mind are deep.

[7]But God will shoot arrows at them;
they will be wounded suddenly.

[8]Because of their tongue God will bring them to ruin;
all who see them will shake with horror.

[9]Then everyone will fear; they will tell what God has brought about,
and ponder what God has done.

[10]Let the righteous rejoice and take refuge in God.
Let all the upright in heart glory. ℟

Psalm 65

Antiphon: Marty Haugen, 1994

℟

1 Praise is due to you, O God, in Zion;
and to you shall vows
be performed,

2 O you who answer prayer!
To you all flesh shall come.

3 When deeds of iniquity overwhelm us,
you forgive our transgressions.

4 Happy are those whom you choose
and bring near to live in your courts.
We shall be satisfied with the
goodness of your house, your
holy temple. ℟

5 By awesome deeds you answer us
with deliverance,
O God of our salvation;

you are the hope of all
the ends of the earth
and of the farthest seas.

6 By your strength you established the
mountains;
you are girded with might.

7 You silence the roaring of the seas,
the roaring of their waves,
the tumult of the peoples. ℟

8 Those who live at earth's farthest
bounds are awed by your signs;
you make the gateways of the
morning and the evening
shout for joy.

9 You visit the earth and water it,
you greatly enrich it;
the river of God is full of water;

you provide the people with grain,
for so you have prepared it.

10 You water its furrows abundantly,
and settle its ridges; ℟

you soften the earth with showers,
and you bless its growth.

11 You crown the year with
your bounty;
your wagon tracks overflow
with richness.

12 The pastures of the wilderness
overflow,
the hills gird themselves with joy,

13 the meadows clothe themselves with
flocks, the valleys deck themselves
with grain,
they shout and sing together
for joy. ℟

Proper 10 [15] A vs. (1–8), 9–13.

Psalm 66

Response *Antiphon: Carolyn Jennings, 1994*

℟

[1]Make a joyful noise to God, all
the earth;
[2]sing the glory of God's name;
give to God glorious praise.

[3]Say to God, "How awesome are
your deeds!
Because of your great power,
your enemies cringe before you.

[4]All the earth worships you;
they sing praises to you,
sing praises to your name."

[5]Come and see what God has done:
God is awesome in deeds
among mortals. ℟

[6]God turned the sea into dry land;
they passed through the river
on foot.

There we rejoiced in God, [7]who
rules by God's might forever,
whose eyes keep watch on the
nations—let the rebellious
not exalt themselves.

[8]Bless our God, O peoples, let the
sound of God's praise be heard,
[9]who has kept us among the
living, and has not let our feet slip.

[10]For you, O God, have tested us;
you have tried us as silver is tried.
℟

[11]You brought us into the net;
you laid burdens on our backs;
[12]you let people ride over our heads;

we went through fire
and through water;
yet you have brought us out to
a spacious place.

[13]I will come into your house
with burnt offerings;
I will pay you my vows [14]that my
lips uttered and my mouth promised
when I was in trouble.

[15]I will offer to you burnt offerings of
fatlings, with the smoke of the
sacrifice of rams;
I will make an offering
of bulls and goats. ℟

[16]Come and hear, all you who fear God,
and I will tell what God
has done for me.
[17]I cried aloud to God,
and extolled God with my tongue.

[18]If I had cherished iniquity in my heart,
God would not have listened.

[19]But truly God has listened;
God has given heed to the words
of my prayer.

20Blessed be God, because God
has not rejected my prayer
or removed God's steadfast
love from me. ℟

Easter 6 A vs. 8–20; Proper 9 [14] C vs. 1–9; Proper 23 [28] C vs. 1–12. (If all verses are used, may be sung with double tone.)

Psalm 67

Antiphon: Peter Niedmann, 1994

℟esponse

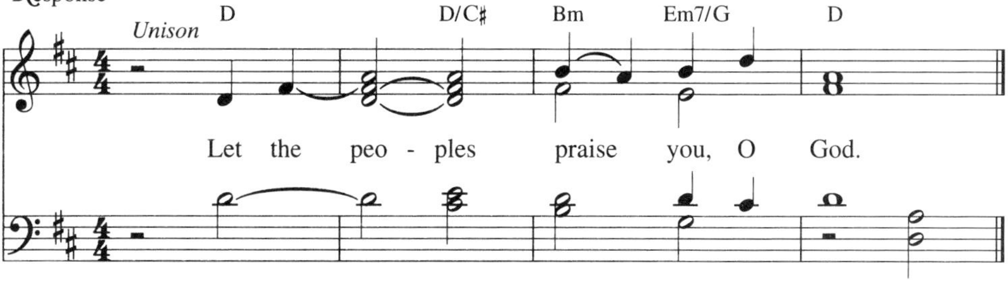

℟

1May God be gracious to us and
bless us
and make God's face to shine
upon us,

2that your way may be known
upon earth,
your saving power
among all nations.

3Let the peoples praise you, O God;
let all the peoples praise you.

4Let the nations be glad and
sing for joy,
for you judge the peoples with
equity and guide the nations
upon earth. ℟

5Let the peoples praise you, O God;
let all the peoples praise you.

6The earth has yielded its increase;
God, our God, has blessed us.

7May God continue to bless us;
let all the ends of the earth
revere God. ℟

Psalm 68

℟ Response *Antiphon: Judy Hunnicutt, 1994*

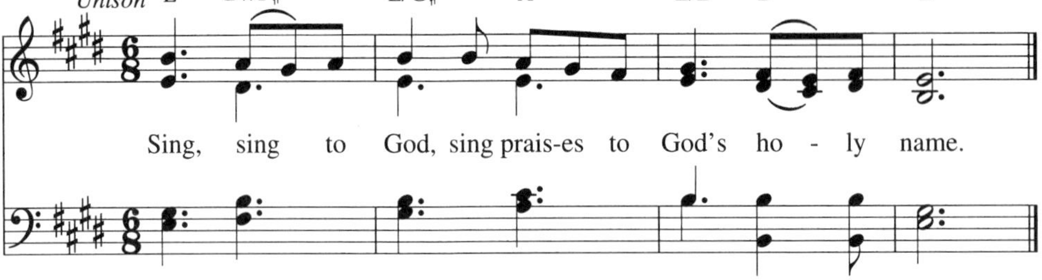

℟

1 Let God rise up, let God's enemies
be scattered;
let those who hate God
flee before God.

2 As smoke is driven away,
so drive them away;
as wax melts before the fire,
let the wicked perish before God.

3 But let the righteous be joyful;
let them exult before God;
let them be jubilant with joy. ℟

4 Sing to God, sing praises
to God's name;
lift up a song to the one who rides
upon the clouds;

be exultant before God
whose name is the Sovereign.

5 Father-Mother of orphans and
protector of widows
is God in God's holy habitation.

6 God gives the desolate a home to
live in; God leads out the prisoners
to prosperity,
but the rebellious live in
a desolate land. ℟

7 O God, when you went out before
your people,
when you marched through the
wilderness, 8 the earth quaked,

the heavens poured down rain at the
presence of God, the God of Sinai,
at the presence of God,
the God of Israel.

9 Rain in abundance, O God, you
showered abroad;
you restored your heritage
when it languished;

10 your flock found a dwelling in it;
in your goodness, O God, you
provided for the needy. ℟

11 God gives the command;
great is the company of those who bore
the tidings:

12 "The rulers of the armies, they flee,
they flee!"
The women at home divide the spoil,

13 though they stay among the sheepfolds
—the wings of a dove are covered with
silver, its pinions with green gold.

14 When the Almighty scattered rulers
there,
snow fell on Zalmon.

15 O mighty mountain, mountain of
Bashan;
O many-peaked mountain, mountain
of Bashan!

℟

16 Why do you look with envy, O many-
peaked mountain,
at the mount that God desired for an
abode to reside there forever?

17 With mighty chariotry, twice ten
thousand, thousands upon thousands,
God came from Sinai into the holy
place.

18 You ascended the high mount, leading
captives in your train and receiving gifts
from people
even from those who rebel against the
Sovereign God's abiding there.

19 Blessed be God, who daily bears us up;
God is our salvation. ℟

20 Our God is a God of salvation,
and to God, the Sovereign, belongs
escape from death.

21 But God will shatter the heads of God's
enemies,
the hairy crown of those who walk in
their guilty ways.

22 God said, "I will bring them back from
Bashan,
I will bring them back from the depths
of the sea,

23 so that you may bathe your feet in
blood,
so that the tongues of your dogs may
have their share from the foe." ℟

24 Your solemn processions are seen, O
God,
the processions of my God, my
Sovereign, into the sanctuary—

25 the singers in front, the musicians last,
between them girls playing
tambourines:

26 "Bless God in the great congregation;
You who are of Israel's fountain,
bless the Sovereign!"

27 There is Benjamin, the least of them,
in the lead,
the princes of Judah in a body, the
princes of Zebulun, the princes of
Naphtali. ℟

28 Summon your might, O God;
show your strength, O God, as you have
done for us before.

29 Rulers bear gifts to you
because of your temple at Jerusalem.

30 Rebuke the wild animals that live
among the reeds,
the herd of bulls with the calves of the
peoples.

Trample under foot those who lust after
tribute;
scatter the peoples who delight in war.

31 Let bronze be brought from Egypt;
let Ethiopia hasten to stretch out its
hands to God. ℟

32 Sing to God, O nations of the earth;
sing praises to God,

33 O rider in the heavens,
the ancient heavens;
listen, God sends out a voice,
a mighty voice.

34 Ascribe power to God, whose
majesty is over Israel;
and whose power is in the skies.

35 Awesome is God in God's sanctuary;
the God of Israel gives power
and strength to God's people.
Blessed be God! ℟

Psalm 69

℟ Response *Unison*

Antiphon: Lee Dengler, 1994

℟

7 It is for your sake that I have
borne reproach,
that shame has covered my face.

8 I have become a stranger to my
kindred,
an alien to my mother's children.

9 It is zeal for your house that has
consumed me;
the insults of those who insult you have
fallen on me. ℟

10 When I humbled my soul with
fasting, they insulted me for doing so.
11 When I made sackcloth my
clothing, I became a
byword to them.

12 I am the subject of gossip for those
who sit in the gate,
and the drunkards make songs
about me.

13 But as for me, my prayer is to
you, O God.
At an acceptable time, O God,
in the abundance of your
steadfast love, answer me.
With your faithful help 14 rescue me
from sinking in the mire;
let me be delivered from my
enemies and from the deep waters.

℟

15 Do not let the flood sweep over me,
or the deep swallow me up,
or the Pit close its mouth over me.

16 Answer me, O God, for your
steadfast love is good;
according to your abundant mercy,
turn to me.

17 Do not hide your face from your
servant, for I am in distress—
make haste to answer me.

18 Draw near to me, redeem me,
set me free because of my enemies.

℟

19 You know the insults I receive, and my
shame and dishonor;
my foes are all known to you.

20 Insults have broken my heart, so that I am ín despair.
I looked for pity, but there was none;
and for comforters, but Í found none.

21 They gave me poíson for food,
and for my thirst they gave me vinegár to drink. ℞

22 Let their table bé a trap for them,
a snare fór their allies.

23 Let their eyes be dimmed so that they cánnot see,
and make their loins tremble continually.

24 Pour out your indignatíon upon them,
and let your burning anger óvertake them.

25 May their camp be a désolation;
let no one live ín their tents.

26 For they persecute those whom you háve struck down,
and those whom you have wounded,
they attáck still more.

27 Add guilt tó their guilt;
may they have no acquittál from you.

28 Let them be blotted out of the book óf the living;
let them not be enrolled amóng the righteous. ℞

29 But I am lowly ánd in pain;
let your salvation, O Gód, protect me.

30 I will praise the name of God wíth a song;
I will magnify God wíth thanksgiving.

31 This will please God more thán an ox,
or more than a bull with hórns and hoofs.

32 Let the oppressed see it ánd be glad;
you who seek God, let your héarts revive. ℞

33 For God héars the needy,
and does not despise God's own that áre in bonds.

34 Let heaven and éarth praise God,
the seas and everything that móves in them.

35 For God will save Zion and rebuild the cíties of Judah;
and God's servants shall live there ánd possess it;

36 the children of God's servants sháll inherit it,
and those who love God's náme shall live in it. ℞

Psalm 70

℟esponse

Antiphon: Elaine Kirkland, 1994

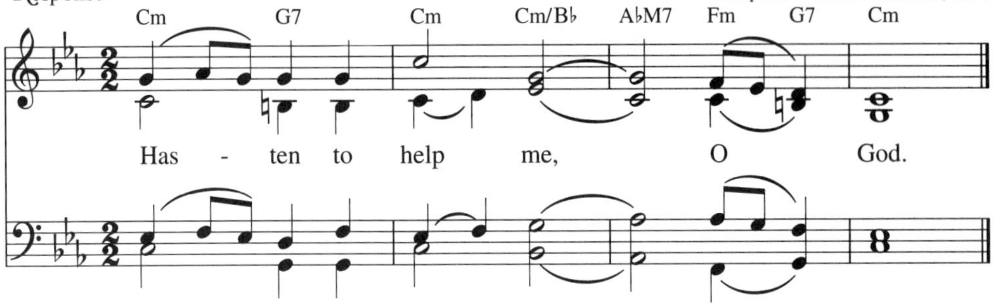

℟

[1]Be pleased, O God, to deliver me.
O God, make haste to help me!

[2]Let those be put to shame and confusion who seek my life.
Let those be turned back and brought to dishonor who desire to hurt me.

[3]Let those who say, "Aha, Aha!"
turn back because of their shame.

[4]Let all who seek you rejoice and be glad in you.
Let those who love your salvation say evermore, "God is great!"

[5]But I am poor and needy; hasten to me, O God!
You are my help and my deliverer; O God, do not delay! ℟

Psalm 71

℟esponse

Antiphon: David Hurd, 1994

℟

[1]In you, O God, I take refuge;
let me never be put to shame.

[2]In your righteousness deliver me and rescue me;
incline your ear to me and save me.

[3]Be to me a rock of refuge, a strong fortress, to save me,
for you are my rock and my fortress.

[4]Rescue me, O my God, from the hand of the wicked,
from the grasp of the unjust and cruel.

[5]For you, O God, are my hope,
my trust, O God, from my youth.
[6]Upon you I have leaned from
my birth;

it was you who took me from my
mother's womb.
My praise is continually of you. ℟

[7]I have been like a portent to many,
but you are my strong refuge.

[8]My mouth is filled with your praise,
and with your glory all day long.

[9]Do not cast me off in the
time of old age;
do not forsake me when my
strength is spent.

[10]For my enemies speak
concerning me,
and those who watch for my
life consult together.

[11]They say, "Pursue and seize that
person whom God has forsaken,
for there is no one to deliver." ℟

[12]O God, do not be far from me;
O my God, make haste to help me!

[13]Let my accusers be put to shame
and consumed;
let those who seek to hurt me be
covered with scorn and disgrace.

[14]But I will hope continually,
and will praise you yet more
and more. ℟

[15]My mouth will tell of your righteous
acts, of your deeds of salvation all day
long,
though their number is past my
knowledge.

[16]I will come praising the mighty deeds of
the Sovereign God,
I will praise your righteousness, yours
alone.

[17]O God, from my youth you have taught
me,
and I still proclaim your wondrous
deeds.

[18]So even to old age and gray hairs, O
God, do not forsake me,
until I proclaim your might to all the
generations to come. ℟

Your power [19]and your righteousness, O
God, reach the high heavens.
You who have done great things, O
God, who is like you?

[20]You who have made me see many
troubles and calamities will revive me
again;
from the depths of the earth you will
bring me up again.

[21]You will increase my honor,
and comfort me once again.

[22]I will also praise you with the harp for
your faithfulness,
O my God; I will sing praises to you
with the lyre, O Holy One of Israel.

[23]My lips will shout for joy when I sing
praises to you;
my soul, which you have rescued, will
also sing for joy.

[24]All day long my tongue will talk of your
righteous help,
for those who tried to do me harm
have been put to shame and disgraced.
℟

Tuesday in Holy Week ABC vs. 1–14; Epiphany 4 [4] C; Proper 16 [21] C vs. 1–6.

Psalm 72

℟esponse

Antiphon: Hyeon Jeong, 1994

℟

1Give the ruler your justice, O God,
and your righteousness
to a ruler's heir.

2May the ruler judge your people
with righteousness,
and your poor with justice.

3May the mountains yield prosperity
for the people,
and the hills, in righteousness. ℟

4May the ruler defend the cause of the
poor of the people,
give deliverance to the needy,
and crush the oppressor.

5May the ruler live while
the sun endures,
and as long as the moon,
throughout all generations.

6May the ruler be like rain
that falls on the mown grass,
like showers that water the earth.

7In the ruler's days may
righteousness flourish
and peace abound, until the
moon is no more. ℟

8May the ruler have dominion from sea
to sea,
and from the River to the ends of the
earth.

9May the foes of the ruler bow down,
and the enemies lick the dust.

10May the monarchs of Tarshish and of
the isles render the ruler tribute,
may the monarchs of Sheba
and Seba bring gifts.

11May all monarchs fall down
before the ruler,
all nations give the ruler service.

12For the ruler delivers the needy
when they call,
the poor and those who have
no helper.

13The ruler has pity on the weak
and the needy,
and saves the lives of the needy.

14From oppression and violence
the ruler redeems their life;
and precious is their blood in
the ruler's sight. ℟

18Blessed be the Sovereign,
the God of Israel,
who alone does wondrous things.

19Blessed be God's glorious name
forever;
may the whole earth be filled
with God's glory.

Amen and Amen.
Amen and Amen. ℟

Epiphany ABC, end with vs. 14; Advent 2 A, omit vs. 10–14.

Psalm 73

℟esponse

Antiphon: Martie McMane, 1994

℟

[1]Truly God is good tó the upright,
to those who are púre in heart.

[2]But as for me, my feet had álmost stumbled;
my steps had ńearly slipped.

[3]For I was envious óf the arrogant;
I saw the prosperity óf the wicked.

[4]For they h́ave no pain;
their bodies are healthý and strong. ℟

[5]They are not in trouble as óthers are;
they are not plagued like óther people.

[6]Therefore pride ís their necklace;
violence covers them ĺike a garment.

[7]Their eyes swell óut with fatness;
their hearts overf́low with follies.

[8]They scoff and śpeak with malice;
loftily they threatén oppression. ℟

[9]They set their mouths ágainst heaven,
and their tongues range óver the earth.

[10]Therefore the people t́urn and praise them,
and find no f́ault in them.

[11]And they say, "How ćan God know?
Is there knowledge in t́he Most High?"

[12]Such áre the wicked;
always at ease, they incŕease in riches. ℟

[13]All in vain I have kept ḿy heart clean
and washed my h́ands in innocence.

[14]For all day long I h́ave been plagued,
and am punished évery morning.

[15]If I had said, "I will talk on ín this way,"
I would have been false to the circle
óf your children.

[16]But when I thought how to únderstand this,
it seemed to me a wearísome task, ℟

[17]until I went into the sanctuarý of God;
then I perceived how t́hey would end.

[18]Truly you set them in ślippery places;
you make them f́all to ruin.

[19]How they are destroyed ín a moment,
swept away utterĺy by terrors!

[20]They are like a dream when óne awakes;
on awaking you deśpise their phantoms. ℟

[21]When my soul ẃas embittered,
when I was pricked ín heart,

[22]I was stupid and ignorant;
toward you I was like á brute beast.

[23]Nevertheless I am continualĺy with you;
you hold me b́y the hand.

℟ God is indeed my refuge and my strength.

24 You guide me with your counsel,
and afterward you will receive me
with honor. ℟

25 Whom have I in heaven but you?
And there is nothing on earth that I
desire other than you.

26 My flesh and my heart may fail,
but God is the strength of my heart
and my portion forever.

27 Indeed, those who are far from you will
perish;
you put an end to those who are false
to you.

28 But for me it is good to be near God;
I have made the Most High God my
refuge, to tell of all your works. ℟

(May be sung with double tone.)

Psalm 74

℟esponse

Antiphon: Elaine Kirkland, 1994

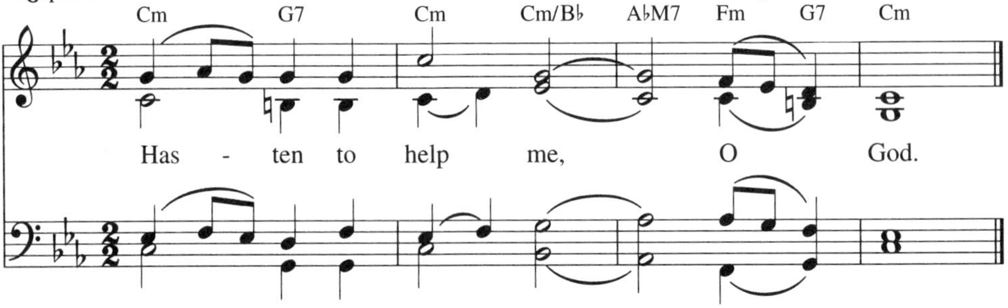

℟

1 O God, why do you cast us off forever?
Why does your anger smoke against
the sheep of your pasture?

2 Remember your congregation, which you
acquired long ago,
which you redeemed to be the tribe
of your heritage.

Remember Mount Zion,
where you came to dwell.

3 Direct your steps to the perpetual ruins;
the enemy has destroyed everything
in the sanctuary. ℟

4 Your foes have roared within your holy
place;
they set up their emblems there.

5 At the upper entrance they hacked the
wooden trellis with axes.

6 And then, with hatchets and hammers,
they smashed all its carved work.

7 They set your sanctuary on fire;
they desecrated the dwelling place of
your name, bringing it to the ground.

8 They said to themselves, "We will
utterly subdue them";
they burned all the meeting places of
God in the land.

9 We do not see our emblems;
there is no longer any prophet, and no
one among us knows how long. ℟

10 How long, O God, is the foe to scoff?
Is the enemy to revile your name
forever?

11 Why do you hold back your hand;
why do you keep your hand in your
bosom?

12 Yet God my sovereign is from of old,
working salvation in the earth.

13 You divided the sea by your might;
you broke the heads of the dragons in the waters.

14 You crushed the heads of Leviathan;
you gave him as food for the creatures of the wilderness. ℟

15 You cut openings for springs and torrents;
you dried up ever-flowing streams.

16 Yours is the day, yours also the night;
you established the luminaries and the sun.

17 You have fixed all the bounds of the earth;
you made summer and winter.

18 Remember this, O God, how the enemy scoffs,
and a godless people reviles your name. ℟

19 Do not deliver the soul of your dove to the wild animals;
do not forget the life of your poor forever.

20 Have regard for your covenant,
for the hidden places of the land are full of the haunts of violence.

21 Do not let the downtrodden be put to shame;
let the poor and needy praise your name.

22 Rise up, O God, plead your cause;
remember how the godless scoff at you all day long.

23 Do not forget the clamor of your foes,
the uproar of your adversaries that goes up continually. ℟

Psalm 75

℟esponse

Antiphon: Judy Hunnicutt, 1994

℟

1 We give thanks to you, O God; we give thanks; your name is near.
People tell of your wondrous deeds.

2 At the set time that I appoint
I will judge with equity.

3 When the earth totters, with all its inhabitants,
it is I who keep its pillars steady.

4 I say to the boastful, "Do not boast,"
and to the wicked, "Do not vaunt your strength;

5 do not lift up your horn on high,
or speak with arrogant voice." ℟

6 For power to raise up comes not from the east or from the west,
nor does it come from the desert;

℟. I will call on God as long as I live (as long as I live).

7 but it is God who exécutes judgment,
putting down one and lifting úp another.

8 For in the hand of God there is a cup with foaming wíne, well mixed;
God will pour a draught from it, and all the wicked of the earth shall drain it down tó the dregs.

9 But I will rejóice forever;
I will sing praises to the Gód of Jacob.

10 All the strength of the wicked I wíll cut off,
but the strength of the righteous shall bé exalted. ℟.

Psalm 76

℟esponse

Antiphon: David Hurd, 1994

℟.

1 In Judah Gód is known,
God's name is gréat in Israel.

2 God's abode has been estáblished in Salem,
God's dwelling pláce in Zion.

3 There God broke the fláshing arrows,
the shield, the sword, and the weapóns of war.

4 Glorióus are you,
more majestic than the everlásting mountains. ℟.

5 The stouthearted were stripped óf their spoil;
they sank into sleep; none of the troops was able to líft a hand.

6 At your rebuke, O Gód of Jacob,
both rider and hórse lay stunned.

7 You indéed are awesome!
Who can stand before you when once your anger ís roused?

8 From the heavens you úttered judgment;
the earth feared ánd was still ℟.

9 when God rose up to estáblish judgment,
to save all the oppressed óf the earth.

10 Human wrath serves ónly to praise you,
when you bind the last bit of your wráth around you.

11 Make vows to the Most High your God, ánd perform them;
let all who surround God bring gifts to the one whó is awesome,

12 who cuts off the spirít of nobles,
who inspires fear in the rulers óf the earth. ℟.

(May be sung with double tone.)

Psalm 77

℟esponse

Antiphon: Emma Lou Diemer, 1994

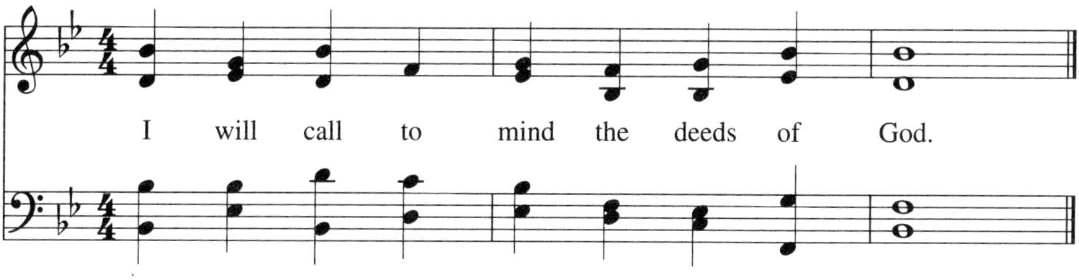

℟

1 I cry alóud to God,
aloud to God, that Gód may
hear me.

2 In the day of my trouble Í seek God;
in the night my hand is stretched
out withóut wearying;
my soul ís not comforted.

3 I think of God, ánd I moan;
I meditate, and my spírit faints.

4 You keep my eyelíds from closing;
I am so troubled that I cánnot speak.
℟

5 I consider the dáys of old,
and remember the years of lóng ago.

6 I commune with my heart ín the night;
I meditate and séarch my spirit:

7 "Will God spurn mé forever,
and never agáin be favorable?

8 Has God's steadfast love céased
forever?
Are God's promises at an end fór all
time? ℟

9 Has God forgotten tó be gracious?
Has God in anger shut up áll
compassion?"

10 And I say, "It ís my grief
that the strong hand of the Most Hígh
is weakened."

11 I will call to mind the déeds of God;
I will remember your
wondérs of old.

12 I will meditate on áll your work;
I will muse on your míghty deeds.
℟

13 Your way, O Gód, is holy.
What god is so great ás our God?

14 You are the God whó works wonders;
you have displayed your might
amóng the peoples.

15 With your strong arm you
redéemed your people,
you redeemed the descendants
of Jacób and Joseph.

16 When the waters saw you, O God,
when the waters saw you,
they wére afraid;
the véry deep trembled. ℟

17 The clouds póured out water;
the skies thundered; your arrows
flashed on évery side.

℟ I will call to mind the deeds of God.

18 The crash of your thunder was
in the whirlwind;
your lightnings lit up the world;
the earth trembled and shook.

19 Your way was through the sea,
your path, through the mighty waters;
yet your footprints were unseen.

20 You led your people like a flock
by the hand of Moses and Aaron. ℟

Psalm 78a

℟esponse

Antiphon: Robert Fryson, 1994

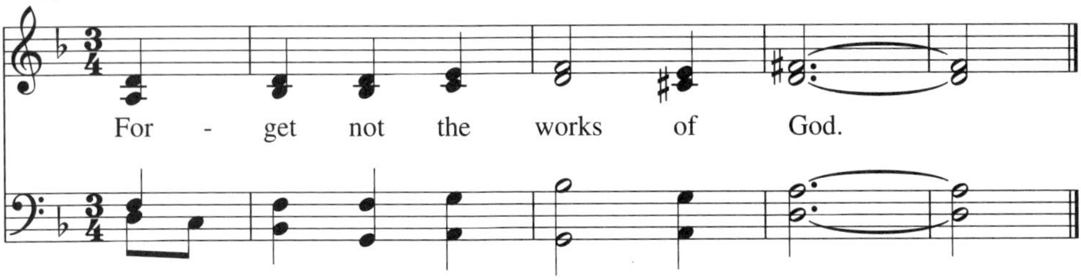

℟

1 Give ear, O my people,
to my teaching;
incline your ears to the words
of my mouth.

2 I will open my mouth in a parable;
I will utter dark sayings
from of old,

3 things that we have heard and known,
that our ancestors have told us.

4 We will not hide them
from their children;
we will tell to the coming
generation the glorious deeds
of God,

we will tell of God's might,
and the wonders that God has done.
℟

5 God established a decree in Jacob,
and appointed a law in Israel,
which God commanded our
ancestors to teach to their children;

6 that the next generation might
know them, the children yet unborn,
that they might rise up and tell
them to their children,

7 so that they should set their
hope in God,
and not forget God's works,
but keep God's commandments. ℟

12 In the sight of their ancestors
God worked marvels in the land
of Egypt, in the fields of Zoan.

13 God divided the sea and let them
pass through it, and made the
waters stand like a heap.

14 In the daytime God led them
with a cloud,
and all night long with
a fiery light.

15 God split rocks open
in the wilderness,
and gave them drink abundantly
as from the deep.

16 God made streams come out of
the rock,
and caused waters to flow
down like rivers. ℟

23Yet God commanded the skies above,
and opened the doors of heaven;

24God rained down on them manna
to eat,
and gave them the grain of heaven.

25Mortals ate of the bread of angels;
God sent them food in abundance.
℟

26God caused the east wind to blow
in the heavens,
and by God's power led out
the south wind;

27God rained flesh upon them like dust,
winged birds like the sand
of the seas;

28God let them fall within their camp, and
all around their dwellings.

29And they ate and were well filled,
for God gave them
what they craved. ℟

32In spite of all this they still sinned;
they did not believe
in God's wonders.

33So God made their days vanish
like a breath,
and their years in terror. ℟

34When God killed them,
they sought for God;
they repented and sought God
earnestly.

35They remembered that God
was their rock,
the Most High God their redeemer.

36But they flattered God
with their mouths;
they lied to God with their tongues.

37Their heart was not steadfast
toward God;
they were not true
to God's covenant.

38Yet God, being compassionate,
forgave their iniquity,
and did not destroy them;
often God was restrained in anger,
and did not stir up all God's wrath.
℟

Proper 21 [26] A vs. 1–4, 12–16; Proper 27 [32] A vs. 1–7; Proper 13 [18] B vs. 23–29; Holy Cross ABC vs. 1–2, 34–38 (Alt.).

(Verses 32 and 33 have been added here to the lectionary verses.)

Psalm 78b

℟

39God remembered that they were but
flesh,
a wind that passes and does not come
again.

40How often they rebelled against God in
the wilderness
and grieved God in the desert!

41They tested God again and again,
and provoked the Holy One of Israel.

42They did not keep in mind God's power,
or the day when God redeemed them
from the foe;

43when God displayed the signs in Egypt,
and the miracles in the fields of Zoan.
℟

44God turned their rivers to blood,
so that they could not drink of their
streams.

℟ Forget not the works of God.

45God sent among them swarms of flies,
which devoured them,
and frogs, which destroyed them.

46God gave their crops to the caterpillar,
and the fruit of their labor to the locust.

47God destroyed their vines with hail,
and their sycamores with frost. ℟

48God gave over their cattle to the hail,
and their flocks to thunderbolts.

49God let loose fierce anger on them—
wrath, indignation, and distress, a company of destroying angels.

50God made a path for God's anger,
and did not spare them from death,
but gave their lives over to the plague.

51God struck all the firstborn in Egypt,
the first issue of their strength in the tents of Ham. ℟

52Then God led out the people like sheep,
and guided them in the wilderness like a flock.

53God led them in safety, so that they were not afraid;
but the sea overwhelmed their enemies.

54And God brought them to God's holy hill,
to the mountain that God's strong hand had won.

55God drove out nations before them;
God apportioned them for a possession and settled the tribes of Israel in their tents. ℟

56Yet they tested and rebelled against the Most High God.
They did not observe God's decrees,

57but turned away and were faithless like their ancestors;
they twisted like a treacherous bow.

58For they provoked God to anger with their high places;
they moved God to jealousy with their idols.

59On hearing, God was full of wrath,
and utterly rejected Israel. ℟

60God abandoned God's dwelling at Shiloh,
the tent where God dwelt among mortals,

61and delivered God's power to captivity,
God's glory to the hand of the foe.

62God gave the people to the sword,
and vented wrath on God's heritage.

63Fire devoured their young men,
and their girls had no marriage song. ℟

64Their priests fell by the sword,
and their widows made no lamentation.

65Then God awoke as from sleep,
like a warrior shouting because of wine.

66God put God's adversaries to rout;
putting them to everlasting disgrace.

67God rejected the tent of Joseph,
and did not choose the tribe of Ephraim,

68but chose the tribe of Judah,
Mount Zion, which God loves. ℟

69God built the sanctuary like the high heavens,
like the earth, which God has founded forever.

70 God chose God's servant David,
and took him from the sheepfolds;
71 God brought David from tending the
nursing ewes
to be the shepherd of God's people
Jacob, of Israel, God's inheritance.
72 With upright heart David tended them,
and guided them with skillful hand. ℟

Psalm 79

℟esponse

Antiphon: Jane Marshall, 1994

℟

1 O God, the nations have come
into your inheritance;
they have defiled your holy temple;
they have laid Jerusalem in ruins.

2 They have given the bodies
of your servants to the birds
of the air for food,
the flesh of your faithful
to the wild animals of the earth.

3 They have poured out their blood like
water all around Jerusalem,
and there was no one to bury them.

4 We have become a taunt
to our neighbors,
mocked and derided by those
around us.

5 How long, O God? Will you
be angry forever?
Will your jealous wrath burn
like fire? ℟

6 Pour out your anger on the nations
that do not know you,
and on the nations that do not
call on your name.

7 For they have devoured Jacob
and laid waste his habitation.

8 Do not remember against us the
iniquities of our ancestors;
let your compassion come speedily
to meet us, for we are brought
very low.

9 Help us, O God of our salvation,
for the glory of your name;
deliver us, and forgive our sins,
for your name's sake. ℟

Psalm 80

℟esponse

Antiphon: Vérne de la Peña, 1994

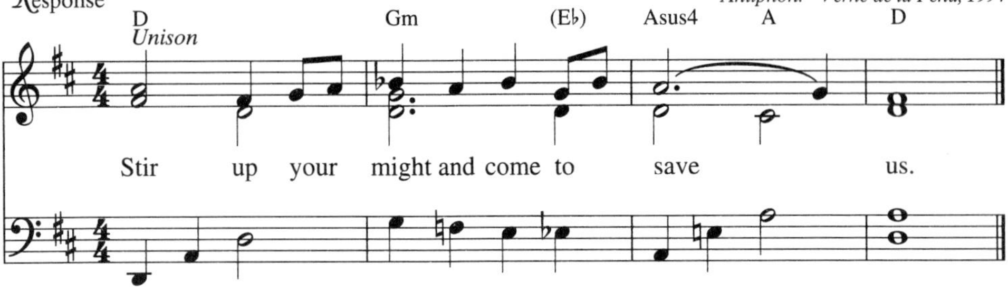

℟

[1]Give ear, O Shepherd of Israel,
you who lead Joseph like a flock!
You who are enthroned upon
the cherubim,

shine forth [2]before Ephraim
and Benjamin and Manasseh.
Stir up your might, and come
to save us!

[3]Restore us, O God;
let your face shine, that
we may be saved.

[4]O Sovereign God of hosts, how long
will you be angry with your
people's prayers?
[5]You have fed them with the
bread of tears, and given them tears
to drink in full measure.

[6]You make us the scorn
of our neighbors;
our enemies laugh
among themselves.

[7]Restore us, O God of hosts;
let your face shine,
that we may be saved. ℟

[8]You brought a vine out of Egypt;
you drove out the nations
and planted it.

[9]You cleared the ground for it;
it took deep root and filled the land.

[10]The mountains were covered
with its shade,
the mighty cedars with its branches;

[11]it sent out its branches to the sea,
and its shoots to the River.

[12]Why then have you broken down
its walls,
so that all who pass along the
way pluck its fruit?

[13]The boar from the forest ravages it,
and all that move in the field
feed upon it. ℟

[14]Turn again, O God of hosts; look
down from heaven, and see;
have regard for this vine,
[15]the stock that your
strong hand planted.

[16]They have burned it with fire,
they have cut it down;
may they perish at the rebuke
of your countenance.

[17]But let your hand be upon the
one at your right hand,
the one whom you made strong
for yourself.

18 Then we will never turn back
from you;
give us life, and we will
call on your name.

19 Restore us, O Sovereign
God of hosts;
let your face shine,
that we may be saved. ℟

Advent 4 A and 1 B vs. 1–7, 17–19; Proper 22 [27] A vs. 7–15; Advent 4 C vs. 1–7 (Alt.); Proper 15 [20] C vs. 1–2, 8–19.

Psalm 81

℟esponse

Antiphon: Jean Slates Hawk, 1994

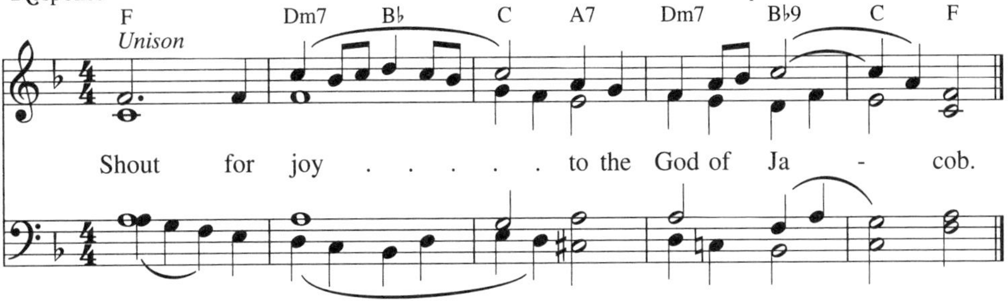

℟

1 Sing aloud to God our strength;
shout for joy to the God of Jacob.

2 Raise a song, sound the tambourine,
the sweet lyre with the harp.

3 Blow the trumpet at the new moon,
at the full moon, on our festal day.

4 For it is a statute for Israel,
an ordinance of the God of Jacob. ℟

5 God made it a decree in Joseph, when
he went out over the land of Egypt.
I hear a voice I had not known:

6 "I relieved your shoulder
of the burden;
your hands were freed
from the basket.

7 In distress you called,
and I rescued you;
I answered you in the secret place
of thunder; I tested you at the
waters of Meribah.

8 Hear, O my people, while I
admonish you;
O Israel, if you would but
listen to me! ℟

9 There shall be no strange god
among you;
you shall not bow down to a
foreign god.

10 I am the Sovereign your God,
who brought you up out of the
land of Egypt.
Open your mouth wide and I
will fill it.

11 But my people did not listen to
my voice;
Israel would not submit to me.

12 So I gave them over to their
stubborn hearts,
to follow their own counsels. ℟

13 O that my people would
listen to me,
that Israel would walk in my ways!

℟ Shout for joy to the God of Jacob.

14 Then I would quickly subdue
their enemies,
and turn my hand against their foes.

15 Those who hate God would
cringe before God,
and their doom would last forever.

16 I would feed you with the finest
of the wheat,
and with honey from the rock
I would satisfy you." ℟

Epiphany 9 [9] B, Proper 4 [9] B vs. 1–10; Proper 17 [22] C vs. 10–16. (If all verses are used, may be sung with double tone.)

Psalm 82

℟esponse

Antiphon: Marty Haugen, 1994

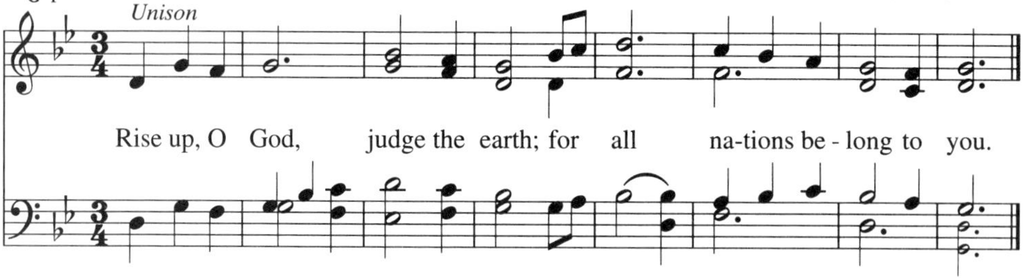

℟

1 In the divine council God has
taken God's place;
God holds judgment in the
midst of the gods:

2 "How long will you judge unjustly
and show partiality to the wicked?

3 Give justice to the weak
and the orphan;
maintain the right of the
lowly and the destitute.

4 Rescue the weak and the needy;
deliver them from the hand of
the wicked." ℟

5 They have neither knowledge
nor understanding, they walk
around in shadows;
all the foundations of the
earth are shaken.

6 I say, "You are gods,
children of the Most High,
all of you;

7 nevertheless, you shall die
like mortals,
and fall like any noble."

8 Rise up, O God, judge the earth;
for all the nations belong to you! ℟

(May be sung with double tone.)

Psalm 83

Antiphon: Vérne de la Peña, 1994

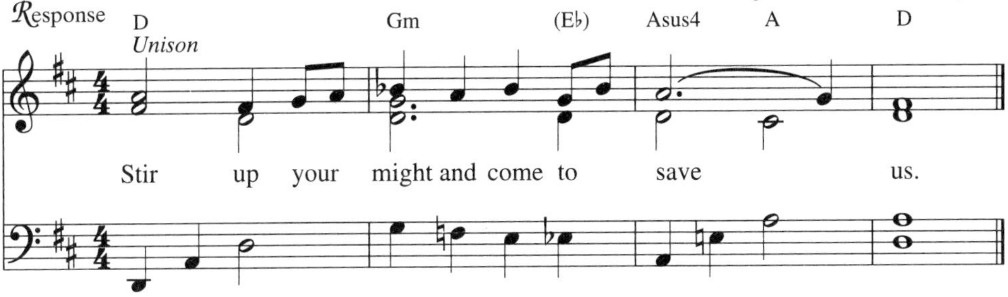

℞

1 O God, do not keep silence;
do not hold your peace or be still, O God!

2 Even now your enemies are in tumult;
those who hate you have raised their heads.

3 They lay crafty plans against your people;
they consult together against those you protect.

4 They say, "Come, let us wipe them out as a nation;
let the name of Israel be remembered no more." ℞

5 They conspire with one accord;
against you they make a covenant—

6 the tents of Edom and the Ishmaelites,
Moab and the offspring of Hagar.

7 Gebal and Ammon and Amalek,
Philistia with the inhabitants of Tyre;

8 Assyria also has joined them,
lending strength to the children of Lot. ℞

9 Do to them as you did to Midian,
as to Sisera and Jabin at the Wadi Kishon,

10 who were destroyed at En-dor,
who became dung for the ground.

11 Make their nobles like Oreb and Zeeb,
all their princes like Zebah and Zalmunna;

12 they said, "Let us take the pastures of God
and make them our own possession." ℞

13 O my God, make them like whirling dust,
like chaff before the wind.

14 As fire consumes the forest,
as the flame sets the mountains ablaze,

15 so pursue them with your tempest
and terrify them with your hurricane.

16 Fill their faces with shame,
so that they may seek your name, O God.

17 Let them be put to shame and dismayed forever;
let them perish in disgrace.

18 Let them know that you alone, whose name is God,
are the Most High over all the earth. ℞

Psalm 84

*R*esponse

Antiphon: Peter Niedmann, 1994

R

1 How lovely is your dwelling place,
O God of hosts!

2 My soul longs, indeed it faints
for the courts of God;
my heart and my flesh sing
for joy to the living God.

3 Even the sparrow finds a home,
and the swallow a nest for herself,

where she may lay her young,
at your altars,
O God of hosts, my Ruler
and my God. *R*

4 Happy are those who live
in your house,
ever singing your praise.

5 Happy are those whose strength
is in you,
in whose heart are the
highways to Zion.

6 As they go through the valley of Baca
they make it a place of springs;
the early rain also covers it
with pools.

7 They go from strength to strength;
the God of gods will be seen
in Zion. *R*

8 O Sovereign God of hosts, hear
my prayer;
give ear, O God of Jacob!

9 Behold our shield, O God;
look on the face of your anointed.

10 For a day in your courts is better than
a thousand elsewhere.
I would rather be a doorkeeper
in the house of my God than live
in the tents of wickedness.

11 For the Sovereign God is a sun
and shield;
God bestows favor and honor.

No good thing does God withhold
from those who walk uprightly.

12 O God of hosts,
happy is everyone who trusts
in you. *R*

Proper 25 [30] C vs. 1–7.

Psalm 85

Antiphon: Carolyn Jennings, 1994

℟

1O God, you were favorable
to your land;
you restored the fortunes of Jacob.

2You forgave the iniquity
of your people;
you pardoned all their sin.

3You withdrew all your wrath;
you turned from your hot anger.

4Restore us again, O God of our
salvation,
and put away your indignation
toward us. ℟

5Will you be angry with us forever?
Will you prolong your anger
to all generations?

6Will you not revive us again,
so that your people may
rejoice in you?

7Show us your steadfast love, O God,
and grant us your salvation. ℟

8Let me hear what God the
Sovereign will speak,
for God will speak peace
to the people;
God will speak to the faithful,
to those who turn to God in
their hearts.

9Surely God's salvation is at hand for
those who fear God,
that God's glory may dwell in
our land. ℟

10Steadfast love and faithfulness
will meet;
righteousness and peace will
kiss each other.

11Faithfulness will spring up
from the ground,
and righteousness will look
down from the sky.

12God will give what is good,
and our land will yield its increase.

13Righteousness will go before God,
and will make a path
for God's steps. ℟

Proper 10 [15] B and Proper 14 [19] A vs. 8–13; Advent 2 B omit vs. 3–7.

Psalm 86

℟esponse

Antiphon: Judy Hunnicutt, 1994

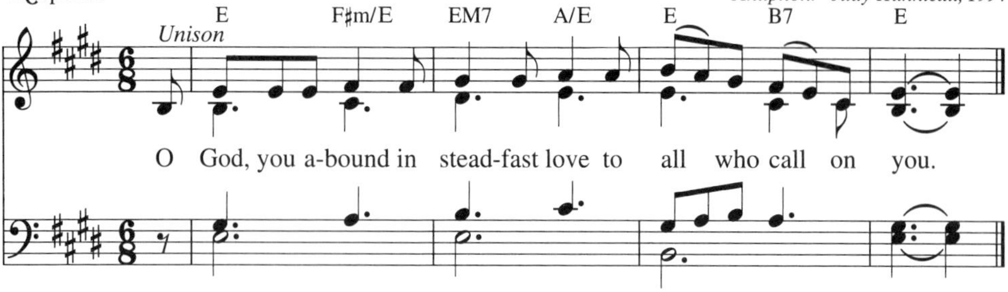

℟

1 Incline your ear, O God,
and ánswer me,
for I am póor and needy.

2 Preserve my life, for I am
devóted to you;
save your servant
who trústs in you.

You áre my God;
3 be gracious to me, O God,
for to you do I cry áll day long.

4 Gladden the soul óf your servant,
for to you, O God,
I lift úp my soul. ℟

5 For you, O God, are good ánd
forgiving,
abounding in steadfast love to
all who cáll on you.

6 Give ear, O God, tó my prayer;
listen to my cry of súpplication.

7 In the day of my trouble
I cáll on you,
for you will ánswer me.

8 There is none like you among
the góds, O God,
nor are there any wórks like yours.

℟

9 All the nations you have made
shall come and bow down
before yóu, O God,
and shall glorífy your name.

10 For you are great and do
wóndrous things;
you alóne are God.

11 Teach me your wáy, O God,
that I may walk ín your truth;
give me an undivided heart to
revére your name.

12 I give thanks to you, O God my God,
with áll my heart,
and I will glorify your náme
forever. ℟

13 For great is your steadfast lóve
toward me;
you have délivered my soul
from the dépths of Sheol.

14 O God, the insolent rise úp
against me;
a band of ruffians seeks my life,
and they do not set yóu
before them.

15 But yóu, O God, are a God
mercíful and gracious,
slow to ánger and abounding
in steadfast lóve and faithfulness.

16 Turn to me and be gracious to me;
give your strength to your servant;
save the child of your servant.

17 Show me a sign of your favor, so
that those who hate me may see it
and be put to shame, because you,
O God, have helped me and
comforted me. ℟

Proper 7 [12] A vs. 1–10, 16–17; Proper 11 [16] A vs. 11–17.

Psalm 87

℟

1 On the holy mount
stands the city God founded;

2 God loves the gates of Zion
more than all the dwellings of Jacob.

3 Glorious things are spoken of you,
O city of God.

4 Rahab and Babylon are among those who
know me. Of Philistia and Tyre, with
Ethiopia,
it is said—"This one was born
there." ℟

5 And of Zion it shall be said, "This one
and that one were born in it";
for the Most High indeed will
establish it.

6 In registering the peoples, God records,
"This one was born there."

7 Singers and dancers alike say,
"All my springs are in you." ℟

Psalm 88

℟esponse

Antiphon: Marty Haugen, 1994

℟

1 O Most High, God of my salvation,
when I cry out in your presence in the night,

2 then let my prayer come before you;
incline your ear to my cry.

3 For my soul is full of troubles,
and my life draws near to Sheol.

4 I am counted among those who go down to the Pit;
I am like those who have no help, ℟

5 like those forsaken among the dead,
like the slain that lie in the grave,

like those whom you remember no more,
for they are cut off from your hand.

6 You have put me in the depths of the Pit,
in the regions deep and hidden.

7 Your wrath lies heavy upon me,
and you overwhelm me with all your waves. ℟

8 You have caused my companions to shun me;
you have made me a thing of horror to them.

I am shut in so that I cannot escape;
9 my eye grows dim through sorrow.

Every day I call on you, O God;
I spread out my hands to you.

10 Do you work wonders for the dead?
Do the shades rise up to praise you? ℟

11 Is your steadfast love declared in the grave,
or your faithfulness in Abaddon?

12 Are your wonders known in the shadows,
or your saving help in the land of forgetfulness?

13 But I, O God, cry out to you;
in the morning my prayer comes before you.

14 O God, why do you cast me off?
Why do you hide your face from me? ℟

15 Wretched and close to death from my youth up,
I suffer your terrors; I am desperate.

16 Your wrath has swept over me;
your dread assaults destroy me.

17 They surround me like a flood all day long;
from all sides they close in on me.

18 You have caused friend and neighbor to shun me;
my companions are far away. ℟

(May be sung with double tone.)

Psalm 89a

Response | *Antiphon: Lee Dengler, 1994*

R.

1 I will sing of your steadfast love,
O God, forever;
with my mouth I will proclaim
your faithfulness to all generations.

2 I declare that your steadfast love
is established forever;
your faithfulness is as firm
as the heavens.

3 You said, "I have made a
covenant with my chosen one,
I have sworn to my servant David:

4 'I will establish your descendants
forever,
and build your throne for all
generations.'" R.

5 Let the heavens praise your wonders, O
God,
your faithfulness in the assembly of
the holy ones.

6 For who in the skies can be compared to
God?
Who among the heavenly beings is
like God,

7 a God feared in the council of the holy
ones,
great and awesome above all that are
around God?

8 O Sovereign God of hosts, who is as
mighty as you, O God?
Your faithfulness surrounds you.

9 You rule the raging of the sea;
when its waves rise, you still them. R.

10 You crushed Rahab like a carcass;
you scattered your enemies with your
mighty arm.

11 The heavens are yours, the earth also is
yours;
the world and all that is in it—you
have founded them.

12 The north and the south—you created
them;
Tabor and Hermon joyously praise
your name.

13 You have a mighty arm;
your hand is powerful, your strong
hand is lifted high.

14 Righteousness and justice are the
foundation of your throne;
steadfast love and faithfulness go
before you. R.

15 Happy are the people who know
the festal shout,
who walk, O God, in the light
of your countenance;

16 they exult in your name all day long, and
extol your righteousness.

17 For you are the glory
of their strength;
by your favor our horn is exalted.

℟ Your steadfast love is established forever.

18 For our shield belongs to God,
our ruler to the Holy One of Israel.
℟

19 Then you spoke in a vision to
your faithful one, and said:
"I have set the crown on one
who is mighty, I have exalted
one chosen from the people.

20 I have found my servant David;
with my holy oil
I have anointed him;

21 my hand shall always remain
with him;
my arm also shall strengthen him.

22 The enemy shall not outwit him,
the wicked shall not humble him.
℟

23 I will crush his foes before him
and strike down those
who hate him.

24 My faithfulness and steadfast love
shall be with him;
and in my name his horn
shall be exalted.

25 I will set his hand on the sea
and his right hand on the rivers.

26 He shall cry to me, 'You are my
Father and Mother,
my God, and the Rock
of my salvation!' ℟

27 I will make him the firstborn,
the highest of the rulers
of the earth.

28 Forever I will keep my steadfast
love for him,
and my covenant with him
will stand firm.

29 I will establish his line forever,
and his throne as long as the
heavens endure. ℟

30 If his children forsake my law
and do not walk according to
my ordinances,

31 if they violate my statutes
and do not keep my
commandments,

32 then I will punish their transgression
with the rod
and their iniquity with scourges;

33 but I will not remove from him
my steadfast love,
or be false to my faithfulness. ℟

34 I will not violate my covenant,
or alter the word that went forth
from my lips.

35 Once and for all I have sworn
by my holiness;
I will not lie to David.

36 His line shall continue forever,
and his throne endure before me
like the sun.

37 It shall be established forever
like the moon,
an enduring witness in the skies."
℟

Proper 8 [13] A vs. 1–4, 15–18; Advent 4 B vs. 1–4, 19–26 (Alt.); Proper 11 [16] B vs. 20–37.

Psalm 89b

℟

38 But now you have spurned and rejected David;
you are full of wrath against your anointed.

39 You have renounced the covenant with your servant;
you have defiled his crown in the dust.

40 You have broken through all his walls;
you have laid his strongholds in ruins.

41 All who pass by plunder him;
he has become the scorn of his neighbors. ℟

42 You have exalted the strong hand of his foes;
you have made all his enemies rejoice.

43 Moreover, you have turned back the edge of his sword,
and you have not supported him in battle.

44 You have removed the scepter from his hand,
and hurled his throne to the ground.

45 You have cut short the days of his youth;
you have covered him with shame.

46 How long, O God? Will you hide yourself forever?
How long will your wrath burn like fire? ℟

47 Remember how short my time is—
for what vanity you have created all mortals!

48 Who can live and never see death?
Who can escape the power of Sheol?

49 O God, where is your steadfast love of old,
which in your faithfulness you swore to David?

50 Remember, O God, how your servant is taunted;
how I bear in my bosom the insults of the peoples,

51 with which your enemies taunt, O God,
with which they taunted the footsteps of your anointed.

52 Blessed be God forever.
Amen and Amen. ℟

Psalm 90

℟esponse

Antiphon: Elaine Kirkland, 1994

℟

1 O God, you have been our dwelling place
in all generations.

2 Before the mountains were brought forth, or ever you had formed the earth and the world,

℟ From everlasting to everlasting, you are God.

from everlasting to everlasting
yóu are God.

3 You turn us báck to dust,
and say, "Turn báck, you mortals."

4 For a thousand years in your sight are
like yesterday when ít is past,
or like a watch ín the night. ℟

5 You sweep them away;
they are líke a dream,
like grass that is renewed ín
the morning;

6 in the morning it flourishes
and ís renewed;
in the evening it fádes and withers.

7 For we are consumed bý your anger;
by your wrath we are óverwhelmed.

8 You have set our iniquíties
before you,
our secret sins in the light óf
your countenance. ℟

9 For all our days pass away
undér your wrath;
our years come to an end
líke a sigh.

10 The days of our life are sevénty years,
or perhaps eighty, if wé are strong;

even then their span is only tóil
and trouble;
they are soon gone,
and we flý away.

11 Who considers the power
óf your anger?
Your wrath is as great as the
fear thát is due you.

12 So teach us to cóunt our days
that we may gain á wise heart. ℟

13 Turn, O Gód! How long?
Have compassion ón your servants!

14 Satisfy us in the morning
with your stéadfast love,
so that we may rejoice
and be glad áll our days.

15 Make us glad as many days as
you háve afflicted us,
and as many years as
we háve seen evil.

16 Let your work be manifest
tó your servants,
and your glorious power
tó their children.

17 Let the favor of the Sovereign our
God be upon us, and prosper for us
the work óf our hands—
O prosper the work óf our hands! ℟

Proper 25 [30] A vs. 1–6, 13–17; Proper 28 [33] A vs. 1–8, (9–11), 12; Proper 23 [28] B vs. 12–17.

Psalm 91

Response

Antiphon: David Hurd, 1994

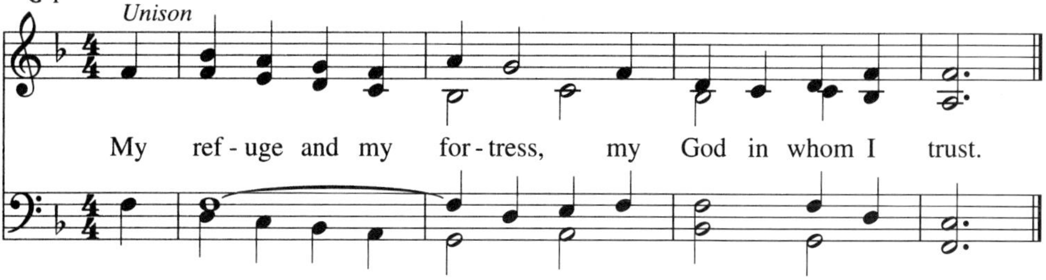

℟

1 You who live in the shelter of
the Most High,
who abide in the shadow of
the Almighty, 2 will say to God,

"My refuge and my fortress;
my God, in whom I trust."

3 For God will deliver you from
the snare of the fowler
and from the deadly pestilence;

4 God will cover you with God's
pinions, and under God's wings
you will find refuge;
God's faithfulness is a shield
and buckler. ℟

5 You will not fear the terror
of the night,
or the arrow that flies by day,

6 or the pestilence that stalks in
the nighttime,
or the destruction that wastes
at noonday.

9 Because you have made God
your refuge,
the Most High your dwelling place,

10 no evil shall befall you,
no scourge come near your tent. ℟

11 For God will command God's angels
concerning you
to guard you in all your ways.

12 On their hands they will bear you up,
so that you will not dash your foot
against a stone.

13 You will tread on the lion
and the adder,
the young lion and the serpent
you will trample under foot.

14 Those who love me, I will deliver;
I will protect those who know
my name.

15 When they call to me,
I will answer them;
I will be with them in trouble,
I will rescue them and honor them.

16 With long life I will satisfy them,
and show them my salvation. ℟

Proper 24 [29] B omit vs. 1–8; Lent 1 C omit vs. 3–8;
Proper 21 [26] C omit vs. 7–13.

Psalm 92

℞esponse

Antiphon: Robert Train Adams, 1994

℞

1 It is good to give thanks to God,
to sing praises to your name,
O Most High;

2 to declare your steadfast love in
the morning,
and your faithfulness by night,

3 to the music of the lute and the harp,
to the melody of the lyre.

4 For you, O God, have made me glad
by your work;
at the works of your hands
I sing for joy. ℞

12 The righteous flourish like the
palm tree,
and grow like a cedar in Lebanon.

13 They are planted in the house of God;
they flourish in the courts
of our God.

14 In old age they still produce fruit;
they are always green
and full of sap,

15 showing that God is upright;
God is my rock, and has
no unrighteousness. ℞

(May be sung with double tone.)

Psalm 93

℟esponse

Antiphon: Emma Lou Diemer, 1994

℟

[1]God is ruler, God is ŕobed in majesty;
the Sovereign is robed,
and is gird́ed with strength.

God has estab́lished the world;
it shall nev́er be moved;

[2]your throne is established f́rom
of old;
you are from éverlasting. ℟

[3]The floods have lifted up, O God,
the floods have lifted úp their voice;
the floods lift úp their roaring.

[4]More majestic than the thunders
of ḿighty waters,
more majestic than the waves
of the sea, majestic on h́igh is God!

[5]Your decrees are v́ery sure;
holiness befits your house,
O God, forévermore. ℟

Psalm 94

℟esponse

Antiphon: Marty Haugen, 1994

℟

[1]O God, you Ǵod of vengeance,
you God of vengeánce, shine forth!

[2]Rise up, O judge óf the earth;
give to the proud what t́hey deserve!

℟ Rise up, O God, judge the earth; for all nations belong to you.

3O God, how long shall the wicked,
how long shall the wicked exult?

4They pour out their arrogant words;
all the evildoers boast. ℟

5They crush your people, O God,
and afflict your heritage.

6They kill the widow and the stranger,
they murder the orphan,

7and they say, "God does not see;
the God of Jacob does not perceive."

8Understand, O dullest of the people;
fools, when will you be wise? ℟

9Does the one who planted the ear not hear?
Does the one who formed the eye not see?

10Does the one who disciplines the nations not chastise—
the one who teaches knowledge to humankind?

11God knows our thoughts,
that they are but an empty breath.

12Happy are those whom you discipline, O God,
and those whom you teach out of your law,

13giving them respite from days of trouble,
until a pit is dug for the wicked. ℟

14For God will not forsake God's people,
and will not abandon God's heritage;

15for justice will return to the righteous,
and all the upright in heart will follow it.

16Who rises up for me against the wicked?
Who stands up for me against evildoers?

17If the God had not been my help,
my soul would soon have lived in the land of silence. ℟

18When I thought, "My foot is slipping,"
your steadfast love, O God, held me up.

19When the cares of my heart are many,
your consolations cheer my soul.

20Can wicked rulers be allied with you,
those who contrive mischief by statute?

21They band together against the life of the righteous,
and condemn the innocent to death.

22But God has become my stronghold,
and my God the rock of my refuge.

23God will repay them for their iniquity
and wipe them out for their wickedness;
the Most High our God will wipe them out. ℟

Psalm 95

Antiphon: Robert Fryson, 1994

Response

R.

[1]O come, let us sing to God;
let us make a joyful noise to
the rock of our salvation!

[2]Let us come into God's presence
with thanksgiving;
let us make a joyful noise to
God with songs of praise!

[3]For God is a great God,
and a great Ruler above all gods.

[4]In God's hand are the depths of the
earth;
the heights of the mountains
are also God's. R.

[5]The sea is God's, for God made it,
and the dry land, which God's hands
have formed.

[6]O come, let us worship and bow
down,
let us kneel before God, our Maker!

[7]For God is our God,
and we are the people of God's
pasture, and the sheep of God's hand.

O that today you would listen to
God's voice!

[8]Do not harden your hearts,
as at Meribah, as on the day at
Massah in the wilderness, R.

[9]when your ancestors tested me,
and put me to the proof, though
they had seen my work.

[10]For forty years I loathed
that generation and said,
"They are a people whose hearts go
astray, and they do not regard my
ways."

[11]Therefore in my anger I swore,
"They shall not enter my rest." R.

Proper 29 [34] A vs. 1–7a.

Psalm 96

Response

Antiphon: Jane Marshall, 1994

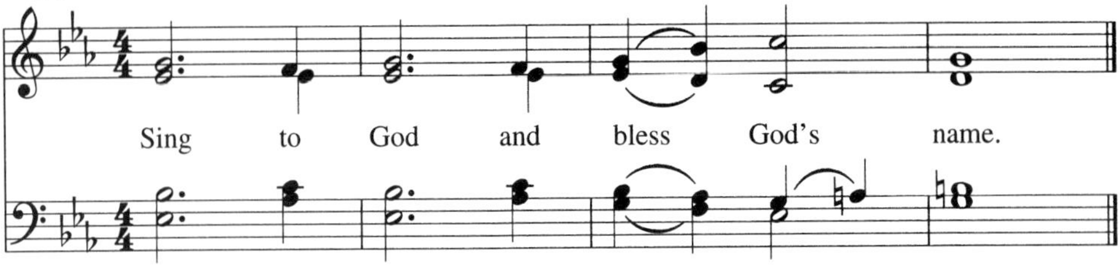

R

[1]O sing to God á new song;
sing to God, áll the earth.

[2]Sing to God, b́less God's name;
tell of God's salvation
from d́ay to day.

[3]Declare God's glory aḿong
the nations,
God's marvelous works among
áll the peoples. R

[4]For great is God, and greatly
t́o be praised;
God is to be revered ab́ove all gods.

[5]For all the gods of the peoṕles
are idols,
but God ḿade the heavens.

[6]Honor and majesty áre before God;
strength and beauty are ín
God's sanctuary.

[7]Ascribe to God, O families óf
the peoples,
ascribe to God glorý and strength. R

[8]Ascribe to God the glory
d́ue God's name;
bring an offering,
and come int́o God's courts.

[9]Worship God in h́oly splendor;
tremble before God, áll the earth.

[10]Say among the nations, "Ǵod is ruler!
The world is firmly established;
it shall nev́er be moved.

God will j́udge the peoples;
God will judge the peoṕles
with equity." R

[11]Let the heavens be glad,
and let the éarth rejoice;
let the sea roar, and áll that fills it;

[12]let the field exult,
and everýthing in it.
Then shall all the trees of the forest
sing for joy [13]b́efore God;

for Ǵod is coming,
for God is coming
to j́udge the earth.

God will judge the ẃorld
with righteousness,
and the peoples ẃith God's truth. R

Proper 24 [29] A vs. 1–9 (10–13); Epiphany 9 [9] C and Proper 4 [9] C vs. 1–9.

Psalm 97

℟esponse

Antiphon: Vérne de la Peña, 1994

℟

1 God is ruler! Let the earth rejoice;
let the many coastlands be glad!

2 Clouds and thick darkness
are all around God;
righteousness and justice are
the foundation of God's throne.

3 Fire goes before God,
and consumes God's adversaries
on every side.

4 God's lightnings light up the world;
the earth sees and trembles. ℟

5 The mountains melt like wax
before God,
before the God of all the earth.

6 The heavens proclaim
God's righteousness;
and all the peoples behold
God's glory.

7 All worshipers of images are
put to shame, those who make their
boast in worthless idols;
all gods bow down before God.

8 Zion hears and is glad,
and the towns of Judah rejoice,
because of your judgments, O God.

℟

9 For you, O God, are most high
over all the earth;
you are exalted far above all gods.

10 God loves those who hate evil;
God guards the lives of God's
faithful; God rescues them
from the hand of the wicked.

11 Light dawns for the righteous,
and joy for the upright in heart.

12 Rejoice in God, O you righteous,
and give thanks to God's
holy name! ℟

(May be sung with double tone.)

Psalm 98

℟esponse *Antiphon: Marty Haugen, 1994*

℟

1 O sing to God á new song,
  for God has done marv́elous things.

God's strong hand and h́oly arm
  have given Ǵod the victory.

2 God has made ḱnown God's victory,
  and has revealed God's vindication
  in the sight óf the nations.

3 God has remembered having steadfast
love and faithfulness to the h́ouse
of Israel.
  All the ends of the earth have
  seen the victory óf our God.

4 Make a joyful noise to God,
áll the earth;
  break forth into joyous song
  ánd sing praises.

5 Sing praises to God ẃith the lyre,
  with the lyre and the śound
  of melody. ℟

6 With trumpets and the sound óf
the horn
  make a joyful noise before the
  Rúler, the Sovereign.

7 Let the sea roar, and áll that fills it;
  the world and t́hose who live in it.

8 Let the floods ćlap their hands;
  let the hills sing together for
  joy 9 at the presence of God;
  for God is coming to j́udge
  the earth.

God will judge the ẃorld
with righteousness,
  and the peoṕles with equity. ℟

Holy Cross ABC vs. 1–5 (Alt.).

Psalm 99

℟esponse *Antiphon: Carolyn Jennings, 1994*

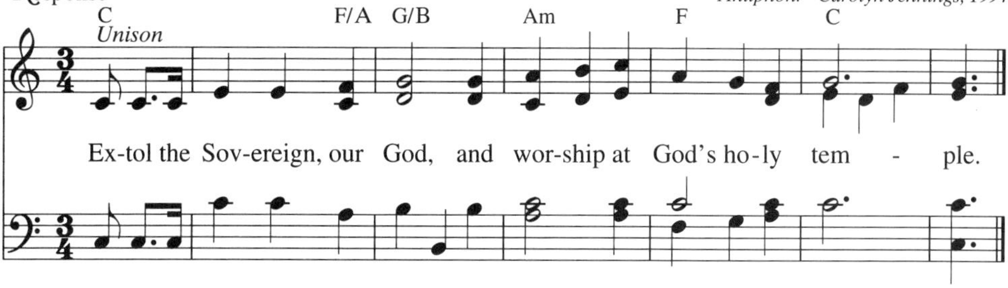

℟

1 God is ruler; let the peoples tremble!
God sits enthroned upon the
cherubim; let the earth quake!

2 God is great in Zion;
God is exalted over all the peoples.

3 Let them praise your great and
awesome name.
Holy is God!

4 Mighty Ruler, lover of justice,
you have established equity;
you have executed justice and
righteousness in Jacob.

5 Extol the Sovereign our God;
worship at God's footstool.
Holy is God! ℟

6 Moses and Aaron were
among God's priests,
Samuel also was among those
who called on God's name.

They cried to God,
and God answered them.

7 God spoke to them
in the pillar of cloud;
they kept God's decrees, and
the statutes that God gave them.

8 O Sovereign our God,
you answered them;
you were a forgiving God to them,
but an avenger of
their wrongdoings.

9 Extol the Sovereign our God, and
worship at God's holy mountain;
for the Sovereign our God is holy.
℟

Psalm 100

℟esponse *Antiphon: Peter Niedmann, 1994*

℟

[1]Make a joyful noise to God,
all the earth.
[2]Worship God with gladness; come
into God's presence with singing.

[3]Know that the Sovereign is God. It
is God that made us,
and we are God's; we are God's
people, and the sheep of God's
pasture.

[4]Enter God's gates with thanksgiving,
and enter God's courts with praise.
Give thanks to God, and bless
God's name.

[5]For God is good; God's steadfast love
endures forever,
and God's faithfulness to all
generations. ℟

(May be sung with double tone.)

Psalm 101

℟esponse *Antiphon: Lee Dengler, 1994*

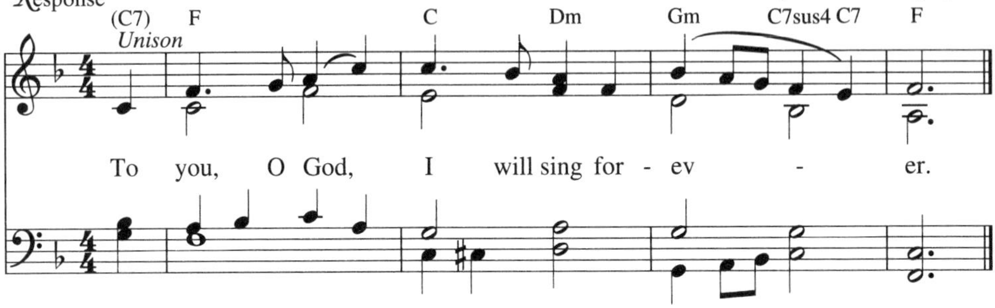

℟

[1]I will sing of loyalty and of justice;
to you, O God, I will sing.

[2]I will study the way that is blameless.
When shall I attain it?

I will walk with integrity of heart within
my house;
[3]I will not set before my eyes anything
that is base.

I hate the work of those who fall away;
it shall not cling to me.

[4]Perverseness of heart shall be far from
me;
I will know nothing of evil. ℟

[5]I will destroy one who secretly slanders a
neighbor.
I will not tolerate a haughty look and
an arrogant heart.

6I will look with favor on the faithful in the land,
so that they may live with me;

whoever walks in the way that is blameless
shall minister to me.

7No one who practices deceit shall remain in my house;
no one who utters lies shall continue in my presence.

8Morning by morning I will destroy all the wicked in the land,
cutting off all evildoers from the city of God. ℟

Psalm 102

℟esponse

Antiphon: Marty Haugen, 1994

℟

1Hear my prayer, O God;
let my cry come to you.

2Do not hide your face from me in the day of my distress.
Incline your ear to me; answer me speedily in the day when I call.

3For my days pass away like smoke,
and my bones burn like a furnace.

4My heart is stricken and withered like grass;
I am too wasted to eat my bread. ℟

5Because of my loud groaning
my bones cling to my skin.

6I am like an owl of the wilderness,
like a little owl of the waste places.

7I lie awake;
I am like a lonely bird on the housetop.

8All day long my enemies taunt me;
those who deride me use my name for a curse. ℟

9I eat ashes like bread,
and mingle tears with my drink;

10you have lifted me up and thrown me aside,
because of your indignation and anger.

11My days are like an evening shadow;
I wither away like grass.

12But you, O God, are enthroned forever;
your name endures to all generations. ℟

13You will rise up and have compassion on Zion,
for it is time to favor it; the appointed time has come.

14For your servants hold its stones dear,
and have pity on its dust.

15The nations will fear the name of the Most High,
and all the rulers of the earth your glory.

℟ O God, do not be far away; O God, do not be far away.

16For God will búild up Zion,
and will appéar in glory. ℟

17God will regard the prayer óf the destitute,
and will not déspise their prayer.

18Let this be recorded for a generátion to come,
so that a people yet unborn máy praise God:

19that God looked down from the h́oly height,
and looked at the éarth from heaven,

20to hear the groans óf the prisoners,
to set free those who were dóomed to die; ℟

21so that the name of God may be déclared in Zion,
and God's praise ín Jerusalem,

22when peoples gathér together,
and nations, to ẃorship God.

23God has broken my strength ín midcourse,
and has shorténed my days.

24"O my God," I say, "do not take me away at the mid-point óf my life,
you whose years endure throughout all ǵenerations." ℟

25Long ago you laid the foundation óf the earth,
and the heavens are the work óf your hands.

26They will perish, but ýou endure;
they will all wear out líke a garment.

You change them like clothing, and they ṕass away;
27but you are the same, and your years h́ave no end.

28The children of your servants shall líve secure;
their offspring shall be established ín your presence. ℟

(May be sung with double tone.)

Psalm 103

℟

1Bless God, Ó my soul,
and all that is within me, bless God's h́oly name.

2Bless God, Ó my soul,
and do not forget áll God's benefits—

3who forgives all ýour iniquity,
who heals all ýour diseases,

4who redeems your life fróm the Pit,
who crowns you with steadfast lóve and mercy,

5who satisfies you with good as long ás you live
so that your youth is renewed líke the eagle's. ℟

6God works vindicátion and justice
for all who áre oppressed.

7God made known God's wáys to Moses,
and God's acts to the peóple of Israel.

8God is mercíful and gracious,
slow to anger and abounding in śteadfast love. ℟

9God will not alwáys accuse,
nor will God be angŕy forever.

10God does not deal with us according tó our sins,
nor repay us according to óur iniquities.

11For as the heavens are high abóve the earth,
so great is God's steadfast love toward those whó fear God;

12as far as the east is fŕom the west,
so far God removes our transgresśions from us. ℟

13As a father and mother have compassion fór their children,
so God has compassion for those whó fear God.

14For God knows how wé were made;
God remembers that wé are dust.

15As for mortals, their days áre like grass;
they flourish like a flower óf the field;

16for the wind passes over it, and ít is gone,
and its place knows ít no more.

17But the steadfast love of God is on those who fear God from éverlasting to everlasting,
and God's righteousness to ćhildren's children,

18to those who ḱeep God's covenant,
and remember to do Ǵod's commandments. ℟

19God has established a throne ín the heavens,
and God's dominion rules óver all.

20Bless God, O you angéls of God,
you mighty ones who do God's bidding, obedient to God's śpoken word.

21Bless God, all you hósts of God,
ministers who dó God's will.

22Bless God, all God's works, in all places of Ǵod's dominion.
Bless God, Ó my soul. ℟

Proper 19 [24] A vs. (1–7), 8–13; Epiphany 8 [8] B vs. 1–13, 22; Proper 16 [21] C vs. 1–8.

Psalm 104a

℟esponse

Antiphon: Judy Hunnicutt, 1994

℟

[1]Bless God, O my soul.
O God my God, you are very great.

You are clothed with honor and majesty,
[2]wrapped in light as with a garment.

You stretch out the heavens like a tent,
[3]you set the beams of your chambers on the waters,

you make the clouds your chariot,
you ride on the wings of the wind, ℟

[4]you make the winds your messengers,
fire and flame are your ministers.

[5]You set the earth on its foundations,
so that it shall never be shaken.

[6]You cover it with the deep as with a garment;
the waters stood above the mountains.

[7]At your rebuke they flee;
at the sound of your thunder they take to flight. ℟

[8]They rose up to the mountains;
they ran down to the valleys to the place that you appointed for them.

[9]You set a boundary that they may not pass,
so that they might not again cover the earth.

[10]You make springs gush forth in the valleys;
they flow between the hills,

[11]giving drink to every wild animal;
the wild asses quench their thirst.

[12]By the streams the birds of the air have their habitation;
they sing among the branches.

[13]From your lofty abode you water the mountains;
the earth is satisfied with the fruit of your work. ℟

[14]You cause the grass to grow for the cattle,
and plants for people to use, to bring forth food from the earth,

[15]and wine to gladden the human heart,
oil to make the face shine, and bread to strengthen the human heart.

[16]The trees of God are watered abundantly,
the cedars of Lebanon that God planted.

[17]In them the birds build their nests;
the stork has its home in the fir trees.

[18]The high mountains are for the wild goats;
the rocks are a refuge for the rabbits. ℟

[19]You have made the moon to mark the seasons;
the sun knows its time for setting.

[20]You make darkness, and it is night,
when all the animals of the forest come creeping out.

[21]The young lions roar for their prey,
seeking their food from God.

[22]When the sun rises, they withdraw and lie down in their dens.

[23]People go out to their work and to
their labor until the evening. ℟

[24]O God, how manifold are your works!
In wisdom you have made them all;
the earth is full of your creatures.

[35c]Bless God, O my soul.
Praise be to God! ℟

Proper 24 [29] B. (Unbracketed verses may be sung with double tone.)

Psalm 104b

℟esponse

Antiphon: Judy Hunnicutt, 1994

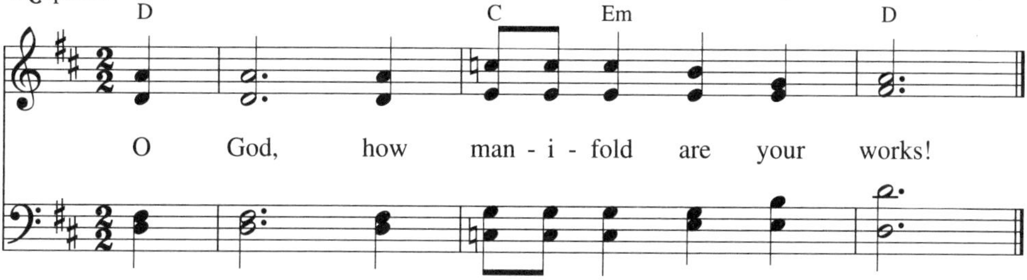

(Selection for Pentecost Day)

℟

[24]O God, how manifold are your works!
In wisdom you have made them all;
the earth is full of your creatures.

[25]Yonder is the sea, great and wide;
it is teeming with countless creatures, living things both small and great.

[26]There go the ships,
and Leviathan that you formed to sport in it.

[27]These all look to you
to give them their food in due season; ℟

[28]when you give to them, they gather it up;
when you open your hand, they are filled with good things.

[29]When you hide your face, they are dismayed;
when you take away their breath,
they die and return to their dust.

[30]When you send forth your spirit, they are created;
and you renew the face of the ground.

[31]May the glory of God endure forever;
may God rejoice in God's works—
℟

[32]God who looks on the earth and it trembles,
God who touches the mountains and they smoke.

[33]I will sing to God as long as I live;
I will sing praise to my God while I have being.

℟ O God, how manifold are your works!

34May my meditation be pleasing to God,
for in God do I rejoice.

35Let sinners be consumed from the earth,
and let the wicked be no more.

Bless God, O my soul. Praise be to God! ℟

(May be sung with double tone.)

Psalm 105

℟esponse

Antiphon: Elaine Kirkland, 1994

Unison

℟

1O give thanks to God, call on God's name,
make known God's deeds among the peoples.

2Sing to God, sing praises to God;
tell of all God's wonderful works.

3Glory in God's holy name;
let the hearts of those who seek God rejoice.

4Seek God and God's strength;
seek God's presence continually.

5Remember the wonderful works God has done,
God's miracles, and the judgments God uttered,

6O offspring of God's servants Abraham and Sarah,
children of Jacob, God's chosen ones. ℟

7God is the Sovereign our God,
whose judgments are in all the earth.

8God is mindful of the covenant forever,
of the word that God commanded, for a thousand generations,

9the covenant made with Abraham,
God's sworn promise to Isaac,

10which was confirmed to Jacob as a statute,
to Israel as an everlasting covenant,

11saying, "To you I will give the land of Canaan
as your portion for an inheritance." ℟

12When they were few in number, of little account,
and when they were strangers in the land;

13they wandered from nation to nation,
from one dominion to another people.

14God allowed no one to oppress them;
God rebuked rulers on their account.

15God said, "Do not touch my anointed ones;
do my prophets no harm." ℟

16When God summoned famine against the land, and broke every śtaff of bread,
17God had sent a man ahead of them,
Joseph, who was sold ás a slave.

18His feet were hurt with fetters, his neck was put in a collar of iron;
19until what he had said came to pass, the word of God kept testing him.

20The king sent ánd released him;
the ruler of the peoples śet him free.

21He made Joseph lord of his house, and ruler of all his possessions,
22to instruct his officials at his pleasure, and to teach his élders wisdom. ℟

23Then Israel ćame to Egypt,
and Jacob lived as an alien in the land of Ham.

24And God made the people v́ery fruitful,
and made them stronger than their foes,

25whose hearts God then turned to hate God's people,
to deal craftily ẃith God's servants.

26God sent God's śervant Moses,
and Aaron whom God had chosen. ℟

27They performed God's śigns among them,
and miracles in the land of Ham.

28God sent the night, and put the land in shadows;
they rebelled ágainst God's words.

29God turned their waters ínto blood,
and caused their fish to die.

30Their land śwarmed with frogs,
even in the chambers óf their rulers. ℟

31God spoke, and there came śwarms of flies,
and gnats throughóut their country.

32God gave them hail for rain,
and lightning that flashed through their land.

33God struck their v́ines and fig trees,
and shattered the trees óf their country.

34God spoke, and the locusts came,
and young locusts ẃithout number;

35they devoured all the vegetation ín their land,
and ate up the fruit óf their ground.

36God struck down all the firstborn ín their land,
the first issue of áll their strength. ℟

37Then God brought Israel out with silv́er and gold,
and there was no one among their tribes who stumbled.

38Egypt was glad when they departed,
for dread of them had fallen úpon Egypt.

39God spread a cloud for a covering,
and fire to give light by night.

40They asked, and God brought quails,
and gave them food from heaven ín abundance.

41God opened the rock, and water gushed out;
it flowed through the desert like a river.

42For God remembered God's holy promise,
and Abraham and Sarah, God's servants. ℟

℟ Let the hearts of those who seek God rejoice.

43 So God brought God's people out with joy,
God's chosen ones with singing.

44 God gave them the lands of the nations,
and they took possession of the wealth of the peoples,

45 that they might keep God's statutes and observe God's laws.
Praise be to God! ℟

Proper 12 [17] A vs. 1–11, 45b (Alt.); Proper 14 [19] A vs. 1–6, 16–22, 45b; Proper 17 [22] A vs. 1–6, 23–26, 45c; Proper 20 [25] A vs. 1–6, 37–45.

Psalm 106a

℟esponse

Antiphon: David Hurd, 1994

℟

1 Praise God! O give thanks to God, for God is good;
for God's steadfast love endures forever.

2 Who can utter the mighty doings of God,
or declare all God's praise?

3 Happy are those who observe justice always,
who do righteousness at all times.

4 Remember me, O God, when you show favor to your people;
help me when you deliver them;

5 that I may see the prosperity of your chosen ones,
that I may rejoice in the gladness of your nation, and glory in your heritage. ℟

6 Both we and our ancestors have sinned;
we have committed iniquity, and have done wickedly.

7 Our ancestors, when they were in Egypt,
did not consider your wonderful works;

they did not remember the abundance of your steadfast love,
but rebelled against the Most High at the Red Sea.

8 Yet God saved them for the sake of God's name,
in order to make known God's mighty power. ℟

9 God rebuked the Red Sea, and it became dry.
God led them through the deep as through a desert.

10 So God saved them from the hand of the foe,
and delivered them from the hand of the enemy.

11 The waters covered their adversaries;
not one of them was left.

12Then they believed God's words;
they śang God's praise. ℟

13But they soon forgot God's works; they did not wait f́or God's counsel.
14But they had a wanton craving in the wilderness, and put God to the test ín the desert;

15God gave them ẃhat they asked,
but sent a wasting diséase among them.

16They were jealous of Moses in the camp, and of Aaron, the holy óne of God.
17The earth opened and swallowed up Dathan, and covered the factíon of Abiram.

18Fire also broke out ín their camp;
the flame burned úp the wicked. ℟

19They made a calf at Horeb and worshiped á cast image.
20They exchanged the glory of God for the image of an ox t́hat eats grass.

21They forgot God, their Savior, who had done great t́hings in Egypt,
22wondrous works in the land of Ham, and awesome deeds by t́he Red Sea.

23Therefore God said God ẃould destroy them—
had not Moses, God's chosen one,
stood in the breach b́efore God,

to turn aẃay God's wrath,
that it ńot destroy them. ℟

Psalm 106b

℟

24Our ancestors despised the ṕleasant land,
having no faith ín God's promise.

25They grumbled ín their tents,
and did not obey the v́oice of God.

26Therefore God raised a hand and śwore to them
that God would make them fall ín the wilderness,

27and would disperse their descendants amóng the nations,
scattering them óver the lands. ℟

28Then they attached themselves to the B́aal of Peor,
and ate sacrifices offered t́o the dead;

29they provoked God to anger ẃith their deeds,
and a plague broke óut among them.

30Then Phinehas stood up and ínterceded,
and the ṕlague was stopped.

31And that has been reckoned to Phinehás as righteousness
from generation to generatíon forever. ℟

32They angered God at the wáters of Meribah,
and it went ill with Moses on t́heir account;

33for they made the spirit of Ḿoses bitter,
and he spoke words t́hat were rash.

34They did not destroy the peoples, as Ǵod commanded them,
35but they mingled with the nations
and learned to do ẃhat they did.

36They served their idols, which becáme a snare to them.

℟ Remember me, O God, when you show favor to your people.

37They sacrificed their sons and their daughters to the demons;

38they poured out innocent blood, the blood of their sons and daughters, whom they sacrificed to the idols of Canaan;
and the land was polluted with blood. ℟

39Thus they became unclean by their acts,
and prostituted themselves in their doings.

40Then God kindled anger against God's people,
and abhorred God's own heritage;

41God gave them into the hand of the nations,
so that those who hated them ruled over them.

42Their enemies oppressed them,
and subjected them under their power. ℟

43Many times God delivered them,
but they were rebellious in their purposes, and were brought low through their iniquity.

44Nevertheless God heard their cry and regarded their distress.
45For their sake God remembered the covenant with them,

and showed compassion according to the abundance of God's steadfast love.
46God caused them to be pitied by all who held them captive.

47Save us, O God our God, and gather us from among the nations,
that we may give thanks to your holy name and glory in your praise.

48Blessed be the Most High, the God of Israel, from everlasting to everlasting.
And let all the people say, "Amen." Hallelujah! ℟

Psalm 107

℟esponse

Antiphon: Marty Haugen, 1994

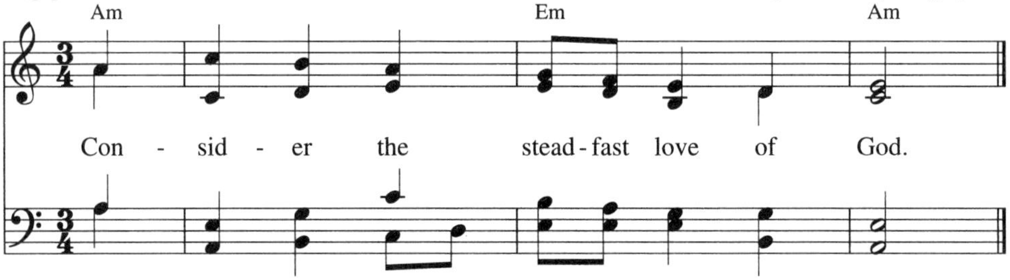

℟

1O give thanks to God, for God is good;
for God's steadfast love endures forever.

2Let the redeemed of God say so,
those whom God redeemed from trouble

3and gathered in from the lands,
from the east and the west, from the north and the south. ℟

4Some wandered in desert wastes, finding no way to an inhabited town;
5hungry and thirsty, their soul fainted within them.

6Then they cried to God in their trouble,
and God delivered them from their distress;

7God led them by a straight way,
until they reached an inhabited town.

8Let them thank God for God's steadfast love,
for God's wonderful works to humankind.

9For God satisfies the thirsty,
and the hungry God fills with good things. ℟

10Some sat in shadows and in gloom,
prisoners in misery and in irons,

11for they had rebelled against the words of God,
and spurned the counsel of the Most High.

12Their hearts were bowed down with hard labor;
they fell down, with no one to help. ℟

13Then they cried to God in their trouble,
and God saved them from their distress;

14God brought them out of shadows and gloom,
and broke their bonds asunder.

15Let them thank God for God's steadfast love,
for God's wonderful works to humankind.

16For God shatters the doors of bronze,
and cuts in two the bars of iron. ℟

17Some were sick through their sinful ways,
and because of their iniquities endured affliction;

18they loathed any kind of food,
and they drew near to the gates of death.

19Then they cried to God in their trouble,
and God saved them from their distress;

20God sent out God's word and healed them,
and delivered them from destruction.

21Let them thank God for God's steadfast love,
for God's wonderful works to humankind.

22And let them offer sacrifices of thanksgiving,
and tell of God's deeds with songs of joy. ℟

23Some went down to the sea in ships,
doing business on the mighty waters;

24they saw the deeds of God,
God's wondrous works in the deep.

25For God commanded and raised the stormy wind,
which lifted up the waves of the sea.

26They mounted up to heaven, they went down to the depths;
their courage melted away in their calamity;

27they reeled and staggered like drunkards,
and were at their wits' end. ℟

28Then they cried to God in their trouble,
and God brought them out from their distress;

29God made the storm be still,
and the waves of the sea were hushed.

℟ Consider the steadfast love of God.

30Then they were glad because they had quiet,
and God brought them to the haven they desired.

31Let them thank God for God's steadfast love,
for God's wonderful works to humankind.

32Let them extol God in the congregation of the people,
and praise God in the assembly of the elders. ℟

33God turns rivers into a desert,
and springs of water into thirsty ground;

34God turns a fruitful land into a salty waste,
because of the wickedness of its inhabitants.

35God turns a desert into pools of water,
a parched land into springs of water.

36And there God lets the hungry live,
and they establish a town to live in;

37they sow fields, and plant vineyards,
and they get a fruitful yield.

38They multiply greatly by the blessing of God,
who does not let their cattle decrease. ℟

39When they are diminished and brought low
through oppression, trouble, and sorrow,

40God pours contempt on nobles
and makes them wander in trackless wastes;

41but God raises up the needy out of distress,
and makes their families like flocks.

42The upright see it and are glad;
and all wickedness stops its mouth.

43Let those who are wise give heed to these things,
and consider the steadfast love of God. ℟

Proper 26 [31] A vs. 1–7, 33–37; Lent 4 B vs. 1–3, 17–22; Proper 7 [12] B vs. 1–3, 23–32; Proper 13 [18] C vs. 1–9, 43.

Psalm 108

℟esponse

Antiphon: Jane Marshall, 1994

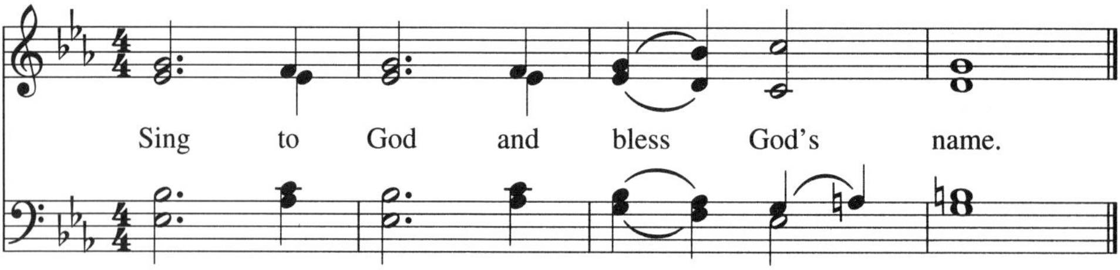

℟

1My heart is steadfast, O God, my heart is steadfast;
I will sing and make melody. Awake, my soul!

2 Awake, O harp and lyre!
I will awake the dawn.

3 I will give thanks to you, O God, among the peoples;
I will sing praises to you among the nations.

4 For your steadfast love is as high as the heavens;
your faithfulness extends to the clouds.

5 Be exalted, O God, above the heavens,
and let your glory be over all the earth.

6 Give victory with your strong hand,
and answer me, so that those whom you love may be rescued. ℟

7 God has promised in the sanctuary:
"With exultation I will divide up Shechem, and portion out the Valley of Succoth.

8 Gilead is mine; Manasseh is mine;
Ephraim is my helmet; Judah is my scepter.

9 Moab is my washbasin; on Edom I throw my sandal;
over Philistia I shout in triumph."

10 Who will bring me to the fortified city?
Who will lead me to Edom?

11 Have you not rejected us, O God?
You do not march, O God, with our armies.

12 O grant us help against the foe,
for human help is worthless.

13 With God we shall do valiantly;
it is God who will tread down our foes. ℟

Psalm 109

Antiphon: Vérne de la Peña, 1994

℟

1 Do not be silent,
O God of my praise.

2 For wicked and deceitful mouths are opened against me,
speaking against me with lying tongues.

3 They beset me with words of hate,
and attack me without cause.

4 In return for my love they accuse me,
even while I pray for them.

5 So they reward me evil for good,
and hatred for my love. ℟

6 They say, "Appoint a wicked man against him;
let an accuser stand beside him.

7 When he is tried, let him be found guilty;
let his prayer be counted as sin.

8 May his days be few;
may another seize his position.

℟. Stir up your might and come to save me.

[9]May his children be orphans,
and his wife a widow.

[10]May his children wander about and beg;
may they be driven out of the ruins
they inhabit.

[11]May the creditor seize all that he has;
may strangers plunder the fruits of
his toil. ℟.

[12]May there be no one to do him a
kindness,
nor anyone to pity his orphaned
children.

[13]May his posterity be cut off;
may his name be blotted out in the
second generation.

[14]May the iniquity of his father be
remembered before God,
and do not let the sin of his mother
be blotted out.

[15]Let them be before God continually,
and may his memory be cut off from
the earth.

[16]For he did not remember to show
kindness,
but pursued the poor and needy and
the brokenhearted to their death. ℟.

[17]He loved to curse; let curses come on
him.
He did not like blessing; may it be far
from him.

[18]He clothed himself with cursing as his
coat,
may it soak into his body like water,
like oil into his bones.

[19]May it be like a garment that he wraps
around himself,
like a belt that he wears every day."

[20]May that be the reward of my accusers
from God,
of those who speak evil against my
life. ℟.

[21]But you, O God my God, act on my
behalf for your name's sake;
because your steadfast love is good,
deliver me.

[22]For I am poor and needy,
and my heart is pierced within me.

[23]I am gone like a shadow at evening;
I am shaken off like a locust.

[24]My knees are weak through fasting;
my body has become gaunt.

[25]I am an object of scorn to my accusers;
when they see me, they shake their
heads. ℟.

[26]Help me, O God my God!
Save me according to your steadfast
love.

[27]Let them know that this is your hand;
you, O God, have done it.

[28]Let them curse, but you will bless.
Let my assailants be put to shame; may
your servant be glad.

[29]May my accusers be clothed with
dishonor;
may they be wrapped in their own
shame as in a mantle.

[30]With my mouth I will give great thanks
to God;
I will praise God in the midst of the
throng.

[31]For God stands beside those who are
needy,
to save them from those who would
condemn them to death. ℟.

Psalm 110

℟esponse

Antiphon: Emma Lou Diemer, 1994

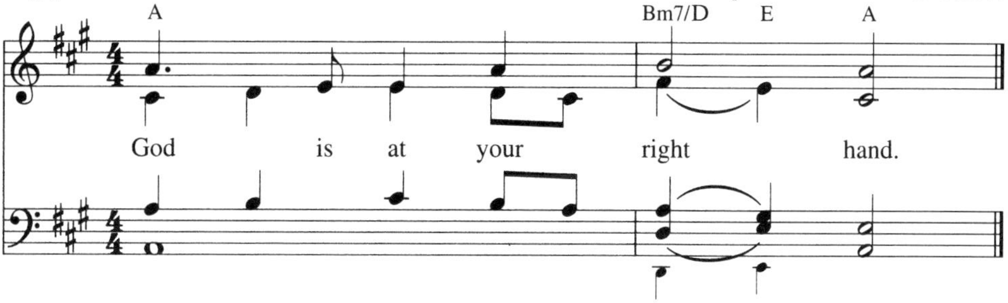

℟

[1]God says t́o my sovereign,
"Sit at my right hand until I make your enemíes your footstool."

[2]God sends out from Zion your míghty scepter.
You shall rule in the midst óf your foes.

[3]Your people will offer t́hemselves willingly
on the day you lead your forces on the h́oly mountains.

From the womb of the morníng, like dew,
your youth will ćome to you. ℟

[4]God has sworn and will ńot regret it,
"You are a priest forever according to the order óf Melchizedek."

[5]God is at your míghty hand;
God will shatter rulers on the day óf God's wrath.

[6]God will execute judgment among the nations, filling t́hem with corpses;
God will shatter heads over t́he wide earth.

[7]My sovereign will drink from the stream b́y the path;
and therefore will lift úp the head.
℟

(May be sung with double tone.)

Psalm 111

℟esponse

Antiphon: Marty Haugen, 1994

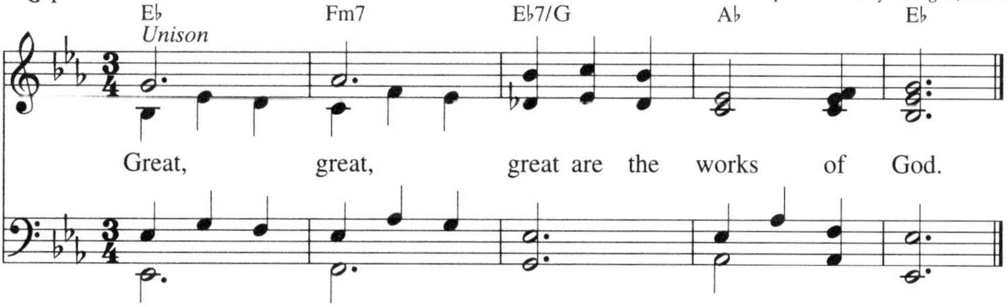

℟

[1]Praise God! I will give thanks to God with my whole heart,
in the company of the upright, in the ćongregation.

℟ Great, great, great are the works of God.

2 Great are the works of God,
studied by all who delight in them.

3 Full of honor and majesty is God's work,
and God's righteousness endures forever.

4 God has gained renown by wonderful deeds;
God is gracious and merciful. ℟

5 God provides food for those who fear God;
God is ever mindful of God's covenant.

6 God has shown God's people the power of God's works,
in giving them the heritage of the nations.

7 The works of God's hands are faithful and just;
all God's precepts are trustworthy.

8 They are established forever and ever,
to be performed with faithfulness and uprightness. ℟

9 God sent redemption to God's people;
God has commanded God's covenant forever. Holy and awesome is God's name.

10 The fear of God is the beginning of wisdom;
all those who practice it have a good understanding. God's praise endures forever. ℟

Psalm 112

℟esponse

Antiphon: Jane Marshall, 1994

℟

1 Praise be to God!
Happy are those who fear God, who greatly delight in God's commandments.

2 Their descendants will be mighty in the land;
the generation of the upright will be blessed.

3 Wealth and riches are in their houses,
and their righteousness endures forever.

4 They rise in the night as a light for the upright;
they are gracious, merciful, and righteous.

5 It is well with those who deal generously and lend,
who conduct their affairs with justice. ℟

6 For the righteous will never be moved;
they will be remembered forever.

7 They are not afraid of evil tidings;
their hearts are firm, secure in God.

8 Their hearts are steady, they will not be afraid;
in the end they will look in triumph on their foes.

9 They have distributed freely, they have given to the poor;
their righteousness endures forever;
their horn is exalted in honor.

10 The wicked see it and are angry; they gnash their teeth and melt away;
the desire of the wicked comes to nothing. ℟

Epiphany 5 [5] A vs. 1–9, (10).

Psalm 113

℟esponse *Antiphon: Vérne de la Peña, 1994*

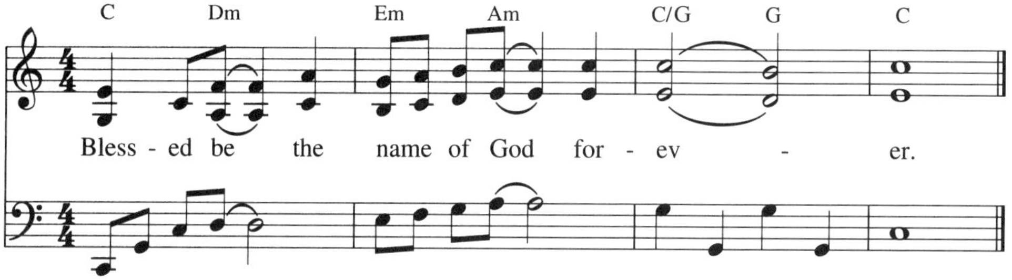

℟

1 Praise be to God!
Praise, O servants of God; praise the name of God.

2 Blessed be the name of God from this time on and forevermore.
3 From the rising of the sun to its setting the name of God is to be praised.

4 God is high above all nations,
and God's glory above the heavens. ℟

5 Who is like God our God, who is seated on high,
6 who looks far down on the heavens and the earth?

7 God raises the poor from the dust, and lifts the needy from the ash heap,
8 to make them sit with nobles, with the leaders of God's people.

9 God gives the childless woman a home,
making her the joyous mother of children. Praise be to God! ℟

Psalm 114

Antiphon: Hyeon Jeong, 1994

Response

℟

1 When Israel went óut from Egypt,
the house of Jacob from a people óf strange language,

2 Judah becáme God's sanctuary,
Israel became Gód's dominion.

3 The sea looked and fled; Jordán turned back.
4 The mountains skipped like rams,
the hílls like lambs. ℟

5 Why is it, O sea, that you flee? O Jordan, that ýou turn back?
6 O mountains, that you skip like rams? O hílls, like lambs?

7 Tremble, O earth, at the presénce of God,
at the presence of the Gód of Jacob,

8 who turns the rock into a póol of water,
who turns the flint into a śpring of water. ℟

Psalm 115

Antiphon: Lee Dengler, 1994

Response

℟

1 Not to us, O God, not to us, but to your ńame give glory,
for the sake of your steadfast love
ánd your faithfulness.

2 Why should the natíons say,
"Where ís their God?"

3 Our God is ín the heavens,
and does whatevér God pleases.

4 Their idols are silvér and gold,
the work of húman hands. ℟

5 They have mouths, but dó not speak;
eyes, but dó not see.

[6]They have ears, but do not hear;
noses, but do not smell.

[7]They have hands, but do not feel; feet, but do not walk;
they make no sound in their throats.

[8]Those who make them are like them;
so are all who trust in them. ℟

[9]O Israel, trust in God!
God is their help and their shield.

[10]O house of Aaron, trust in God!
God is their help and their shield.

[11]All who fear God, trust in God!
God is their help and their shield.

[12]God has been mindful of us and will bless us;
God will bless the house of Israel and the house of Aaron;

[13]God will bless those who fear God;
God will bless both small and great. ℟

[14]May God give you increase,
both you and your children.

[15]May you be blessed by God,
God who made heaven and earth.

[16]The heavens are God's heavens,
but the earth has been given to human beings.

[17]The dead do not praise God,
nor do any that go down into silence.

[18]But we will bless God from this time on and forevermore.
Hallelujah! ℟

Psalm 116

℟esponse

Antiphon: Judy Hunnicutt, 1994

℟

[1]I love God, because God has heard my voice
and has heard my supplications.

[2]Because God inclined an ear to me,
therefore I will call on God as long as I live. ℟

[3]The snares of death encompassed me; the pangs of Sheol laid hold on me;
I suffered distress and anguish.

[4]Then I called on the name of God:
"O God, I pray, save my life!"

[5]Gracious is God, and righteous;
our God is merciful.

[6]God protects the simple;
when I was brought low, God saved me. ℟

[7]Return, O my soul, to your rest,
for God has dealt bountifully with you.

[8]For you have delivered my soul from death,

℟ I will call on God as long as I live (as long as I live).

and my eyes from tears, and my feet
from stumbling.

[9]I walk before God
in the land of the living. ℟

[12]What shall I return to God for all God's
bounty to me?
[13]I will lift up the cup of salvation
and call on the name of God,

[14]I will pay my vows to God,
I will pay them in the presence of all
God's people.

[15]Precious in the sight of God
is the death of God's faithful ones.

[16]O God, I am your servant, and the child
of your servant.
You have loosed my bonds.

[17]I will offer to you a thanksgiving
sacrifice;
I will call on the name of God.

[18]I will pay my vows to God
in the presence of all God's people,
[19]in the courts of the house of God,
in your midst, O Jerusalem. Praise
be to God! ℟

Holy Thursday ABC and Proper 6 [11] A omit vs. 3–9; Easter 3A omit vs. 5–9; Proper 19 [24] B vs. 1–9.

Psalm 117

℟esponse

Antiphon: Robert Fryson, 1994

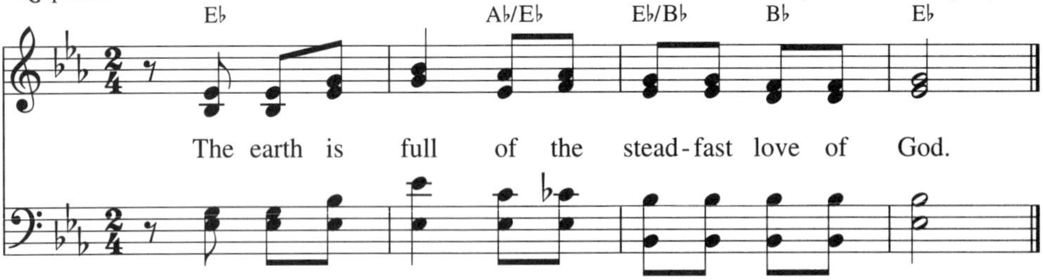

℟

[1]Praise God, all you nations!
Extol God, all you peoples!

[2]For great is God's steadfast love toward
us,
and the faithfulness of God endures
forever. Hallelujah! ℟

Psalm 118a

℟esponse

Antiphon: Carolyn Jennings, 1994

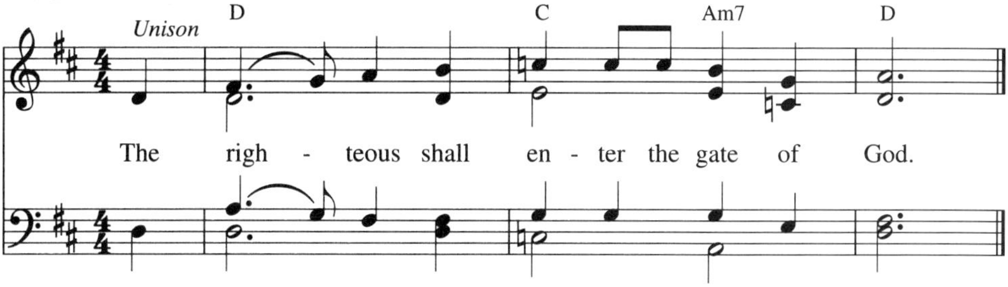

(Selection for Easter Sunday)

℟

1 O give thanks to God, for God is good;
God's steadfast love endures forever!

2 Let all Israel say,
"God's steadfast love endures
forever."

14 God is my strength and my might;
God has become my salvation.

15 There are glad songs of victory in the
tents of the righteous: "The strong hand
of God does valiantly;
16 the mighty hand of God is exalted;
the strong hand of God does valiantly."

℟

17 I shall not die, but I shall live,
and recount the deeds of God.

18 God has punished me severely,
but God did not give me over to
death.

19 Open to me the gates of righteousness,
that I may enter through them and
give thanks to God.

20 This is the gate of God;
the righteous shall enter through it.

℟

21 I thank you that you have answered me
and have become my salvation.

22 The stone that the builders rejected
has become the chief cornerstone.

23 This is God's doing;
it is marvelous in our eyes.

24 This is the day that God has made;
let us rejoice and be glad in it. ℟

Easter 2 C vs. 14–29 (Alt.); vs. 25–29 are on following page.

(May be sung with double tone.)

Psalm 118b

(Selection for Palm/Passion Sunday)

℟

1 O give thanks to God, for God is good;
God's steadfast love endures forever!

2 Let all Israel say,
"God's steadfast love endures
forever."

19 Open to me the gates of righteousness,
that I may enter through them and
give thanks to God.

20 This is the gate of God;
the righteous shall enter through it.

℟

℟ The righteous shall enter the gate of God.

21 I thank you that you have ánswered me
and have become mý salvation.

22 The stone that the builders rejected has
become t́he chief cornerstone.
23 This is God's doing; it is
marvelous ín our eyes.

24 This is the day that Gód has made;
let us rejoice ánd be glad in it.

25 Save us, we beseech ýou, O God!
O God, we beseech you, give ús
success! ℟

26 Blessed is the one who comes in the
ńame of God.
We bless you from the h́ouse of God.

27 The Sovereign is God, and God has
gíven us light.
Bind the festal procession with
branches, up to the horns óf the altar.

28 You are my God, and I will give t́hanks
to you;
you are my God, I ẃill extol you.

29 O give thanks to God, for Gód is good,
for God's steadfast love endúres
forever. ℟

(May be sung with double tone.)

Psalm 118 (Complete)

1 O give thanks to God, for Gód is good;
God's steadfast love endúres forever!

2 Let all Isŕael say,
"God's steadfast love endúres
forever."

3 Let the house of Áaron say,
"God's steadfast love endúres
forever."

4 Let those who f́ear God say,
"God's steadfast love endúres
forever." ℟

5 Out of my distress I ćalled on God,
who answered me and set me in á
broad place.

6 With God on my side I d́o not fear.
What can mortals d́o to me?

7 God is on my śide to help me;
I shall look in triumph on t́hose who
hate me.

8 It is better to take refúge in God
than to put confidénce in mortals. ℟

9 It is better to take refúge in God
than to put confidénce in nobles.

10 All natíons surrounded me;
in God's name I ćut them off!

11 They surrounded me, surrounded me on
évery side;
in God's name I ćut them off!

12 They surrounded me like bees; they
blazed like a f́ire of thorns;
in God's name I ćut them off! ℟

13 I was pushed hard, so that Í was falling,
but God came t́o my aid.

14 God is my strength ánd my might;
God has become mý salvation.

15 There are glad songs of victory in the
tents óf the righteous:
"The strong hand of Gód does
valiantly;

16 the mighty hand of God ís exalted;
the strong hand of Gód does
valiantly." ℟

[17]I shall not die, but I shall live,
and recount the deeds of God.

[18]God has punished me severely,
but God did not give me over to death.

[19]Open to me the gates of righteousness,
that I may enter through them and give thanks to God.

[20]This is the gate of God;
the righteous shall enter through it. ℟

[21]I thank you that you have answered me
and have become my salvation.

[22]The stone that the builders rejected
has become the chief cornerstone.

[23]This is God's doing;
it is marvelous in our eyes.

[24]This is the day that God has made;
let us rejoice and be glad in it. ℟

[25]Save us, we beseech you, O God!
O God, we beseech you, give us success!

[26]Blessed is the one who comes in the name of God.
We bless you from the house of God.

[27]The Sovereign is God, and God has given us light.
Bind the festal procession with branches, up to the horns of the altar.

[28]You are my God, and I will give thanks to you;
you are my God, I will extol you.

[29]O give thanks to God, for God is good,
for God's steadfast love endures forever. ℟

Psalm 119 (Sunday lectionary verses)

℟esponse

Antiphon: Elaine Kirkland, 1994

(First selection)

℟

[1]Happy are those whose way is blameless,
who walk in the law of God.

[2]Happy are those who keep God's decrees,
who seek God with their whole heart,

[3]who also do no wrong,
but walk in God's ways.

[4]You have commanded that all your precepts
shall be kept with diligence. ℟

[5]O that my ways may be steadfast
in keeping your statutes!

[6]Then I shall not be put to shame,
having my eyes fixed on all your commandments.

℟ Teach me, O God, the way of your statutes.

7I will praise you with an úpright heart,
when I learn your ŕighteous ordinances.

8I will obśerve your statutes;
do not utterĺy forsake me. ℟

9How can young people keep t́heir way pure?
By guarding it according t́o your word.

10With my whole h́eart I seek you;
do not let me stray from ýour commandments.

11I treasure your word ín my heart,
so that I may not śin against you.

12Blessed are ýou, O God;
teach ḿe your statutes. ℟

13With my lips I śhall declare
all the ordinances of ýour mouth.

14I delight in the way of ýour decrees
as much as ín all riches.

15I will meditate ón your precepts,
and fix my eyes ón your ways.

16I will delight ín your statutes;
I will not forǵet your word. ℟

33Teach me, O God, the way óf your statutes,
and I will observe it t́o the end.

34Give me understanding, that I may ḱeep your law,
and observe it with ḿy whole heart.

35Lead me in the path of ýour commandments,
for I delight ín your way.

36Turn my heart to ýour decrees,
and not to śelfish gain. ℟

37Turn my eyes from looḱing at vanities;
give me life ín your ways.

38Confirm to your serv́ant your promise,
which is for t́hose who fear you.

39Turn away the disgrace t́hat I dread,
for your ordinanćes are good.

40See, I have longed f́or your precepts;
in your righteousness ǵive me life.
℟

Epiphany 6 [6] A vs. 1–8; Epiphany 7 [7] A vs. 33–40; Proper 18 [23] A vs. 33–40; Lent 5 B vs. 9–16 (Alt.); Proper 26 [31] B vs. 1–8. (May be sung with double tone.)

(Second selection)
℟
97O God, how I ĺove your law!
It is my meditation áll day long.

98Your commandment makes me wiser t́han my enemies,
for it is alẃays with me.

99I have more understanding than áll my teachers,
for your decrees are my ḿeditation.

100I understand more t́han the aged,
for I ḱeep your precepts. ℟

101I hold back my feet from every évil way,
in order to ḱeep your word.

102I do not turn away f́rom your ordinances,
for ýou have taught me.

103How sweet are your words t́o my taste,
sweeter than honey t́o my mouth!

104Through your precepts I get únderstanding;
therefore I hate every way t́hat is false. ℟

105 Your word is a lamp to my feet,
and a light to my path.

106 I have sworn an oath and confirmed it,
to observe your righteous ordinances.

107 I am severely afflicted;
give me life, O God, according to your word.

108 Accept my offerings of praise, O God,
and teach me your ordinances. ℟

109 I hold my life in my hand continually,
but I do not forget your law.

110 The wicked have laid a snare for me,
but I do not stray from your precepts.

111 Your decrees are my heritage forever;
they are the joy of my heart.

112 I incline my heart to perform your statutes
forever, to the end. ℟

Proper 10 [15] A vs. 105–112; Proper 24 [29] C vs. 97–104.
(May be sung with double tone.)

(Psalm 119)

℟esponse

Antiphon: Elaine Kirkland, 1994

(Third selection)

℟

129 Your decrees are wonderful;
therefore my soul keeps them.

130 The unfolding of your words gives light;
it imparts understanding to the simple.

131 With open mouth I pant,
because I long for your commandments.

132 Turn to me and be gracious to me,
as is your custom toward those who love your name. ℟

133 Keep my steps steady according to your promise,
and never let iniquity have dominion over me.

134 Redeem me from human oppression,
that I may keep your precepts.

135 Make your face shine upon your servant,
and teach me your statutes.

136 My eyes shed streams of tears
because your law is not kept. ℟

137 You are righteous, O God,
and your judgments are right.

138 You have appointed your decrees in righteousness
and in all faithfulness.

℟ Teach me, O God, the way of your statutes.

139My zeal consumes me
because my foes forget your words.

140Your promise is well tried,
and your servant loves it. ℟

141I am small and despised,
yet I do not forget your precepts.

142Your righteousness is an everlasting righteousness,
and your law is the truth.

143Trouble and anguish have come upon me,
but your commandments are my delight.

144Your decrees are righteous forever;
give me understanding that I may live. ℟

Proper 12 [17] A vs. 129–136; Proper 26 [31] C vs. 137–144. (May be sung with double tone.)

Psalm 119 (Complete)

℟

1Happy are those whose way is blameless,
who walk in the law of God.

2Happy are those who keep God's decrees,
who seek God with their whole heart,

3who also do no wrong,
but walk in God's ways.

4You have commanded that all your precepts
shall be kept with diligence. ℟

5O that my ways may be steadfast
in keeping your statutes!

6Then I shall not be put to shame,
having my eyes fixed on all your commandments.

7I will praise you with an upright heart,
when I learn your righteous ordinances.

8I will observe your statutes;
do not utterly forsake me. ℟

9How can young people keep their way pure?
By guarding it according to your word.

10With my whole heart I seek you;
do not let me stray from your commandments.

11I treasure your word in my heart,
so that I may not sin against you.

12Blessed are you, O God;
teach me your statutes. ℟

13With my lips I declare
all the ordinances of your mouth.

14 I delight in the way of your decrees
as much as in all riches.

15I will meditate on your precepts,
and fix my eyes on your ways.

16I will delight in your statutes;
I will not forget your word. ℟

17Deal bountifully with your servant,
so that I may live and observe your word.

18Open my eyes,
so that I may behold wondrous things out of your law.

19I live as an alien in the land;
do not hide your commandments from me.

[20]My soul is consumed at all times
with longing for your ordinances. ℟

[21]You rebuke the insolent, accursed ones,
who wander from your commandments;

[22]take away from me their scorn and contempt,
for I have kept your decrees.

[23]Even though nobles sit plotting against me,
your servant will meditate on your statutes.

[24]Your decrees are my delight,
they are my counselors. ℟

[25]My soul clings to the dust;
revive me according to your word.

[26]When I told of my ways, you answered me;
teach me your statutes.

[27]Make me understand the way of your precepts,
and I will meditate on your wondrous works.

[28]My soul melts away for sorrow;
strengthen me according to your word. ℟

[29]Put false ways far from me;
and graciously teach me your law.

[30]I have chosen the way of faithfulness;
I set your ordinances before me.

[31]I cling to your decrees, O God;
let me not be put to shame.

[32]I run the way of your commandments
for you enlarge my understanding. ℟

[33]Teach me, O God, the way of your statutes,
and I will observe it to the end.

[34]Give me understanding, that I may keep your law,
and observe it with my whole heart.

[35]Lead me in the path of your commandments,
for I delight in your way.

[36]Turn my heart to your decrees,
and not to selfish gain. ℟

[37]Turn my eyes from looking at vanities;
give me life in your ways.

[38]Confirm to your servant your promise,
which is for those who fear you.

[39]Turn away the disgrace that I dread,
for your ordinances are good.

[40]See, I have longed for your precepts;
in your righteousness give me life. ℟

[41]Let your steadfast love come to me, O God,
your salvation according to your promise.

[42]Then I shall have an answer for those who taunt me,
for I trust in your word.

[43]Do not take the word of truth utterly out of my mouth,
for my hope is in your commandments.

[44]I will keep your law continually,
I will keep it forever and ever. ℟

[45]I shall walk at liberty,
for I have sought your precepts.

[46]I will also speak of your decrees before rulers,
and shall not be put to shame;

[47]I find my delight in your commandments,
because indeed I love them.

℟ Teach me, O God, the way of your statutes.

48 I revere your commandments, which I love,
and I will meditate on your statutes. ℟

49 Remember your word to your servant,
in which you have given me hope.

50 This is my comfort in my distress,
that your promise gives me life.

51 The arrogant utterly deride me,
but I do not turn away from your law.

52 When I think of your ordinances from of old,
I take comfort, O God.

53 Hot indignation seizes me because of the wicked,
those who forsake your law.

54 Your statutes have been my songs
wherever I make my home. ℟

55 I remember your name in the night, O God,
and I keep your law.

56 This blessing has fallen to me,
for I have kept your precepts.

57 You, O God, are my portion;
I promise to keep your words.

58 I implore your favor with all my heart;
be gracious to me according to your promise. ℟

59 When I think of your ways,
I turn my feet to your decrees;

60 I hurry and do not delay
to keep your commandments.

61 Though the cords of the wicked ensnare me,
I do not forget your law.

62 At midnight I rise to praise you,
because of your righteous ordinances.

63 I am a companion of all who fear you,
of those who keep your precepts.

64 The earth, O God, is full of your steadfast love;
teach me your statutes. ℟

65 You have dealt well with your servant,
O God, according to your word.

66 Teach me good judgment and knowledge,
for I believe in your commandments.

67 Before I was humbled I went astray,
but now I keep your word.

68 You are good and do good;
teach me your statutes. ℟

69 The arrogant smear me with lies,
but with my whole heart I keep your precepts.

70 Their hearts are fat and gross,
but I delight in your law.

71 It is good for me that I was humbled,
so that I might learn your statutes.

72 The law of your mouth is better to me
than thousands of gold and silver pieces. ℟

73 Your hands have made and fashioned me;
give me understanding that I may learn your commandments.

74 Those who fear you shall see me and rejoice,
because I have hoped in your word.

75 I know, O God, that your judgments are right,
and that in faithfulness you have humbled me.

76 Let your steadfast love become my comfort
according to your promise to your servant. ℟

77 Let your mercy come to me, that I may live;
for your law is my delight.

78 Let the arrogant be put to shame, because they have destroyed me with guile;
as for me, I will meditate on your precepts.

79 Let those who fear you turn to me,
so that they may know your decrees.

80 May my heart be blameless in your statutes,
so that I may not be put to shame. ℟

81 My soul languishes for your salvation;
I hope in your word.

82 My eyes fail with watching for your promise;
I ask, "When will you comfort me?"

83 Though shrunken like a wineskin in the smoke,
I have not forgotten your statutes.

84 How long must your servant endure?
When will you judge those who persecute me? ℟

85 The arrogant have dug pitfalls for me;
they flout your law.

86 All your commandments are enduring;
help me, I am persecuted without cause;

87 They have almost made an end of me on earth;
but I have not forsaken your precepts.

88 In your steadfast love spare my life,
so that I may keep the decrees of your mouth. ℟

89 God exists forever;
your word is firmly fixed in heaven.

90 Your faithfulness endures to all generations;
you have established the earth, and it stands fast.

91 By your appointment they stand today,
for all things are your servants.

92 If your law had not been my delight,
I would have perished in my misery. ℟

93 I will never forget your precepts,
for by them you have given me life.

94 I am yours, O God;
save me, for I have sought your precepts.

95 The wicked lie in wait to destroy me,
but I consider your decrees.

96 I have seen a limit to all perfection,
but your commandment is exceedingly broad. ℟

97 Oh God, how I love your law!
It is my meditation all day long.

98 Your commandment makes me wiser than my enemies,
for it is always with me.

99 I have more understanding than all my teachers,
for your decrees are my meditation.

100 I understand more than the aged,
for I keep your precepts. ℟

101 I hold back my feet from every evil way,
in order to keep your word.

102 I do not turn away from your ordinances,
for you have taught me.

103 How sweet are your words to my taste,
sweeter than honey to my mouth!

104 Through your precepts I get understanding;

℟ *Teach me, O God, the way of your statutes.*

therefore I hate every way that is false. ℟

105 Your word is a lamp to my feet,
and a light to my path.

106 I have sworn an oath and confirmed it,
to observe your righteous ordinances.

107 I am severely afflicted;
give me life, O God, according to your word.

108 Accept my offerings of praise, O God,
and teach me your ordinances. ℟

109 I hold my life in my hand continually,
but I do not forget your law.

110 The wicked have laid a snare for me,
but I do not stray from your precepts.

111 Your decrees are my heritage forever;
they are the joy of my heart.

112 I incline my heart to perform your statutes
forever, to the end. ℟

113 I hate the double-minded,
but I love your law.

114 You are my hiding place and my shield;
I hope in your word.

115 Go away from me, you evildoers,
that I may keep the commandments of my God.

116 Uphold me according to your promise, that I may live,
and let me not be put to shame in my hope. ℟

117 Hold me up, that I may be safe
and have regard for your statutes continually.

118 You spurn all who go astray from your statutes;
for their cunning is in vain.

119 All the wicked of the earth you count as dross;
therefore I love your decrees.

120 My flesh trembles for fear of you,
and I am afraid of your judgments. ℟

121 I have done what is just and right;
do not leave me to my oppressors.

122 Guarantee your servant's well-being;
do not let the godless oppress me.

123 My eyes fail from watching for your salvation,
and for the fulfillment of your righteous promise.

124 Deal with your servant according to your steadfast love,
and teach me your statutes. ℟

125 I am your servant; give me understanding,
so that I may know your decrees.

126 It is time for God to act,
for your law has been broken.

127 Truly I love your commandments more than gold,
more than fine gold.

128 Truly I direct my steps by all your precepts;
I hate every false way. ℟

129 Your decrees are wonderful;
therefore my soul keeps them.

130 The unfolding of your words gives light;
it imparts understanding to the simple.

131 With open mouth I pant,
because I long for your commandments.

132 Turn to me and be gracious to me,
as is your custom toward those who love your name. ℟

133 Keep my steps steady according tó your promise,
and never let iniquity have dominion óver me.

134 Redeem me from huḿan oppression,
that I may ḱeep your precepts.

135 Make your face shine upón your servant,
and teach ḿe your statutes.

136 My eyes shed śtreams of tears
because your law ís not kept. ℟

137 You are rightéous, O God,
and your judgḿents are right.

138 You have appointed your dećrees in righteousness
and ín all faithfulness.

139 My źeal consumes me
because my foes forǵet your words.

140 Your promise ís well tried,
and your śervant loves it. ℟

141 I am small ánd despised,
yet I do not forǵet your precepts.

142 Your righteousness is an everĺasting righteousness,
and your law ís the truth.

143 Trouble and anguish have ćome upon me,
but your commandments are ḿy delight.

144 Your decrees are rightéous forever;
give me understanding that Í may live. ℟

145 With my whole ĥeart I cry;
answer me, O God. I will ḱeep your statutes.

146 I cry to ýou to save me,
that I may observe ýour decrees.

147 I rise before dawn and ćry for help;
I put my hope ín your words.

148 My eyes are awake before each watch óf the night,
that I may meditate ón your promise. ℟

149 In your steadfast love ĥear my voice;
O God, in your justice preśerve my life.

150 Those who persecute me with evil purṕose draw near;
they are far ḟrom your law.

151 Yet you are ńear, O God,
and all your commandḿents are true.

152 Long ago I learned from ýour decrees
that you have established ́them forever. ℟

153 Look on my miserý and rescue me,
for I do not forǵet your law.

154 Plead my cause ánd redeem me;
give me life according tó your promise.

155 Salvation is far ḟrom the wicked,
for they do not śeek your statutes.

156 Great is your merćy, O God;
give me life according tó your justice. ℟

157 Many are my persecutors ánd my adversaries,
yet I do not swerve from ýour decrees.

158 I look at the faithless ẃith disgust,
because they do not keep ýour commands.

159 Consider how I ĺove your precepts;
preserve my life according to your śteadfast love.

160 The sum of your ẃord is truth;
and every one of your righteous ordinances endúres forever. ℟

℟ Teach me, O God, the way of your statutes.

161 Nobles persecute me without cause,
but my heart stands in awe of your words.

162 I rejoice at your word
like one who finds great spoil.

163 I hate and abhor falsehood,
but I love your law.

164 Seven times a day I praise you,
I praise you for your righteous ordinances. ℟

165 Great peace have those who love your law;
nothing can make them stumble.

166 I hope for your salvation, O God,
and I fulfill your commandments.

167 My soul keeps your decrees;
I love them exceedingly.

168 I keep your precepts and decrees,
for all my ways are before you. ℟

169 Let my cry come before you, O God;
give me understanding according to your word.

170 Let my supplication come before you;
deliver me according to your promise.

171 My lips will pour forth praise,
because you teach me your statutes.

172 My tongue will sing of your promise,
for all your commandments are right. ℟

173 Let your hand be ready to help me,
for I have chosen your precepts.

174 I long for your salvation, O God,
and your law is my delight.

175 Let me live that I may praise you,
and let your ordinances help me.

176 I have gone astray like a lost sheep;
seek out your servant, for I do not forget your commandments. ℟

Psalm 120

Response

Antiphon: Lee Dengler, 1994

℟

1 In my distress I cry to God,
that God may answer me:

2 "Deliver me, O God, from lying lips,
from a deceitful tongue."

3 What shall be given to you?
And what more shall be done to you,
you deceitful tongue?

4 A warrior's sharp arrows,
with glowing coals of the broom tree! ℟

5 Woe is me, that I am an alien in Meshech,
that I must live among the tents of Kedar.

6 Too long have I had my dwelling
among those who hate peace.

7 I am for peace;
but when I speak, they are for war.
℟

Psalm 121

℟esponse

Antiphon: David Hurd, 1994

℟

1 I lift up my eyes to the hills—
from where will my help come?

2 My help comes from God,
who made heaven and earth.

3 God will not let your foot be moved;
God who keeps you will not slumber.

4 God who keeps Israel
will neither slumber nor sleep. ℟

5 God is your keeper;
God is your shade at your side.

6 The sun shall not strike you by day,
nor the moon by night.

7 God will keep you from all evil;
God will keep your life.

8 God will keep your going out and your coming in
from this time on and forevermore. ℟

(May be sung with double tone.)

Psalm 122

℟esponse

Antiphon: Emma Lou Diemer, 1994

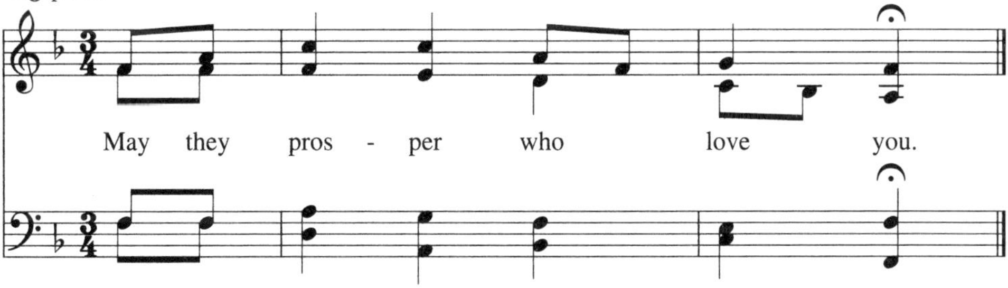

℟

1 I was glad when they said to me,
"Let us go to the house of God!"

2 Our feet are standing within your gates,
O Jerusalem.

℟ May they prosper who love you.

3Jerusalem—built as a city that is
bound firmly together.

4To it the tribes go up, the tribes of God,
as was decreed for Israel,
to give thanks to the name of God.

5For there the thrones for judgment were
set up,
the thrones of the house of David. ℟

6Pray for the peace of Jerusalem:
"May they prosper who love you.

7"Peace be within your walls,
and security within your towers."

8For the sake of my relatives and friends
I will say,
"Peace be within you."

9For the sake of the house of the
Sovereign our God,
I will seek your good. ℟

(May be sung with double tone.)

Psalm 123

℟esponse

Antiphon: Robert Train Adams, 1994

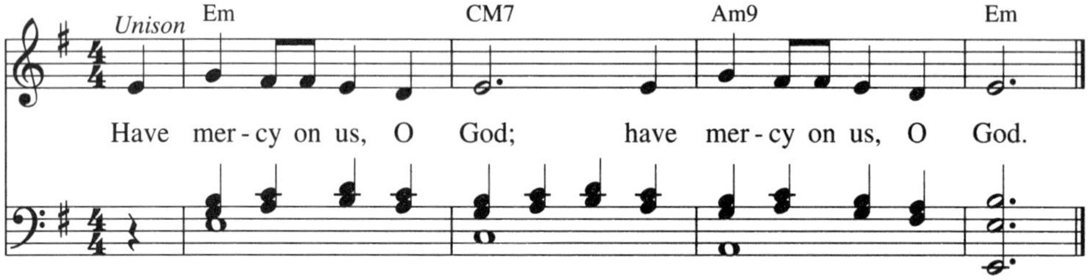

℟

1To you I lift up my eyes,
O you who are enthroned in
the heavens!

2As the eyes of subjects look to the hand
of their ruler,
so our eyes look to the Sovereign
our God, until God has mercy upon
us.

3Have mercy upon us, O God, have
mercy upon us,
for we have had more than enough of
contempt.

4Our soul has had more than its fill of
the scorn of those who are at ease,
and its fill of the contempt of the
proud. ℟

(May be sung with double tone.)

Psalm 124

Antiphon: Jane Marshall, 1994

Response

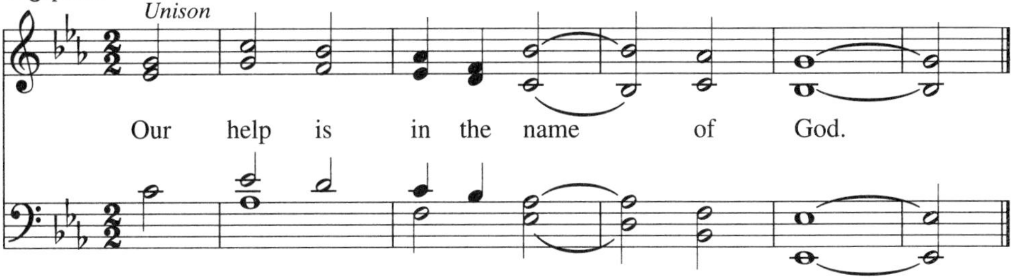

℟

[1]If it had not been God who was ón our side
—let Israél now say—

[2]if it had not been God who was ón our side,
when our enemíes attacked us,

[3]then they would have swallowed us úp alive,
when their anger was kińdled against us;

[4]then the flood would have swept ús away,
the torrent would have gone over us;

[5]then over us would have gone the ŕaging waters. ℟

[6]Blessed be the Sovereígn, our God,
who has not given us as prey t́o their teeth.

[7]We have escaped like a bird from the snare óf the fowlers;
the snare is broken, and we h́ave escaped.

[8]Our help is in the ńame of God,
who made heaven and earth. ℟

Psalm 125

Antiphon: Vérne de la Peña, 1994

Response

℟

[1]Those who trust in God are ĺike Mount Zion,
which cannot be moved, but abídes forever.

[2]As the mountains surŕound Jerusalem,
so God surrounds the people, from this time on and forévermore.

℟ Do good, O God, to those who are good.

3For the scepter of wickedness shall not rest on the land allotted to the righteous,
so that the righteous might not stretch out their hands to do wrong.

4Do good, O God, to those who are good,
and to those who are upright in their hearts.

5But those who turn aside to their own crooked ways,
God will lead them away with evildoers. Peace be upon Israel! ℟

Psalm 126

℟esponse

Antiphon: Martie McMane, 1994

℟

1When God restored the fortunes of Zion,
we were like those who dream.

2Then our mouth was filled with laughter,
and our tongue with shouts of joy;

then it was said among the nations,
"God has done great things for them."

3God has done great things for us,
and we rejoiced. ℟

4Restore our fortunes, O God,
like the watercourses in the Negeb.

5May those who sow in tears
reap with shouts of joy.

6Those who go out weeping, bearing the seed for sowing,
shall come home with shouts of joy,
carrying their sheaves. ℟

Psalm 127

Antiphon: Robert Fryson, 1994

℟esponse

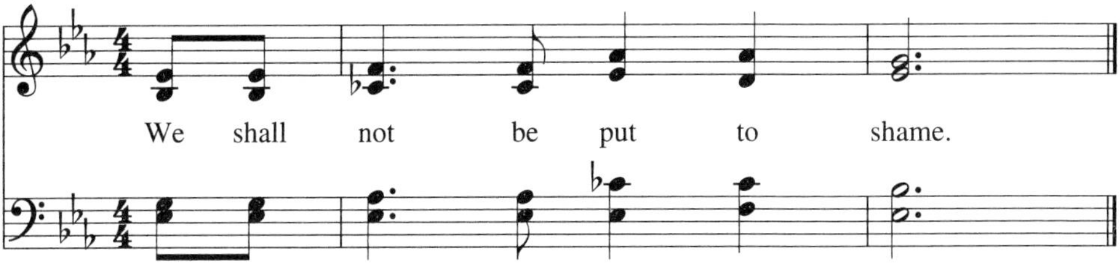

℟

¹Unless God builds the house,
 those who build it labor in vain.

Unless God guards the city,
 the guard keeps watch in vain.

²It is in vain that you rise up early and go late to rest, eating the bread of anxious toil;
 for God gives sleep to God's beloved. ℟

³Sons and daughters are indeed a heritage from God,
 the fruit of the womb is a reward.

⁴Like arrows in the hand of a warrior
 are the offspring of one's youth.

⁵Happy is the person whose quiver is full of them,
 who shall not be put to shame
 speaking with enemies in the gate. ℟

Psalm 128

Antiphon: Carolyn Jennings, 1994

℟esponse

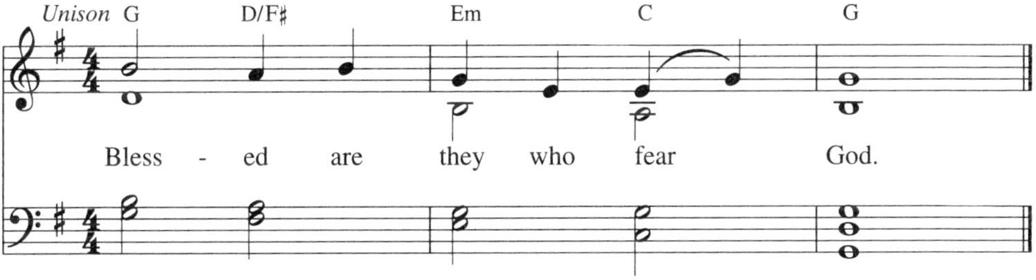

℟

¹Happy is everyone who fears God,
 and who walks in God's ways.

²You shall eat the fruit of the labor of your hands;
 you shall be happy, and it shall go well with you.

³Your spouse will be like a fruitful vine within your house;
 your children will be like olive shoots around your table. ℟

⁴Thus shall the one be blessed who fears God.
 ⁵May God bless you from Zion.

May you see the prosperity of Jerusalem all the days of your life.
 ⁶May you see your children's children. Peace be upon Israel! ℟

Psalm 129

℟esponse

Antiphon: Emma Lou Diemer, 1994

℟

[1]"Often have they attacked me from my youth"
—let Israel now say—

[2]"often have they attacked me from my youth,
yet they have not prevailed against me.

[3]The plowers plowed on my back;
they made their furrows long."

[4]The Most High is righteous,
and has cut the cords of the wicked. ℟

[5]May all who hate Zion
be put to shame and turned backward.

[6]Let them be like the grass on the housetops
that withers before it grows up,

[7]with which reapers do not fill their hands
or binders of sheaves fill their arms,

[8]while those who pass by do not say,
"The blessing of God be upon you! We bless you in the name of the Most High!" ℟

(May be sung with double tone.)

Psalm 130

℟esponse

Antiphon: Judy Hunnicutt, 1994

℟

[1]Out of the depths I cry to you, O God.
[2]O God, hear my voice!

Let your ears be attentive to the voice of my supplications!
[3]If you, O God, should mark iniquities, who could stand? ℟

[4]But there is forgiveness with you, so that you may be revered.
[5]I wait for God, my soul waits, and in God's word I hope;

[6]my soul waits for God more than those who watch for the morning,

more than those who watch for the morning.

7O Israel, hope in God!
For with God there is steadfast love.

With God is great power to redeem;
8It is God who will redeem Israel
from all its iniquities. ℟

Psalm 131

℞esponse

Antiphon: Elaine Kirkland, 1994

May be sung as a round the last time.

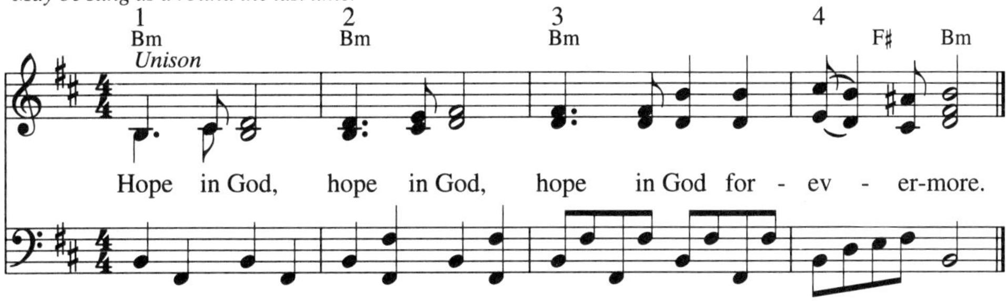

℟

1O God, my heart is not lifted up,
my eyes are not raised too high;

I do not occupy myself with things too great
or things too marvelous for me.

2But I have calmed and quieted my soul,
like a weaned child with its mother;

my soul is like the weaned child
that stays with me.

3O Israel, hope in God
from this time on and forevermore. ℟

Psalm 132

℞esponse

Antiphon: David Hurd, 1994

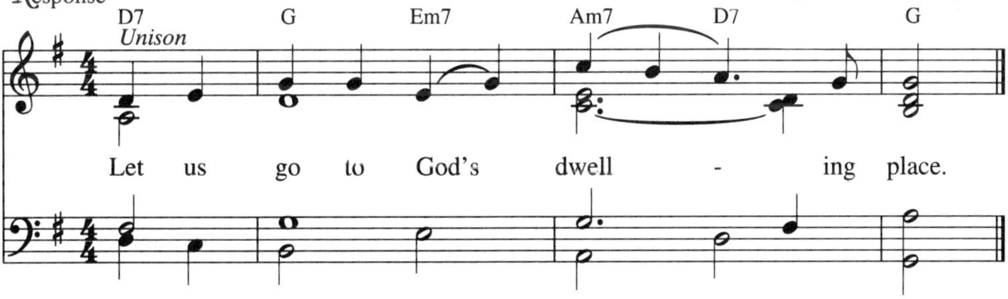

℟

1O God, remember in David's favor
all the hardships he endured;

2how David swore to God
and vowed to the Mighty One of Jacob,

℟ Let us go to God's dwelling place.

3"I will not enter my house or get into my bed;
4I will not give sleep to my eyes or slumber to my eyelids,

5until I find a place for God,
a dwelling place for the Mighty One of Jacob." ℟

6We heard of it in Ephrathah;
we found it in the fields of Jaar.

7"Let us go to God's dwelling place;
let us worship at God's footstool."

8Rise up, O God, and go to your resting place,
you and the ark of your might.

9Let your priests be clothed with righteousness,
and let your faithful shout for joy. ℟

10For your servant David's sake
do not turn away the face of your anointed one.

11God swore to David a sure oath and will not turn back on it:
"One of the offspring of your body I will set on your throne.

12If your offspring keep my covenant and my decrees that I shall teach them,
their offspring also shall sit on your throne forevermore." ℟

13For God has chosen Zion;
God has desired it for a habitation:

14"This is my resting place forever;
here I will reside, for I have desired it.

15I will abundantly bless its provisions;
I will satisfy its poor with bread.

16Its priests I will clothe with salvation,
and its faithful will shout for joy. ℟

17There I will cause a horn to sprout up for David;
I have prepared a lamp for my anointed one,

18whose enemies I will clothe with disgrace,
but upon my anointed a crown will gleam."

℟

Psalm 133

℟esponse

Antiphon: Hyeon Jeong, 1994

℟

1How very good and pleasant it is
when kindred live together in unity!

2It is like the precious oil on the head,
running down upon the beard,
upon the beard of Aaron,
running down over the collar of his robes.

3It is like the dew of Hermon,
which falls on the mountains of Zion.

For there God ordained the blessing,
the blessing of life forevermore. ℟

Psalm 134

℟esponse

Antiphon: Vérne de la Peña, 1994

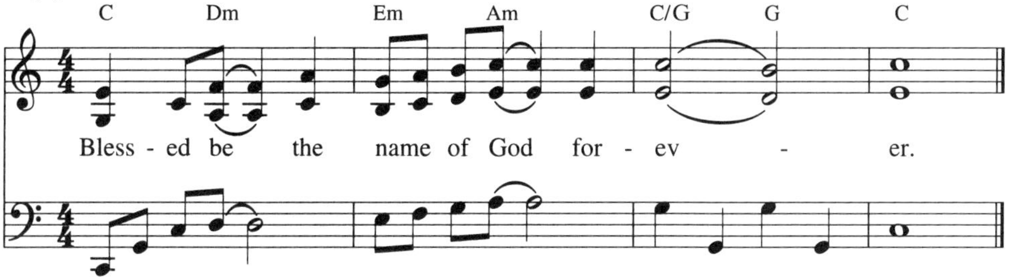

℟

1Come, bless God, all you servants of God,
who stand by night in the house of God!

2Lift up your hands to the holy place,
and bless the Most High.

3May God, maker of heaven and earth,
bless you out of Zion. ℟

Psalm 135

℟esponse

Antiphon: Peter Niedmann, 1994

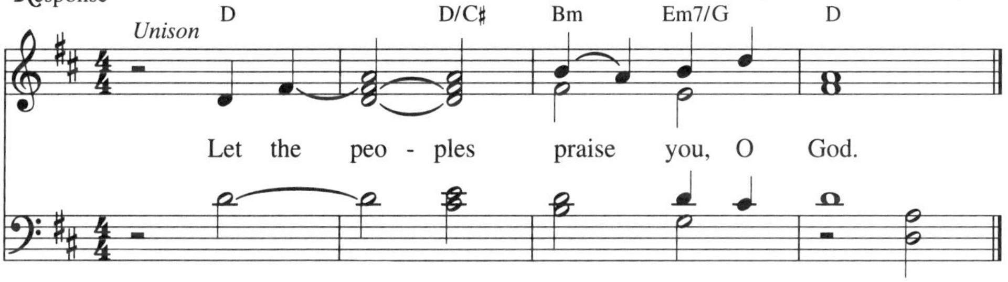

℟

1Hallelujah! Praise the name of God;
give praise, O servants of the Most High,

2you that stand in the house of God,
in the courts of the house of our God.

3Praise God, for God is good;
sing to God's name, for God is gracious.

4For God has chosen Jacob as God's,
Israel as God's own possession. ℟

5For I know that God is great;
our God is above all gods.

6Whatever God pleases God does,
in heaven and on earth, in the seas and all deeps.

℟ Let the peoples praise you, O God.

7 It is God who makes the clouds rise at the end of the earth;
God makes lightnings for the rain and brings out the wind from God's storehouses.

8 It was God who struck down the firstborn of Egypt,
striking down both human beings and animals;

9 God sent signs and wonders into your midst, O Egypt,
against Pharaoh and all his servants. ℟

10 God struck down many nations
and killed mighty rulers—

11 Sihon, king of the Amorites, and Og, king of Bashan,
and all the kingdoms of Canaan—

12 and gave their land as a heritage,
a heritage to God's people Israel.

13 Your name, O God, endures forever,
your renown, O God, throughout all ages. ℟

14 For God will vindicate God's people,
and have compassion on God's servants.

15 The idols of the nations are silver and gold,
the work of human hands.

16 They have mouths, but they do not speak;
they have eyes, but they do not see;

17 they have ears, but they do not hear,
and there is no breath in their mouths. ℟

18 Those who make them and all who trust them
shall become like them.

19 Bless God, O house of Israel!
Bless God, O house of Aaron!

20 Bless God, O house of Levi!
Bless God, all you that fear God!

21 From Zion, blessed be God—the one who resides in Jerusalem.
Hallelujah! ℟

Psalm 136

℟esponse

Antiphon: Emma Lou Diemer, 1994

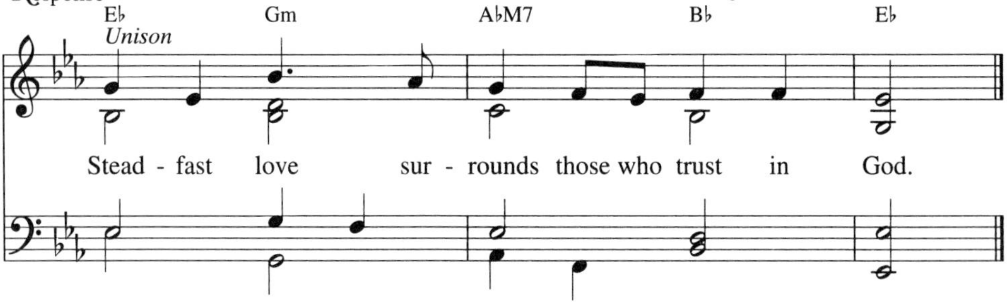

℟

1 O give thanks to God, for God is good,
for God's steadfast love endures forever.

2 O give thanks to the God of gods,
for God's steadfast love endures forever.

[3]O give thanks to the Sovereign of sovereigns,
for God's steadfast love endures forever;

[4]who alone does great wonders,
for God's steadfast love endures forever; ℟

[5]who by understanding made the heavens,
for God's steadfast love endures forever;

[6]who spread out the earth on the waters,
for God's steadfast love endures forever;

[7]who made the great lights,
for God's steadfast love endures forever;

[8]the sun to rule over the day,
for God's steadfast love endures forever; ℟

[9]the moon and stars to rule over the night,
for God's steadfast love endures forever.

[10]who struck Egypt through their firstborn,
for God's steadfast love endures forever;

[11]and brought Israel out from among them,
for God's steadfast love endures forever;

[12]with a strong hand and an outstretched arm,
for God's steadfast love endures forever; ℟

[13]who divided the Red Sea in two,
for God's steadfast love endures forever;

[14]and made Israel pass through the midst of it,
for God's steadfast love endures forever;

[15]but overthrew Pharaoh and his army in the Red Sea,
for God's steadfast love endures forever;

[16]who led the people through the wilderness,
for God's steadfast love endures forever; ℟

[17]who struck down great rulers,
for God's steadfast love endures forever;

[18]and killed famous rulers,
for God's steadfast love endures forever;

[19]Sihon, king of the Amorites,
for God's steadfast love endures forever;

[20]and Og, king of Bashan,
for God's steadfast love endures forever;

[21]and gave their land as a heritage,
for God's steadfast love endures forever;

[22]a heritage to God's servant Israel,
for God's steadfast love endures forever. ℟

[23]It is God who remembered us in our low estate,
for God's steadfast love endures forever;

[24]and rescued us from our foes,
for God's steadfast love endures forever;

℟ Steadfast love surrounds those who trust in God.

25who gives food tó all flesh,
for God's steadfast love endúres forever;

26O give thanks to the Gód of heaven,
for God's steadfast love endúres forever. ℟

Psalm 137

℟esponse

Antiphon: Jonathan McNair, 1994

℟

1By the rivers of Babylon—there wé sat down
and we wept when we remémbered Zion.

2And so we hung úp our harps,
there upón the willows.

3For there our captors asked us for songs,
and our tormentors ásked for mirth,
saying, "Sing us one of the sóngs of Zion!"

4How could we sing God's song in a fóreign land?
5If I forget you, O Jerusalem, let my ríght hand wither! ℟

6Let my tongue cling to the roof of my mouth, if I do nót remember you,
if I do not set Jerusalem above my híghest joy.

7Remember, O God, against the Edomites the day of Jerúsalem's fall,
how they said, "Tear it down!
Tear it down to íts foundations!"

8O city of Babýlon, you devastator!
Happy shall they be whó pay you back what you have dóne to us!

9Happy shall they be who táke your little ones
and dash them agáinst the rock! ℟

(May be sung with double tone.)

Psalm 138

℟esponse

Antiphon: Emma Lou Diemer, 1994

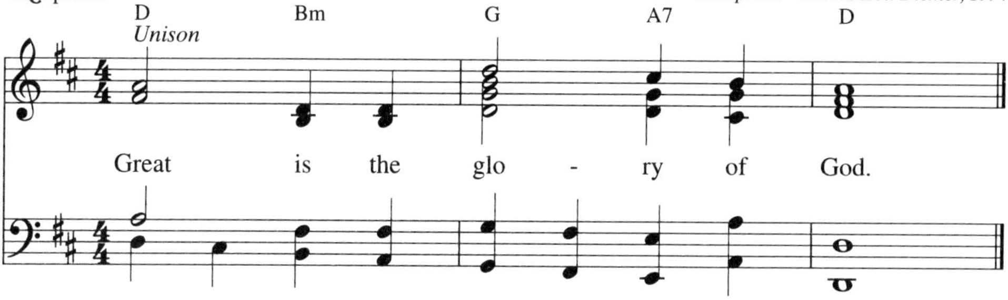

℟

1 I give you thanks, O God, with my whole heart;
before the gods I sing your praise;

2 I bow down toward your holy temple and give thanks to your name
for your steadfast love and your faithfulness;

for you have exalted your name
and your word above everything.

3 On the day I called, you answered me,
you increased my strength of soul. ℟

4 All the rulers of the earth shall praise you, O God,
for they have heard the words of your mouth.

5 They shall sing of the ways of God,
for great is the glory of God.

6 For though God is high, God regards the lowly;
but the haughty, God perceives from far away.

7 Though I walk in the midst of trouble,
you preserve me against the wrath of my enemies;

you stretch out your hand,
and your right hand delivers me.

8 God will fulfill God's purpose for me;
your steadfast love, O God, endures forever. Do not forsake the work of your hands. ℟

Psalm 139

℟esponse

Antiphon: Jane Marshall, 1994

℟

1 O God, you have searched me and known me.

2 You know when I sit down and when I rise up; you discern my thoughts from far away.

℟ *Search me, O God, and know my heart.*

3You search out my path and my lying down,
and are acquainted with all my ways. ℟

4Even before a word is on my tongue,
O God, you know it completely.

5You hem me in, behind and before,
and lay your hand upon me.

6Such knowledge is too wonderful for me;
it is so high that I cannot attain it. ℟

7Where can I go from your spirit?
Or where can I flee from your presence?

8If I ascend to heaven, you are there;
if I make my bed in Sheol, you are there. ℟

9If I take the wings of the morning
and settle at the farthest limits of the sea,

10even there your hand shall lead me,
and your right hand shall hold me fast.

11If I say, "Surely the shadows shall cover me,
and the light around me become night,"

12even the night is not without light to you; the night is as bright as the day,
for the night is as light to you. ℟

13For it was you who formed my inward parts;
you knit me together in my mother's womb.

14I praise you, for I am fearfully and wonderfully made.
Wonderful are your works; that I know very well. ℟

15My frame was not hidden from you,
when I was being made in secret,
intricately woven in the depths of the earth.

16Your eyes beheld my unformed substance.
In your book were written all the days that were formed for me
before they existed.

17How weighty to me are your thoughts, O God!
How vast is the sum of them!

18I try to count them—they are more than the sand;
I come to the end—I am still with you. ℟

19O that you would kill the wicked, O God,
and that the bloodthirsty would depart from me—

20those who speak of you maliciously,
and lift themselves up against you for evil!

21Do I not hate those who hate you, O God?
And do I not loathe those who rise up against you?

22I hate them with perfect hatred;
I count them my enemies.

23Search me, O God, and know my heart;
test me and know my thoughts.

24See if there is in me any wicked way,
and lead me in the way everlasting. ℟

Proper 11 [16] A vs. 1–12, 23–24; Epiphany 2 [2] B vs. 1–6, 13–18; Proper 4 [9] B and Proper 18 [23] C vs. 1–6, 13–18.

Psalm 140

℟esponse

Antiphon: Robert Train Adams, 1994

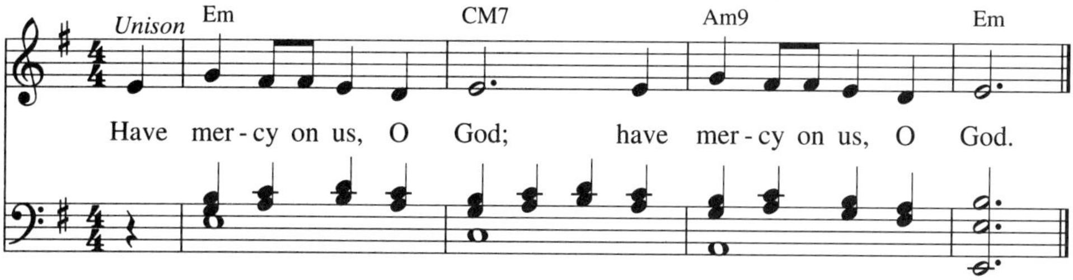

℟

1 Deliver me, O God, from evildoers;
protect me from those who are violent,

2 who plan evil things in their minds
and stir up wars continually.

3 They make their tongue sharp as a snake's,
and under their lips is the venom of vipers.

4 Guard me, O God, from the hands of the wicked;
protect me from the violent who have planned my downfall. ℟

5 The arrogant have hidden a trap for me,
and with cords they have spread a net,
along the road they have set snares for me.

6 I say to God, "You are my God;
give ear, O God, to the voice of my supplications."

7 O God, my God, my strong deliverer,
you have covered my head in the day of battle.

8 Do not grant, O God, the desires of the wicked;
do not further their evil plot. ℟

9 Those who surround me lift up their heads;
let the mischief of their lips overwhelm them!

10 Let burning coals fall on them!
Let them be flung into pits, no more to rise!

11 Do not let the slanderer be established in the land;
let evil speedily hunt down the violent!

12 I know that God maintains the cause of the needy ones,
and executes justice for those who are poor.

13 Surely the righteous shall give thanks to your name;
the upright shall live in your presence. ℟

Psalm 141

℟esponse

Antiphon: Jonathan McNair, 1994

℟

1 I call upon you, O God; come quickly to me;
give ear to my voice when I call to you.

2 Let my prayer be counted as incense before you,
and the lifting up of my hands as an evening sacrifice.

3 Set a guard over my mouth, O God;
keep watch over the door of my lips.

4 Do not turn my heart to any evil, to busy myself with wicked deeds with those who work iniquity;
do not let me eat of their delicacies. ℟

5 Let the righteous strike me;
let the faithful correct me.

Never let the oil of the wicked anoint my head,
for my prayer is continually against their wicked deeds.

6 When they are given over to those who shall condemn them,
then they shall learn that my words were pleasant.

7 Like a rock that one breaks apart and shatters on the land,
so shall their bones be strewn at the mouth of Sheol. ℟

8 But my eyes are turned toward you, O God, my God;
in you I seek refuge; do not leave me defenseless.

9 Keep me from the trap that they have laid for me,
and from the snares of evildoers.

10 Let the wicked fall into their own nets,
while I alone escape. ℟

Psalm 142

℟esponse

Antiphon: Marty Haugen, 1994

℟

[1]With my voice I cry to God;
with my voice I make supplication to God.

[2]Before God I pour out my complaint;
Before God I tell my trouble.

[3]When my spirit is faint, you know my way.
In the path where I walk they have hidden a trap for me.

[4]Look beside me and see
—there is no one who takes notice of me; ℟

no refuge remains to me;
there is no one who cares for me.

[5]I cry to you, O God; I say,
"You are my refuge, my portion in the land of the living."

[6]Give heed to my cry, for I am brought very low.
Save me from my persecutors, for they are too strong for me.

[7]Bring me out of prison, so that I may give thanks to your name.
The righteous will surround me, for you will deal bountifully with me. ℟

(May be sung with double tone.)

Psalm 143

℟esponse

Antiphon: Marty Haugen, 1994

℟

[1]Hear my prayer, O God; give ear to my supplications in your faithfulness;
answer me in your righteousness.

[2]Do not enter into judgment with your servant,
for no one living is righteous before you.

℟ *My soul thirsts for you, my soul thirsts for you like a parched land.*

3 For the enemy has pursued me, crushing my life to the ground,
making me sit in the shadows like those long dead.

4 Therefore my spirit faints within me;
my heart within me is appalled. ℟

5 I remember the days of old, I think about all your deeds,
I meditate on the works of your hands.

6 I stretch out my hands to you;
my soul thirsts for you like a parched land.

7 Answer me quickly, O God; my spirit fails.
Do not hide your face from me, or I shall be like those who go down to the Pit.

8 Let me hear of your steadfast love in the morning, for in you I put my trust.
Teach me the way I should go, for to you I lift up my soul. ℟

9 Save me, O God, from my enemies;
I have fled to you for refuge.

10 Teach me to do your will, for you are my God.
Let your good spirit lead me on a level path.

11 For your name's sake, O God, preserve my life.
In your righteousness bring me out of trouble.

12 In your steadfast love cut off my enemies, and destroy all my adversaries,
for I am your servant. ℟

(May be sung with double tone.)

Psalm 144

℟esponse *Antiphon: Robert Train Adams, 1994*

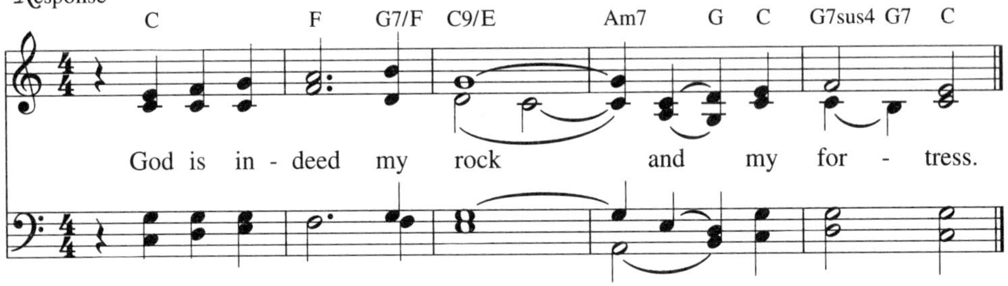

℟

1 Blessed be God, my rock,
who trains my hands for war, and my fingers for battle;

2 my rock and my fortress, my stronghold and my deliverer,
my shield, in whom I take refuge, who subdues the peoples under me.

3 O God, what are human beings that you regard them,
or mortals that you think of them?

4 They are like a breath;
their days are like a passing shadow. ℟

5 Bend your heavens, O God, and come down;
touch the mountains so that they smoke.

6 Make the lightning flash and scatter them;
send out your arrows and rout them.

7 Stretch out your hand from on high;
set me free and rescue me from the mighty waters,

Rescue me from the hand of aliens,
8 whose mouths speak lies, and whose right hands are false. ℟

9 I will sing a new song to you, O God;
upon a ten-stringed harp I will play to you,

10 the one who gives victory to rulers,
who rescues David, God's servant.

11 Rescue me from the cruel sword, and deliver me from the hand of aliens,
whose mouths speak lies, and whose right hands are false. ℟

12 May our sons in their youth be like plants full grown,
our daughters like corner pillars, cut for the building of a palace.

13 May our barns be filled with produce of every kind;
may our sheep increase by thousands, by tens of thousands in our fields,

14 and may our cattle be heavy with young.
May there be no breach in the walls, no exile, and no cry of distress in our streets.

15 Blessed are the people to whom such blessings fall;
blessed are the people whose God is the Most High. ℟

Psalm 145

℟esponse *Antiphon: Vérne de la Peña, 1994*

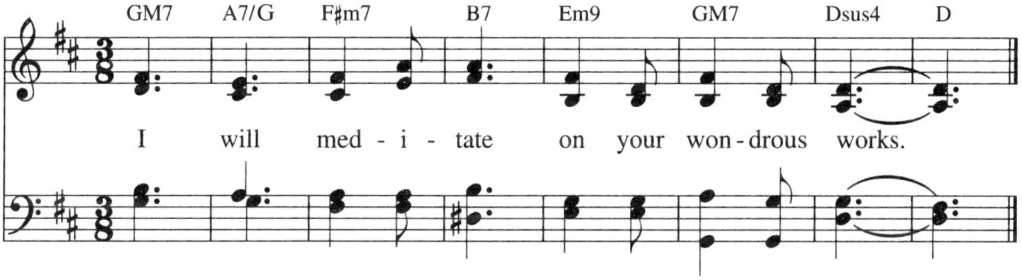

℟

1 I will extol you, my God and Ruler,
and bless your name forever and ever.

2 Every day I will bless you,
and praise your name forever and ever.

3 Great is God, and greatly to be praised;
God's greatness is unsearchable.

4 One generation shall laud your works to another,
and shall declare your mighty acts. ℟

5 On the glorious splendor of your majesty,
and on your wondrous works, I will meditate.

6 The might of your awesome deeds shall be proclaimed,
and I will declare your greatness.

7 They shall celebrate the fame of your abundant goodness,
and shall sing aloud of your righteousness.

℟ I will meditate on your wondrous works.

8God is gracious and merciful,
slow to anger and abounding in steadfast love. ℟

9God is good to all,
and God's compassion is over all that God has made.

10All your works shall give thanks to you, O God,
and all your faithful shall bless you.

11They shall speak of the glory of your dominion,
and tell of your power,

12to make known to all people your mighty deeds,
and the glorious splendor of your dominion. ℟

13Your reign is an everlasting reign,
and your dominion endures throughout all generations.

God is faithful in every word,
and gracious in every deed.

14God upholds all who are falling,
and raises up all who are bowed down.

15The eyes of all look to you,
and you give them their food in due season.

16You open your hand to all,
satisfying the desire of every living thing. ℟

17In every way God is just,
and kind in every action.

18God is near to all who call,
to all who call on God in truth.

19God fulfills the desire of all who fear God;
God also hears their cry, and saves them.

20God watches over all who love God,
but will destroy all the wicked.

21My mouth will speak the praise of God,
and all flesh will bless God's holy name forever and ever. ℟

Proper 9 [14] A vs. 8–14; Proper 13 [18] A vs. 8–9, 14–21; Proper 20 [25] A vs. 1–8; Proper 12 [17] B vs. 10–18; Proper 27 [32] C vs. 1–5, 17–21 (Alt.).

Psalm 146

℟esponse

Antiphon: Judy Hunnicutt, 1994

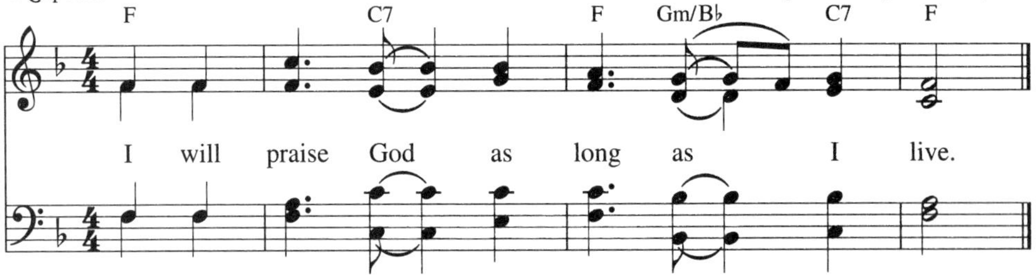

℟

1Praise be to God!
Praise God, O my soul!

2I will praise God as long as I live;
I will sing praises to my God all my life long.

3 Do not put your trust in nobles, in mortals,
in whom there is no help.

4 When their breath departs, they return to the earth;
on that very day their plans shall perish. ℟

5 Happy are those whose help is the God of Jacob,
whose hope is in the Sovereign their God,

6 who made heaven and earth, the sea, and all that is in them;
who keeps faith forever;

7 who executes justice for the oppressed;
who gives food to the hungry. ℟

God sets the prisoners free;
8 God opens the eyes of those who cannot see.

God lifts up those who are bowed down;
God loves those who are righteous.

9 God watches over the strangers, and upholds the orphan and the widow,
but the way of the wicked God brings to ruin.

10 The Sovereign will reign forever, your God, O Zion, for all generations.
Praise be to God! ℟

Advent 3 A vs. 5–10 (Alt.).

Psalm 147

℟esponse

Antiphon: Elaine Kirkland, 1994

℟

1 Praise God! How good it is to sing praises to our God;
for God is gracious, and a song of praise is fitting.

2 God builds up Jerusalem;
God gathers the outcasts of Israel.

3 God heals the brokenhearted,
and binds up their wounds.

4 God determines the number of the stars;
God gives to all of them their names.

5 Great is our God, and abundant in power,
whose understanding is beyond measure. ℟

6 God lifts up the downtrodden;
God casts the wicked to the ground.

7 Sing to God with thanksgiving;
make melody to our God on the lyre.

8 God covers the heavens with clouds, prepares rain for the earth,
and makes grass grow on the hills.

℟ Great is our God, and abundant in power.

9 God gives to the animals their food,
and to the young ravens when they cry.

10 God has no delight in the strength of the horse,
nor pleasure in the speed of a runner;

11 but God takes pleasure in those who fear God,
in those who hope in God's steadfast love. ℟

12 Praise God, O Jerusalem!
Praise your God, O Zion!

13 For God strengthens the bars of your gates;
God blesses your children within you.

14 God grants peace within your borders;
God fills you with the finest of wheat.

15 God sends out a command to the earth;
God's word runs swiftly. ℟

16 God gives snow like wool;
God scatters frost like ashes.

17 God hurls down hail like crumbs—
who can stand before God's cold?

18 God sends out a word, and melts them;
God makes a wind blow, and the waters flow.

19 God declares the word to Jacob,
and declares God's statutes and ordinances to Israel.

20 God has not dealt thus with any other nation; they do not know God's ordinances.
Praise be to God! ℟

Christmas 2 ABC vs. 12–20 (Alt.); Epiphany 5 [5] B vs. 1–11, 20c.

Psalm 148

℟esponse

Antiphon: David Hurd, 1994

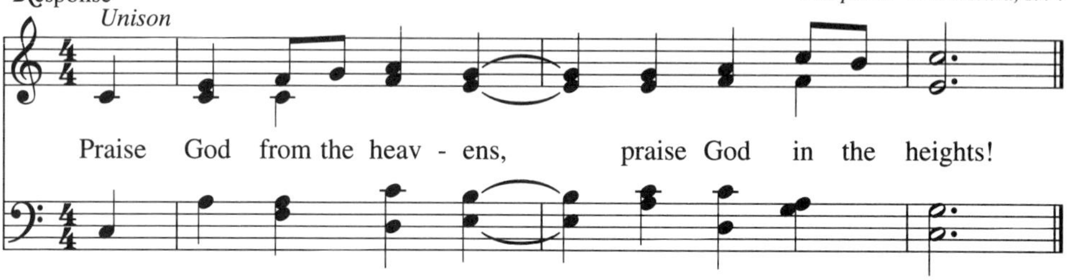

℟

1 Praise God! Praise God from the heavens;
praise God in the heights!

2 Praise God, all you angels of God;
praise God, all you host of heaven!

3 Praise God, you sun and moon;
praise God, all you shining stars!

4 Praise God, you highest heavens,
and you waters above the heavens! ℟

5 Let them praise the name of God,
for God commanded and they were created.

6 God established them forever and ever;
God fixed their bounds, which cannot be passed.

7 Praise God from the earth, you sea monsters and all deeps,

8 fire and hail, snow and frost, stormy
wind fulfilling God's command!

9 Mountains and all hills, fruit trees and
all cedars!
10 Beasts of the forest and all cattle,
crawling things and flying birds! ℟

11 Rulers of the earth and all peoples,
nobles and all leaders of the earth!

12 Young men and women alike,
old and young together!

13 Let them praise the name of the
Sovereign,
whose name alone is exalted, whose
glory is above earth and heaven.

14 God has raised up a horn for the people,
and praise for all the faithful,
for the people of Israel who are close
to God. Praise be to God! ℟

(May be sung with double tone.)

Psalm 149

℟esponse

Antiphon: Robert Train Adams, 1994

℟

1 Praise God! Sing to God a new song;
sing God's praise in the assembly of
the faithful.

2 Let Israel be glad in its Maker;
let the children of Zion rejoice in
their Ruler.

3 Let them praise God's name with
dancing,
making melody to God with
tambourine and lyre.

4 For God takes pleasure in the people;
God adorns the humble with victory. ℟

5 Let the faithful exult in glory;
let them sing for joy on their
couches.

6 Let the high praises of God be in their
throats,
and two-edged swords in their hands,

7 to execute vengeance on the nations
and punishment on the peoples,

8 to bind their rulers with fetters and their
nobles with chains of iron,
9 to execute on them the judgment
decreed.

This is glory for all God's faithful ones.
Praise be to God! ℟

Psalm 150

Response

Antiphon: Emma Lou Diemer, 1994

R

1 Praise be to God! Praise God in Gód's own sanctuary;
praise God in the míghty firmament!

2 Praise God for God's míghty deeds;
praise God according to God's surpássing greatness! R

3 Praise God with trúmpet sound;
praise God with lúte and harp!

4 Praise God with tambouríne and dance;
praise God with stríngs and pipe!

5 Praise God with clánging cymbals;
praise God with loud cláshing cymbals!

6 Let everything that bréathes praise God!
Praise bé to God! R

Canticles, Ancient Songs, and Psalm Settings

Psalm 51A

Chant setting: Henry Purcell (1659–1695)

1 Have mercy on me, O God, according to your stead-fast love; according to your abundant mercy blot out my trans-gressions.

2 Wash me thoroughly from my in - iquity, and cleanse me from my sin.

3 For I know 'my trans-'gressions, "and my 'sin is 'ever be - 'fore me.

4 Against you, you alone, have I sinned, and done what is e - vil in your sight,

so that you are justified 'in your 'sentence "and blame-less 'when you 'pass . . . 'judgment.

5 Indeed, I was born guilty, a sinner when my mother con - ceived me.

6 You desire truth in the 'in - ward 'being; "therefore teach me 'wisdom in my 'se - cret 'heart.

7 Purge me with hyssop, and I shall be clean; wash me, and I shall be purer than snow.

8 Let me hear 'joy and 'gladness; "let the bones that 'you have 'crushed re - 'joice.

9 Hide your face from my sins, and blot out all my in - iquities.

10 Create in me a clean 'heart, O 'God, "and put a 'new and right 'spirit with - 'in me.

11 Do not cast me a - way from your presence, and do not take your ho - ly spir - it from me.

12 Restore to me the 'joy of your sal-'vation, "and sus-'tain in me a 'will - ing 'spirit.

13 Then I will teach trans - gressors your ways, and sinners will re-turn to you.

14 Deliver me from bloodshed, O God, O 'God of my sal-'vation, "and my tongue will sing a - 'loud of 'your de - 'liverance.

15 O God, open my lips, and my mouth will de-clare your praise.

16 For you have no de - 'light in 'sacrifice; "if I were to give a burnt offering, 'you would 'not be 'pleased.

17 The sacrifice acceptable to God is a trou - bled spirit; a broken and contrite heart, O God, you will not de - spise.

(May be sung as a double chant. See next page.)

Psalm 63A

Chant setting: Thomas Morley (c. 1557–1603)

2 So I have looked upon |you in the |sanctuary, ||be - |holding your |power and |glory.

3 Because your steadfast love is better than life, my lips will praise . . . you.

4 So I will bless you as |long as I |live; ||I will lift up my |hands and |call on your |name.

5 My soul is satisfied as with a rich feast, and my mouth praises you with joy - ful lips

6 when I think of |you on my |bed, ||and meditate on |you in the |watches of the |night;

7 for you have been my help, and in the shadow of your wings I sing for joy.

8 My soul |clings to |you; ||your |might - y |hand up - |holds me.

O God, you are my God, I seek you, my soul . . . . thirsts for you.

(May be sung as a double chant. See below.)

Cambridge Chant

Daniel Hathaway, 1994

Psalm 67A

Chant setting: Vincent No ello (1781–1861)

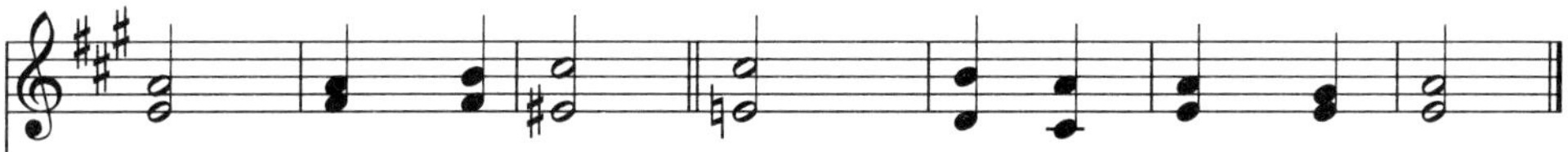

[1] May God be gracious to | us and bless us, | and make God's | face to | shine up - on us.
[2] That your way may be known up-on | earth, | your saving | power a - | mong all | nations.

[3] Let the peoples ˈpraise you, O ˈGod; ˈˈlet ˈall the ˈpeo - ples ˈpraise you.
[4] Let the nations be glad and | sing for | joy, | for you judge the peoples with equity and | guide the | nations upon | earth.
[5] Let the peoples ˈpraise you, O ˈGod; ˈˈlet ˈall the ˈpeo - ples ˈpraise you.
[6] The earth has | yielded its | increase; | God, our | God, has | blessed . . . | us.
[7] May God con - ˈtinue to ˈbless us; ˈˈlet all the ˈends of the ˈearth re-vere ˈGod.

Joseph Barnby (1838–1896)

Jonathan McNair, 1994

Psalm 95A

Chant setting: Richard Farrant (c. 1530–1580)

1 O come, let us sing to God; let us make a joyful noise to the rock of our sal - vation!

2 Let us come into God's presence with thanks - giving; let us make a joyful noise to God with songs of praise!

3 For God is a |great . . . |God, ||and a great |Ruler a - |bove all |gods.

4 In God's hand are the depths of the earth; the heights of the mountains are al - so God's.

5 The sea is |God's, for God |made it, ||and the dry land, which |God's . . . hands have |formed.

6 O come, let us worship and bow down, let us kneel before God, our Maker!

7 For |God is our |God, ||and we are the people of God's |pasture, and the |sheep of God's |hand.

O that to - day you would lis - ten to God's voice!

(May be sung as a double chant. See below.)

James Turle (1802–1882)

Daniel Hathaway, 1994

Psalm 100A

Chant setting: William Byrd (1538–1623)

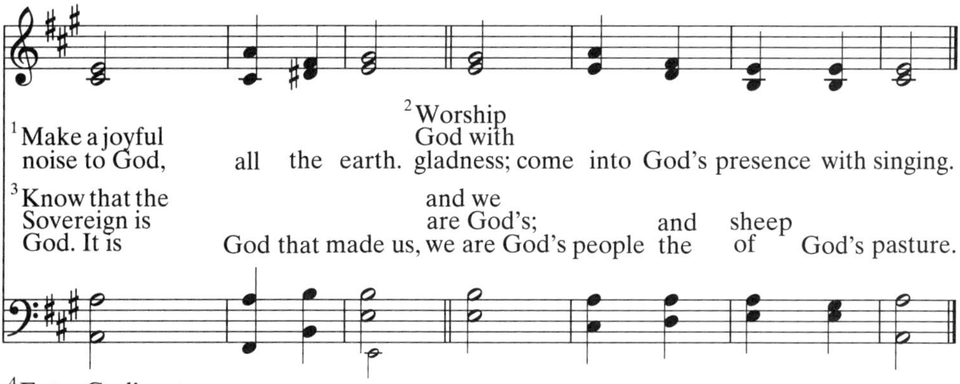

1 Make a joyful noise to God, all the earth. 2 Worship God with gladness; come into God's presence with singing.

3 Know that the Sovereign is God. It is God that made us, and we are God's; we are God's people and the sheep of God's pasture.

4 Enter God's gates with thanksgiving, and enter God's ˡcourts with ˡpraise. ǁGive thanks to ˡGod and ˡbless God's ˡname.

5 For God is good; God's steadfast love en - dures for - ever, and God's faithful-ness to all gene-rations.

(May be sung as a single or double chant. See below.)

Daniel Hathaway, 1994

Bruce Neswick, 1994

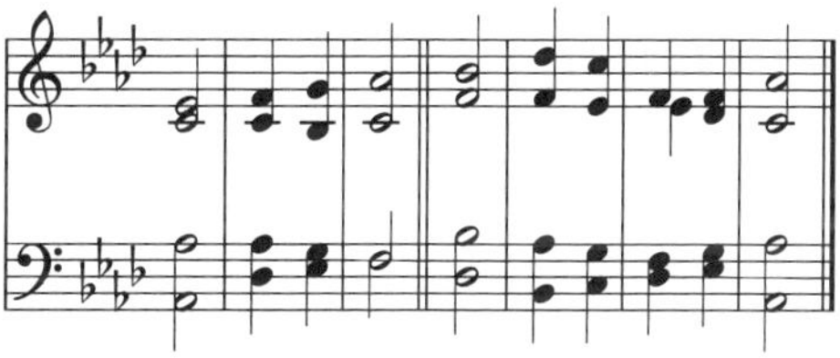

Bruce Neswick, 1994

Psalm 121A

Chant setting: James Turle (1802–1882)

1 I lift up my eyes to the hills— from where will my help come?
2 My help comes from God, the God who made heaven and earth.

3 God will not let your |foot be |moved; ||God who |keeps you |will not |slumber.
4 God who keeps Israel will nei - ther slumber nor sleep.
5 God |is your |keeper; ||God is your |shade . . . |at your |side.
6 The sun shall not strike you by day, nor shall the moon by night.
7 God will |keep you from all |evil; ||and |God will |keep your |life.
8 God will keep your going out and your com - ing in from this time on and for - ev - er - more.

(May be sung as a double chant. See below.)

John Robinson (1682–1762)

Bruce Neswick, 1994

Psalm 141A

Chant setting: William Croft (1678–1727)

[1] I call upon you, O God; come quickly to me; give ear to my voice when I call to you.

[2] Let my prayer be counted as incense be - fore you, and the lifting up of my hands as an eve - ning sacrifice.

[3] Set a guard over my ꞌmouth, O ꞌGod; ꞌꞌkeep ꞌwatch over the ꞌdoor of my ꞌlips.

[4] Do not turn my heart to any evil, to busy my - self with wick - ed deeds;

with those who work in - iquity, do not let me eat of their delicacies.

[5] Let the ꞌrigh - teous ꞌstrike me; ꞌꞌand ꞌlet the ꞌfaithful cor - ꞌrect me.

Never let the oil of the wicked a - noint my head, for my prayer is continually a - gainst their wick - ed deeds.

[6] When they are then given over to those who ꞌshall con-ꞌdemn them, ꞌꞌthey shall ꞌlearn that my ꞌwords were ꞌpleasant.

[7] Like a rock that one breaks apart and shatters on the land, so shall their bones be strewn at the mouth of Sheol.

[8] But my eyes are turned toward you, O ꞌGod, my ꞌGod; ꞌꞌin you I seek refuge; ꞌdo not ꞌleave me de - ꞌfenseless.

[9] Keep me from the trap that they have laid for me, and keep me from the snares of those who do evil.

[10] Let the wicked fall into ꞌtheir own ꞌnets, ꞌꞌwhile ꞌI a - ꞌlone es - ꞌcape.

(May be sung as a double chant. See below.)

Henry Purcell (1659–1695)
Arr. James Turle (1802–1882)

Canticle of Mary
(Magnificat)

℟ Response *Antiphon: Carolyn Jennings, 1994*

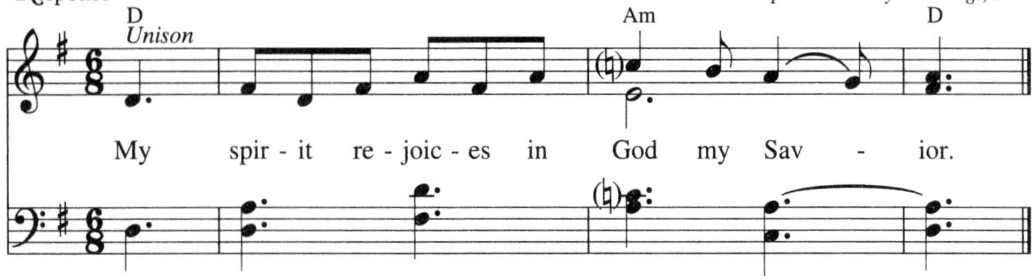

Luke 1:46–55

℟

My soul magnifies the Sovereign,
and my spirit rejoices in God my Savior;

for God has looked with favor on the lowliness of God's servant.
Surely, from now on all generations will call me blessed;

for the Mighty One has done great things for me,
the Mighty One whose name is holy. ℟

God's mercy is for those who fear God
from generation to generation.

God has shown great strength;
and has scattered the proud in the thoughts of their hearts.

God has brought down the powerful from their thrones,
and lifted up the lowly;

God has filled the hungry with good things,
and sent the rich away empty. ℟

God has helped God's servant Israel,
in remembrance of God's mercy,

according to the promise made to our ancestors,
to Abraham and Sarah and to their descendants forever. ℟

Canticle of Zechariah

(Benedictus)

℟esponse

Antiphon: Robert Fryson, 1994

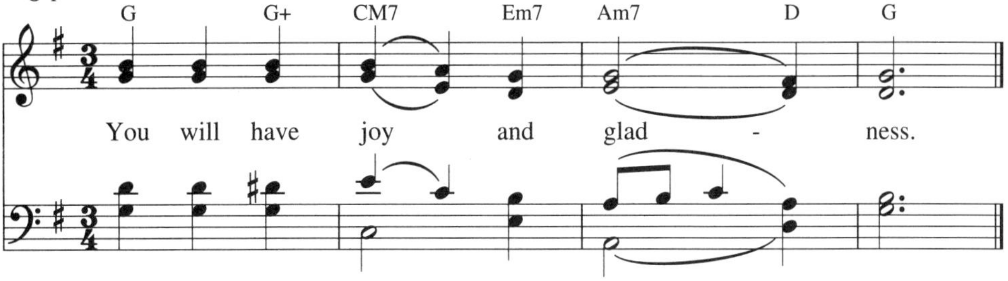

Luke 1:68–79

℟

Blessed be the Sovereign God of Israel,
who has looked favorably on the people and redeemed them.

God has raised up a mighty savior for us
in the house of God's servant David;

as God spoke through the mouth of the holy prophets from of old,
that we would be saved from our enemies and from the hand of all who hate us. ℟

Thus God has shown the mercy
promised to our ancestors,

and has remembered God's holy covenant,
the oath that God swore to our ancestor Abraham,

to grant us that we, being rescued from the hands of our enemies,
might serve God without fear,
in holiness and righteousness
before God all our days. ℟

And you, child, will be called the prophet of the Most High,
for you will go before God
to prepare God's ways;

to give knowledge of salvation to the people
by the forgiveness of their sins.

By the tender mercy of our God,
the dawn from on high will break upon us,

to give light to those who sit in night and in the shadow of death,
to guide our feet into the way of peace. ℟

Canticle of Simeon

(Nunc Dimittis)

℟esponse

Antiphon: Arthur G. Clyde, 1994

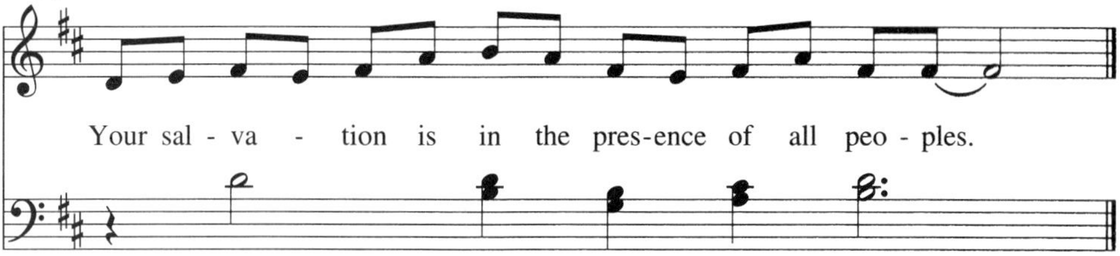

Luke 2:29–32

℟

O God, now you are dismissing your servant in peace,
according to your word;

for my eyes have seen your salvation,

which you have prepared in the presence of all peoples,

a light for revelation to the Gentiless
and for glory to your people Israel. ℟

Second Canticle of Isaiah

℟esponse

Antiphon: Vérne de la Peña, 1994

Isa. 55:6–11

℟

Seek God while God may be found,
call upon God while God is near;

let the wicked forsake their way,
and the unrighteous their thoughts;

let them return to God, that God may have mercy on them,
and to our God, for God will abundantly pardon. ℟

For my thoughts are not your thoughts,
nor are your ways my ways, says God.

For as the heavens are higher
than the earth,
so are my ways higher than
your ways and my thoughts than
your thoughts.

For as the rain and the snow come
down from heaven,
and do not return there until
they have watered the earth,

making it bring forth and sprout,
giving seed to the sower and
bread to the eater,

so shall my word be that goes out
from my mouth;
it shall not return to me empty,

but it shall accomplish that which
I purpose,
and succeed in the thing for
which I sent it. ℟

Col. 1:15–20

℟

Canticle to the Lamb

℟esponse

Antiphon: Robert Train Adams, 1994

Rev. 4:11; 5:9–10, 12, 13

℟

You are worthy, our Sovereign
and God,
to receive glory and honor and
power,

for you created all things,
and by your will they existed
and were created. ℟

You are worthy, O Christ, for you
were slaughtered,
and by your blood you
ransomed saints for God

from every tribe and language
and from every people and
nation;

you have made them to be a
dominion and priests serving
our God,
and they will reign on earth. ℟

Worthy is the Lamb that was
slaughtered to receive power and
wealth and wisdom,
and might and honor and glory
and blessing!

To the one seated on the throne
and to the Lamb be blessing and
honor,
and glory and might forever and
ever! ℟

Canticle to Christ

℟ Response

Antiphon: Marty Haugen, 1994

Col. 1:15–20

Christ is the image of the invisible God,
  the firstborn of all creation;

for in Christ all things in heaven and on earth were created,
  things visible and invisible,

whether thrones or dominions or rulers or powers —
  all things have been created through Christ and for Christ.

Christ, indeed, is before all things,
  and in Christ all things hold together. ℟

Christ is the head of the body,
  which is the church;

Christ is the beginning, the firstborn from the dead,
  so that Christ might come to have first place in everything.

For in Christ all the fullness of God
  was pleased to dwell,

and through Christ God was pleased to reconcile to God all things,
  whether on earth or in heaven,
  by making peace through the blood of the cross. ℟

Canticle of the Mystery Revealed in Flesh

℟esponse

Antiphon: Hyeon Jeong, 1994

1 Tim. 3:16; 6:15, 16

℟

Christ was revealed in flesh,
vindicáted in spirit,
  seen by angels, proclaimed
  ámong Gentiles,

believed in throughóut the world,
  taken úp in glory.

At the right time God will bring
about the manifestátion of Christ—
  God who is the blessed and
  only Sovereign, the Ruler of
  rulers and Sovéreign of
  sovereigns.

It is God alone who has
ímmortality
  and dwells in unapproachāble
  light,

whom no one has ever seen ór can
see—
  to God be honor and
  eternal dominíon. Amen. ℟

Canticle of the Three

(Benedicite omnia opera)

℟esponse *Antiphon: Arthur G. Clyde, 1993*

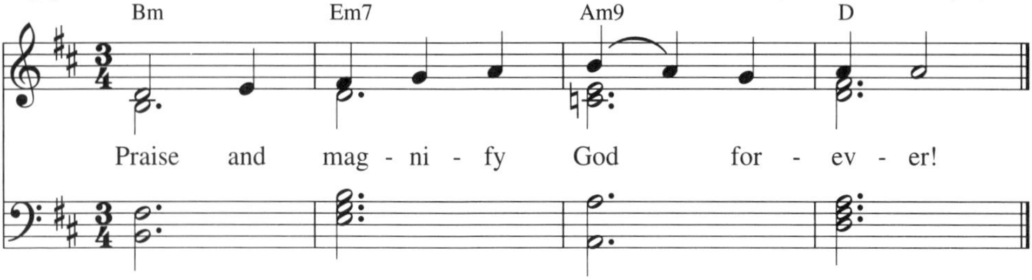

Prayer of Azariah 35–65

℟

All you works of God, bless your God;
you angels of God, bless your God;

you heavens, bless your God;
all the waters above the heavens, bless your God; ℟

You powers of God, bless your God;
you sun and moon, bless your God;

stars of the heaven, bless your God;
all rain and dew, bless your God; ℟

All the winds, bless your God;
you fire and heat, bless your God;

you winter cold and summer heat, bless your God;
you dews and falling snow, bless your God; ℟

You ice and cold, bless your God;
you frosts and snows, bless your God;

nights and days, bless your God;
you light and darkness, bless your God; ℟

Lightnings and clouds, bless your God;
let the earth bless God;

you mountains and hills, bless your God;
all that grows in the ground, bless your God; ℟

You running waters, bless your God;
you seas and rivers, bless your God;

you whales and all that move in the waters, bless your God;
all you birds of the air, bless your God; ℟

All you animals and cattle, bless your God;
all you people on earth, bless your God;

O Israel, bless your God;
you priests of God, bless your God; ℟

all you who serve God, bless your God;
you spirits and souls of the righteous, bless your God;

you holy and humble in heart, bless your God;
Blessed are you, O God in the dome of heaven. ℟

(May be sung with double tone.)

O Holy Radiance, Joyous Light

(Phos Hilaron)

Col. 3:16–17; Isa. 60:19–20; John 1:1–5

Greek, 2nd–4th century C.E.
Transl. The New Century Hymnal, *1994*

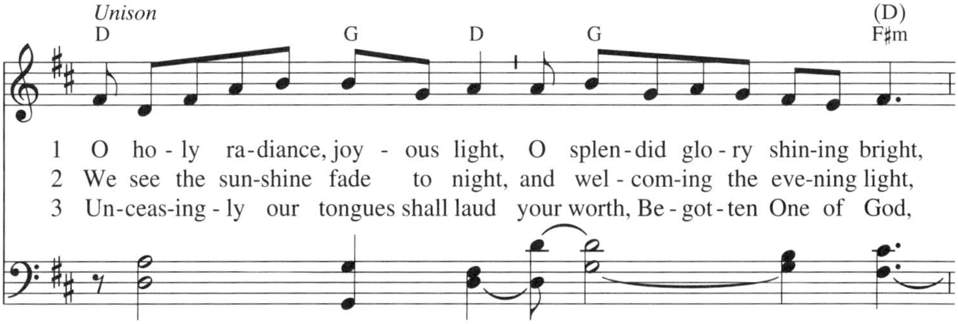

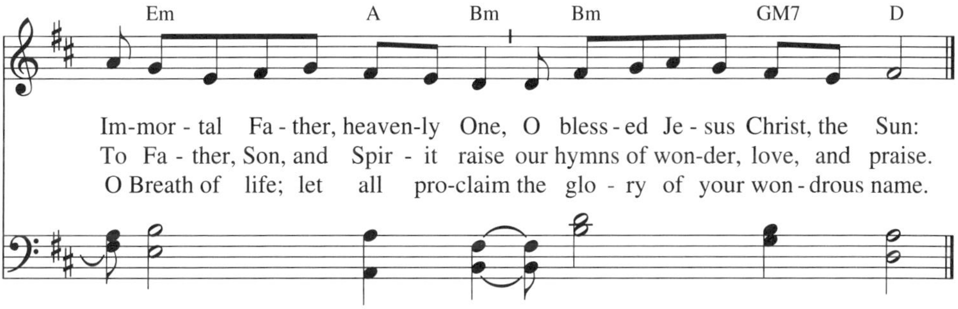

Known as "The Candlelight Hymn" or "Phos Hilaron," this hymn was sung in the ancient church at the Lighting of Lamps for Vespers. St. Basil, who died in 379 C.E., referred to it as being of uncertain date and authorship. Its original tune is also unknown.

Tune: CONDITOR ALME SIDERUM L.M.
ancient Sarum plainsong, Mode IV
Harm. The New Century Hymnal, *1994*
Alternate tune: TALLIS' CANON

O Wisdom, Breathed from God

(O Sapientia)

St. 1, 2, "O Antiphons," Latin, 6th–7th century,
Transl. The New Century Hymnal, *1994*
St. 3, The New Century Hymnal, *1994*

Sir. 24:1–6; Wisd. 7:25, 8:1, 7; Luke 1:78–79;
John 8:12; Mal. 4:2

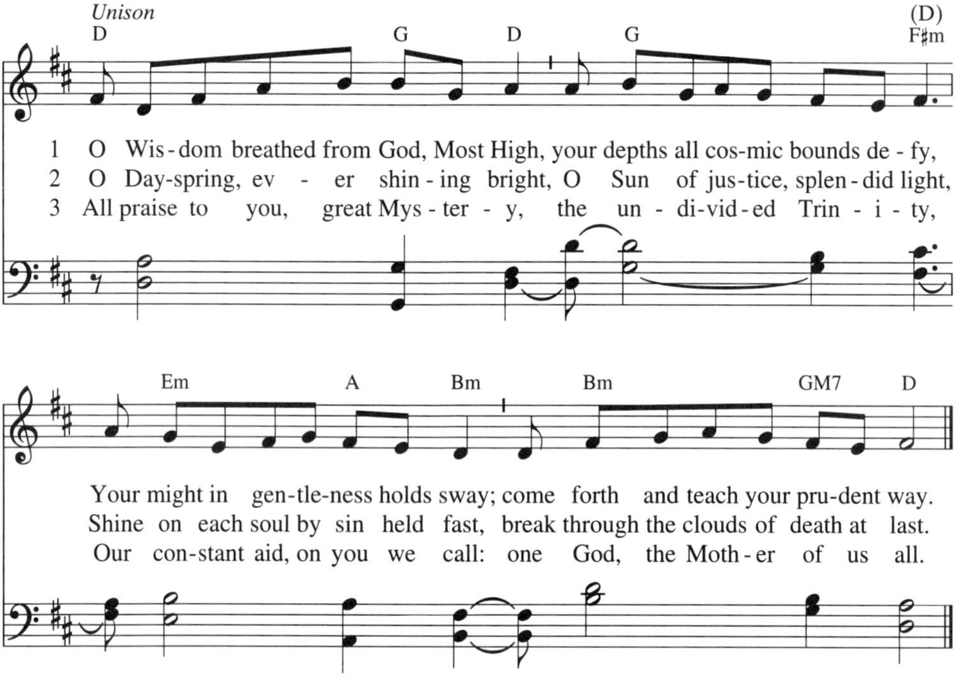

"Sophia" *may be substituted for* "O Wisdom" *in stanza 1.*

The first two stanzas of this hymn are a translation of two of the seven ancient "O Antiphons" used at vespers, one for each of the seven days before Christmas. The first of these is "O Sapientia" (O Wisdom). The third stanza includes ideas from the writings of Julian of Norwich and phrases from the early prayer services of the Western church.

Tune: CONDITOR ALME SIDERUM L.M.
ancient Sarum plainsong, Mode IV
Harm. The New Century Hymnal, *1994*
Alternate tune: TALLIS' CANON

Singing Psalms

Singing the Psalms and Canticles in Corporate Worship

Psalms and Canticles

Psalms were originally intended for singing, and the late twentieth century has witnessed a revival of this ancient custom. *The New Century Psalter* presents the psalms in their biblical form, with verses arranged in balance for antiphonal use. They are pointed to be sung to simple tunes, or tones. The format also allows for their use as readings in corporate or private meditation. The same is true for the canticles, Bible texts that were traditionally sung but taken from sources other than the book of Psalms.

Using the Psalms and Canticles in Worship

The psalms and canticles in this psalter can be used in a variety of ways.

- They may be read by an individual for private devotions.
- They may be sung responsively:
  a solo voice (cantor) alternating with the congregation;
  choir alternating with congregation;
  one part of the congregation alternating with another part of the congregation.
- They may be sung through entirely by the congregation, without alternating.
- They may be read responsively (when reading, the points [ʹ] are ignored):
  leader alternating with the congregation;
  two sides of the congregation alternating;
  alternating by half couplet or whole couplet.

Singing the Psalms and Canticles Using a Psalm Tone and Points

The psalms and canticles have been arranged into couplets, each with an A phrase and a B phrase (indented), to match the melody of a *tone*. The point (ʹ) in the text is positioned to indicate exactly where the melody note changes. If the choice is to have a cantor alternate with congregation, the cantor sings the first couplet as follows:

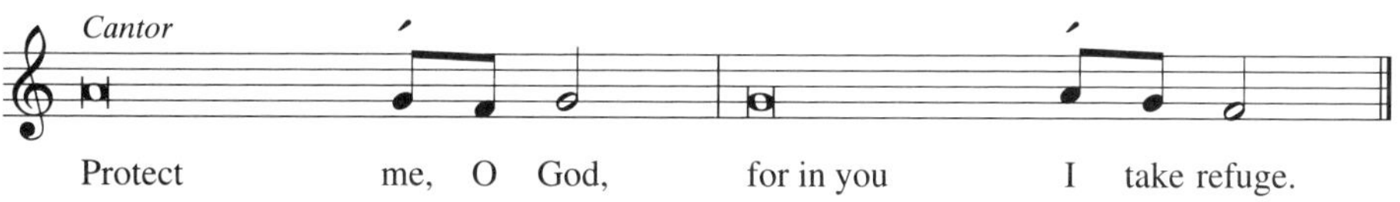

The congregation then answers with the indented couplet, repeating the same melody (tone) "by ear," and observing the point as the place to change the note.

This alternating continues for the desired number of verses.

Using the Response (℟)

The symbol ℟ indicates the singing, by all, of the response. If the psalm or canticle is read responsively, instead of being sung, the response may be spoken or sung by all at the designated places.

One Way to Use a Psalm or Canticle in Worship

1. The response is played through once.
2. The response is sung by all.
3. The tone is played.
4. The first couplet is sung by the cantor or choir, accompanied by the tone.
5. The second couplet is sung by the congregation, accompanied by the tone.
6. Continue alternating couplets. Where indicated, the response is played and sung (with no musical introduction).
7. The singing of the psalm or canticle continues as before.
8. The response is sung by all at the end (with no introduction).

Additional Helps

1. The points are always placed so that an accented syllable will fall on the last note of musical phrase A or B in the tone. If there are extra syllables, they are also sung on the last note.

2. The psalms and canticle texts are to be sung in a natural speech rhythm, at a comfortable pace, and with minimal (if any) pause for punctuation.

3. Several tones have been provided here. These, plus additional tones, will be found in the accompanist edition in various transpositions.

4. This form of psalm singing can be learned with little difficulty, and the same tone may be used for any psalm.

5. Double tones are designed to carry the text of two couplets. The above guidelines for singing will apply, except that two couplets will be matched with phrases A, B, C, and D of the tone. Thus, alternating may be accomplished by having the cantor sing the first *two* couplets, with the congregation responding with the next *two* couplets. Or the congregation, by itself, may sing the entire selection to the double tone, and with the designated response.

Psalm Tones and Matching Tones with Antiphons

Psalm tones, beginning on page 226, are provided in varied keys. The Psalm Tone Index beginning on page 224 will prove helpful in selecting a tone that is appropriate in key and style to the antiphon and the mood of the psalm. When beginning the practice of psalm singing in worship, it is recommended that the number of different tones used be kept to a minimum. Later, when the basic pattern is established, new tones may be introduced more frequently.

Creating Psalm Tones

The tones shown here are merely harmonic sequences with easy melodies that work well to support the sung recitation of words. New tones may be developed by keeping some simple concepts in mind. A single tone is comprised of:

a) a beginning chanting note (harmonized), two moving notes, and a half-cadence note (harmonized), followed by
b) a second chanting note (harmonized), two moving notes, and a cadence note (harmonized).

The chanting notes and cadence notes are supported with harmonies, whereas the moving notes usually are not. Thus, four simple chords are used to make a single tone.

The Pointing of Psalms

An understanding of how psalms are pointed will help in teaching congregations and choirs to sing them. Each phrase to be chanted has a point near the end. The point is placed by locating where the last strong accent occurs in the spoken phrase, then counting back two syllables. This is where the point is placed. This will be the syllable that coincides with the first of the changing notes. The entire phrase preceding the point is sung on the chanting tone. Thus in the phrase

and God has dominion over it

the **o** in "**o**-ver" is the last strong accent. Counting back two syllables, the point is placed on do-mín-ion. The result is a phrase that can be sung very naturally, in speech rhythm.

and God has do -	**min** -	ion	**o**ver it
chanting tone	*changing notes*		*cadence note*

As can be seen in this instance, sometimes there will be more than one syllable to be sung on the last note. These words will be sung with natural emphasis, starting with the strong syllable (in this case "**o**"), with the rest trailing off.

Do congregations need to have all this information? In most cases it would not be very helpful. It is, however, useful for the person responsible for leading the music in worship to have an understanding of the structure of psalm pointing.

This is a suggested sequence for accompanying the singing of a psalm:

- Play the antiphon through in the tempo in which it is to be sung (in the manner of a hymn introduction).
- Play it again as all join in singing the antiphon.
- Immediately play through the tone.
- Play the tone again to support the singing of the first couplet by the cantor.
- Follow the text rhythms used by the cantor.
- Play the tone again to support the singing of the next couplet by all.
- Continue the pattern of alternating couplets between cantor and all.
- Play the antiphon (or response) when ℟ appears.
- Continue playing the tone as the cantor sings the first couplet of the next section.
- Continue the tone as all join in singing the next couplet.
- Continue as above.

Further suggestions for accompanying the singing of psalms include:

- Successful psalm singing always depends on an awareness of speech rhythms.
- Preceding the antiphons (responses) marked ℟ there is no need to play a chord or give a pitch to start. This would intrude on the flow of text. The routine, once established, will flow naturally.
- If using a pattern of cantor alternating couplets with choir and congregation, try playing the melody alone with the cantor, adding harmony for the next couplet sung by choir and congregation. Always be aware of the spoken voice rhythms, and let the accompaniment be very flexible.
- Another option for organists is to accompany the cantor, complete with harmony, but played on a softer manual (8′ + 4′ flutes), shifting to a louder manual (8′ + 4′ diapason + flutes) for the couplets sung by all.
- The moving notes (eighth notes) should never be stressed or held; the emphasis of the phrase is always on the chords. If accompanying with guitar, observe only the four chord points (see "Creating Psalm Tones"); there is no need to play or accompany the moving notes.

It is well established that in earliest times, psalms were accompanied, sometimes in elaborate fashion. Throughout the Christian era, accompaniment has varied, as has the style of psalm tone. In some settings psalms have been sung unaccompanied, and this too could be an option, especially in an intimate setting such as morning or evening prayer. Once the fundamentals of singing and accompanying psalms are established, there is no limit to applying musical innovations such as the following:

- The basic reciting chords of the psalm tone sounded with handbells (or hand chimes/choir chimes).
- Flute played ad lib.
- Finger cymbals played at the beginning of each couplet.

The Cantor

The word "cantor" means singer. It is used here to indicate the person who will be the song leader for the singing of the psalms. Performing the role of cantor does not require extensive musical training. The basic requirements are a pleasant singing voice, a good ear for melody, and the ability to sing the texts in a natural speech rhythm.

- Members of the choir could alternate as cantors for each Sunday.
- A child can be a cantor.
- It is appropriate for a minister leading worship to serve also in the role of cantor.

Whoever takes the responsibility, it is essential that she or he take time to prepare. A rehearsal, however brief, with the accompanist is recommended. One final suggestion about the cantor's singing of the psalm: usually the text is sung in a straightforward way, with neither greatly varied dynamics nor dramatic emphasis. An overall evenness of performance will enhance the meditative intent of the psalm text.

The "Hallel" Psalms

The psalter contains what are known as the "Hallel" (Praise), the name given in Rabbinical writings to six psalms, 113–118. These six psalms are also called the "Egyptian Hallel" ("When Israel went out from Egypt," 114:1) to distinguish them from Psalm 136, known as the "Great Hallel," and from Psalms 146–148, which were also regarded as a kind of Hallel because of their many references to praise.

In these psalms "Yahweh," the name of God given by God to Moses (Exodus 6:2–3), is praised many times. The English phrase often found in these psalms, "Praise the Lord" or "Praise God," is a translation of the Hebrew "Hallelujah," which combines "Hallel" with "Yah" ("Jah"). In other translations of these psalms, however, "hallelujah" is simply transliterated from the Hebrew.

All of these "Hallel" psalms as they appear in *The New Century Psalter* have been matched with antiphons taken from the psalm. As an alternative to the printed antiphons, these psalms may appropriately be sung substituting "Hallelujah!" as the antiphon. (It is a common practice in many traditions to avoid singing "Hallelujah!" during the season of Lent.)

At the point in the service when the psalm will be sung, or in the bulletin for the service, announce that the antiphon (or response) is "Hallelujah! Hallelujah!" The antiphon will be sung to the same tone that is chosen for the psalm. For example:

(Any of the single tones may be used in this way.)

The following is a simple way of using the "Hallelujah!" antiphon in worship.

- The psalm tone is played.
- All sing "Hallelujah! Hallelujah!" to the psalm tone.
- The cantor immediately begins the psalm using the same tone.
- The congregation continues with the next couplet, etc.
- Subsequently, the "Hallelujah! Hallelujah!" response is repeated wherever the symbol ℛ for the antiphon (or response) appears.

The "Hallelujah!" response may be spoken, if the psalm is read responsively.

Another option for the response is to use one of the musical settings of "Alleluia" provided in this Accompanist Edition. The method described above, however, should prove much easier for congregations to learn.

Psalms at Morning and Evening Prayer

In Morning Prayer, there is usually a morning psalm and another psalm of praise. There is also a canticle from the Old Testament. In Evening Prayer, there are two evening psalms and a canticle from the New Testament. Also, for either Morning or Evening Prayer additional psalms may be used. For a cycle of selected psalms for weekday use, consult a daily lectionary. Psalms are the heart of Morning and Evening Prayer, intended for meditation. This is why it is recommended that they be sung while seated, and that silence follow each psalm. This practice may be one to which worshipers are not accustomed, and it may seem more comfortable to omit or shorten this time. Bear in mind, however, that this can be a time to meditate on the Word of God. Once established as a regular practice, the use of psalm and silence will become an act of prayer consistent with the intent of the order for worship. These orders for daily prayer can be adapted to a variety of settings, including individual and small-group devotions. The musical approach should be appropriate to the occasion. For a small group, unaccompanied singing or use of a guitar might prove very satisfying. For larger groups, organ or piano accompaniment might work better.

For Morning Prayer, in addition to the pointed versions, Anglican-style settings of Psalms 51, 63, 67, 95, and 100 are provided (see 51A, 63A, 67A, 95A, and 100A and at the end of the psalms). Other psalms of praise or Hebrew scripture canticles found in the Psalter section may be added. A lectionary will prove helpful. The Canticle of Zechariah is always a part of Morning Prayer, and is provided in pointed form on page 207.

For Evening Prayer, the constant psalm is 141. It is provided in two settings in this psalter: as a pointed psalm and in Anglican chant style (141A). The constant canticle is the Canticle of Mary, or Magnificat. It is presented in pointed form on page 206. Other psalms and canticles may be used. The pointed setting of Psalm 121, page 173, and the Anglican version, 121A, are particularly appropriate for evening. As in Morning Prayer, a lectionary will prove helpful in selecting additional psalms.

Psalms in the Easter Vigil

Liturgies for Easter Vigil vary in the choice of readings, but usually follow a pattern of readings alternating with psalms and canticles. *The New Century Psalter* should prove an excellent resource for Easter Vigil, as spoken word alternates with the singing of psalms. In some traditions the Canticle of the Three, found on page 212, is used after the final Hebrew Scripture reading.

INDEX TO PSALM TONES COORDINATED WITH ANTIPHONS

PSALM TONES WITH TRANSPOSITIONS

1 1, 2F, 3C, 5, 7F, 8C
2 2, 4G, 5G, 6G, 7, 11G, 14, 15
3 7, 10, 13Gm
4 5, 7, 11, 14F, 15
5 5, (6), 7F, 9Dm, 10Dm, 11
6 (2A♭), 3E♭, 4A♭, 5E♭, 6, 7, 8
7 1D, 2, 3, 4, 6A, 8D, 12D
8 1, 2F, 4F, 5, 6, 11, 14F, 15B♭
9 (5), 6, 8, 14E♭, 15B♭
10 1D, 2, 3, 4, 6A, 8D, 14, 15
11 7D♭ or A♭, 9Cm, 10
12 1, 2F, 3C, 4B♭, 5, 6, 7F, (11), 14C, 15B♭
13 7F, 9, 13
14 6, 7, 8, 14E♭
15 1D, 2, (3), 6G, 7F, 8D, 11, 14, 15
16 1D, 2, 3, 4, 4G, 8D, 11, 14
17 (1), 7G, 9, 13
18 1D, 2, 3, 4, 6A, 7F, 8D
19 1, 2, 3, 4G, 5G, 6G, 7G, 8D
20 1, 5G, 7G, 9, (11G), 13, 15
21 4B♭, 5, 6, 12B♭
22 7, 10, 13Gm
23 1E♭, 2A♭, 3E♭, 4A♭, 6A♭, 7, 8
24 (1), 2F, 4F, 7, 12C
25 1D, 2, 3, 4G, 5G, 6G, 8D
26 1D, 2, 3, 4G, 5G, 6G, 8D, 11, 14
27 9Dm, 10Dm, 5, 7F, 11, 13
28 1D, 2, 3, 4, 6A, 7F, 8D
29 1, 5, 7F, 8C, 12C, 14, 15
30 1D, (2), 3, 4, 5D, (6G), 8D, 11
31a 1, 2F, 3C, 4F, 6G, 8C, 9
31b 5, 5C, 7, 9, 11E♭, 15
32 1E♭, 2A♭, 3E♭, 4A♭, 6A♭, 7, 8, 14E♭, 15B♭
33 1E♭, 2A♭, 3E♭, 4A♭, 5E♭, 6A♭, 7, 8
34a 12 (C or F), 1, 2F, 3C, 4F, 5, 8C
34b 1D, 2, 3, 4, 6G, 8D
35 7, 10, 13Gm
36 1D, 2, 3, 4, 5D, 8D, 9Bm, 10Bm
37 1E, 2A, 3E, 4, 5E, 6A, 8E, 11G, 14E
38 7, 10, 13Gm
39 5, (6), 7F, 9Dm, 10Dm, 11
40 1D, 2, 3, 4, 5D, 6G, 8D
41 12D, 1D, 2, 3, 4, 6G, 8D, 11, 14, 15
42 7D♭ or A♭, 9Cm, 10
43 7D♭ or A♭, 9Cm, 10
44 7D♭ or A♭, 9Cm, 10
45 2A, 3, 4, 6A, 7A, 8D, 11G, 12D, 12E, 14, 15
46 1E♭, 2A♭, 3E♭, 4A♭, 5E♭, 6A♭, 7, 8
47 1E♭, 2A♭, 3E♭, 4A♭, 5E♭, 6A♭, 8
48 1, 2, 3, 4G, 5G, 6G, 7, 8D
49 1, (2), 3C, 4G, 6G, 7, 8C, 9
50 5G, 7G, 9, 13Bm
51 1, 2F, 3C, 4G, 6G, 7, 8C, 9, 11E♭, 12C, 14C, 15
52 7F, 9, 13
53 6, 7, 8, 14E♭
54 1, 2, 3C, 4G, 5G, 6G, 8C
55 12D, 1D, 2, 3, 4, 5D, 6A, 7F, 8D
56 1E♭, 2A♭, 3E♭, 4A♭, 6A♭, 7, 8, 14E♭, 15B♭
57 1, 2, 3, 4G, 5G, 8C
58 7, 10, 13Gm
59 1E♭, 2A♭, 3E♭, 4A♭
60 7, 9Dm, 10, 13Gm
61 2, 4G, 5G, 7, 8, 10
62 1E, 2A, 3E, 4, 6A, 8A
63 2, 4G, 5G, 7, 8, 10
64 1, 2F, 3C, 4B♭, 5, 6
65 1D, 2, 3, 4, 6A, 8D, 12D
66 1, 2, 4G, 5G, 6G, (8C), 11E♭, 15
67 1D, 2, 3, 4, 4G, 8D
68 1E, 2A, 3E, 4, 5E, 6A, 8E
69 2, 4G, 6G, 7G
70 9Cm, 10, 13Gm
71 1, 2, 3C, 5G, 6G, 8C, 9
72 12D, 1D, 2, 3, 4, 5D, 6A, 7F, 8D
73 5, (6), 7F, 9Dm, 10Dm, 11
74 9Cm, 10, 13Gm
75 4B♭, 5, 6, 12B♭
76 1, 5, 7F, 8C, 12C, 14, 15
77 1E♭, 3E♭, 4B♭, 6, 8
78 12D, 2, 5, 7F, 9Dm, 13
79 7, 9Dm, 10, 13Gm
80 12D, 1D, 2, 3, 4, 5D, 8D
81 3F, 4B♭, 5, 6, 14F, 15B♭
82 7, 10, 13Gm
83 12D, 1D, 2, 3, 4, 5D, 8D
84 1, 2, 3, 4G, 6G
85 1E♭, 2A♭, 3E♭, 4A♭, 5E♭, 6A♭, 7, 8
86 1E, 3E, 5E, 6E
87 1, 5G, 7G, 9, (11G), 13, 15
88 7, 10, 13Gm
89 1E, 4, 6A, 7G, 9, 13
90 2F, 3C, 4B♭, 5, 6
91 1, 2F, 3C, 4B♭, 5, 6
92 1E♭, 2A♭, 3E♭, 4A♭, 6, 8, 14E♭, 15B♭
93 1, 4G, 5G, 6C, 7, 8C
94 7, 10, 13Gm
95 1D, 2, 3, 4G, 5D, 8D
96 2, 3E♭, 5E♭, 6, 7, 8
97 (4B♭), 5, (7F), 11, 14F, 15B♭
98 1, 2, 3, 4G, 5G, 8C

99 1, 2F, 3C, 4G, 7
100 2F, 4B♭, 5, 6, 15B♭
101 1, 2F, 3C, 5, 8C, 14C, 14F, 15B♭
102 7, 10, 13Gm
103 1, 2F, 3C, 5, 8C, 14C, 14F, 15B♭
104 1D, 2, 3, 4, 6A, 7F, 8D, 12D, 11, 14, 15
105 1, 3C, 4G, (7), 8C
106 1D, 2, 3, 4, 5D, 6A
107 1, 7F, 8C, 9, (12D), 13
108 2, 3E♭, 5E♭, 6, 7, 8
109 12D, 1D, 2, 3, 4, 5D, 8D
110 1D, 3, 4, 6A, 7F, 8D, 11, 14E, 15
111 4A♭, 5E♭, 6, 6A♭, 7, 8
112 5, 7, 9Dm, 13
113 1, 3C, 4G, 5C, 8C
114 1D, 2A, 3, 4, 6A, 7F, 8D
115 1, 2F, 3C, 5, 8C, 14C, 14F, 15B♭
116 4B♭, 5, 6, 12B♭
117 1E♭, 2A♭, 3E♭, 4A♭, 5E♭, 6A♭, 7, 8
118 1D, 2, 3, 4, 6A, 7F, 8D, 11, 12D, 14, 15
119 1D, 2, 3, 4, 6A, 8D, 14
120 9Dm, 10Dm, 5, 7F, 11, 13
121 1D, 2, 3, 4, 6A, 8D, 14, 15
122 1, 2F, 3C, 4B♭, 5, 6, 7F, (11), 14C, 15B♭
123 2, 4G, 9, 11G, 13
124 (1E♭), 2A♭, (3E♭), 4A♭, 5E♭, 6, 7, 8, 10
125 2, 3C, 4G, 5G, 7G, 9
126 1, 2F, 3C, 4F, 5, 8C
127 (2A♭), 3E♭, 4A♭, 5E♭, 6, 7, 8
128 2, 3, 4G, 5G, 6G, 8D
129 1, 2F, 3C, 4B♭, 5, 6, 7F, (11), 14C, 15B♭
130 9, 13
131 7D or G, 10Bm, 13Bm
132 1, 2, 3, 4G, 5G, 8D
133 1D, 3, 4, 6A, 8D
134 1, 3C, 4G, 5C, 8C
135 1D, 2, 3, 4, 4G, 8D
136 1E♭, 3E♭, 4A♭, 5E♭, 6, 7, 8
137 13
138 1D, 2, 3, 4, 6A, 7F, 8D
139 1, 3C, 7F, 9, 13
140 2, 4G, 9, 11G, 13
141 1, 2, 3C, 4G, 5C, 6G, 9
142 7, 10, 13Gm
143 9, 11, 13
144 1, 2F, 3C, 4F, 6G, 8C, 9
145 1D, 2, 3, 4, 5D, 6A, 8D
146 2F, 4B♭, 5, 6
147 1, 2, 4G, 5G, 7G, 9
148 1, 4G, 14C, 15
149 1, 2, 3C, 4G, 6G, 7
150 2F, 4B♭, 5, 6, 7F

CANTICLE TONES

of Mary 12, 1D, 2, 3, 4, 7F, 8D
of Zechariah 2, 3, 4G, 5G, 6G
of Simeon 1D, 3, 4, 8D, 13Bm
of Isaiah, Second 1, 3C, 5G, 9
to the Lamb 12E♭, 1E♭, 4A♭, 6A♭, 7, 8
to Christ 4B♭, 5, 6, (7)
of the Mystery Revealed in Flesh 1E♭, 3E♭, 4B♭, 5E♭, 6, 7, 8
of the Three 1D, 2, 3, 4, 5D, 7F, 8D, 11, 14

Key to Using This Index

On the following pages, each tone is presented first in its original key or mode, followed by transpositions of the tone as possible, with melodic range taken into consideration. In this Index, the suggested tones are referenced by number; transpositions are referenced by number and key. For example, "2F" refers to tone 2 transposed to F major. "9Dm" refers to tone 9 transposed to D minor. For some antiphons, tones in *related* keys are suggested in addition to tones in the *same* key. Tones in parentheses are possible, but may prove less suited to link with the antiphon.

PSALM TONES WITH TRANSPOSITIONS

Tones 1, 8: May Schwarz; 2, 3, 4, 7, 9, 10, 12, 13, 14: Jonathan McNair; 5: Jeffrey Radford; 6, 11, 15: Arthur G. Clyde.

4
A/C♯ C♯m D A
4G
G/B Bm C G
4F
F/A Am B♭ F
4B♭
B♭/D Dm E♭ B♭
4A♭
A♭/C Cm D♭ A♭
5
Dm7 G C7 F Em7(♭5) A7
Interlude between verses
5C
Am7 D G7 C Bm7(♭5) E7
5G
Em7 A D7 G F♯m7(♭5) B7
5D
Bm7 E A7 D C♯m7(♭5) F♯7
5E
C♯m7 F♯ B7 E D♯m7(♭5) G♯7
5E♭
Cm7 F B♭7 E♭ Dm7(♭5) G7

6 B♭ E♭2/G F7 B♭
6A♭ A♭ D♭2/F E♭7 A♭
6G G C2/E D7 G
6A A D2/F♯ E7 A
7 E♭ B♭ Cm G
7A♭ A♭ E♭ Fm C
7D♭ D♭ A♭ B♭m F
7F F C Dm A
7G G D Em B
7E E B C♯m G♯
8 E♭ E♭/G A♭ E♭
8C C C/E F C

PSALM TONES WITH TRANSPOSITIONS

11G (Double tone)
G A7/G Am7(♭5)/G G Em F♯m7/E Bm7 E
12 (Single tone)
D Am C D
12E
E Bm D E
12C
C Gm B♭ C
12B♭
B♭ Fm A♭ B♭
12E♭
E♭ B♭m D♭ E♭
12D
D Am C D
13
Am G Dm Am
13Bm
Bm A Em Bm
13Gm
Gm F Cm Gm
14 (Double tone)
GM7 F♯7 Em9/7 CM7 FM7 B♭M7 Asus7 DM7

PSALM TONES WITH TRANSPOSITIONS

14E (Double tone)

14C (Double tone)

14F (Double tone)

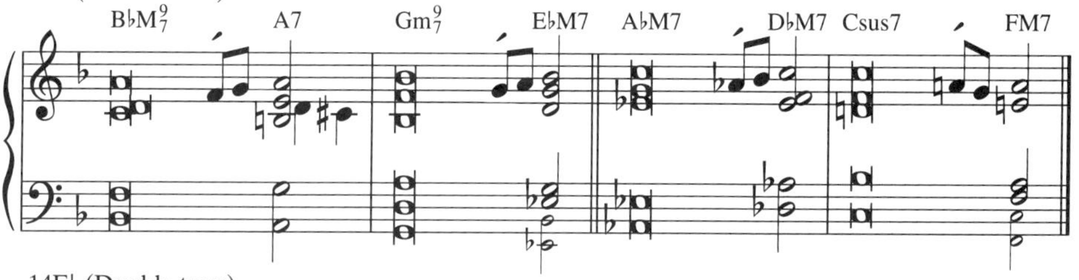

14E♭ (Double tone)

15 (Double tone)

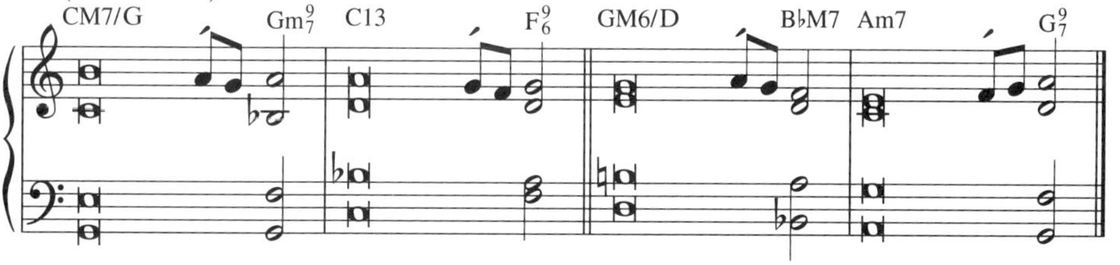

15B♭ (Double tone)